GORILLA DREAMS:
The Legacy of Dian Fossey

GORILLA DREAMS:
The Legacy of Dian Fossey

Georgianne Nienaber

iUniverse, Inc.

New York Lincoln Shanghai

GORILLA DREAMS: The Legacy of Dian Fossey

Copyright © 2006 by Georgianne Nienaber

iUniverse books may be ordered through booksellers or by contacting:

iUniverse
2021 Pine Lake Road, Suite 100
Lincoln, NE 68512
www.iuniverse.com
1-800-Authors (1-800-288-4677)

ISBN-13: 978-0-595-37669-8 (pbk)
ISBN-13: 978-0-595-82053-5 (ebk)
ISBN-10: 0-595-37669-X (pbk)
ISBN-10: 0-595-82053-0 (ebk)

Printed in the United States of America

For Nyiramacyibili

"Bitter pain seized her heart, and she rent the covering upon her divine hair with her dear hands: her dark cloak she cast down from both her shoulders and sped, like a wild bird, over the firm land and yielding sea, seeking her child. But no one would tell her the truth, neither god nor mortal men; and of the birds of omen none came with true news for her. Then for nine days queenly Deo wandered over the earth with flaming torches in her hands, so grieved that she never tasted ambrosia and the sweet draught of nectar, nor sprinkled her body with water."

—The Homeric Hymns. ll. 40-53

Contents

Chronology of Important Events in Dian Fossey's Life

1932   Born in California

1949   Begins studies at Marin Junior College

1950   Begins pre-veterinary studies at the University of California, Davis

1954   Graduates from San Jose State College with a B.A. in occupational therapy

1956   Hired by Kosair Children's Hospital in Louisville, Kentucky
        Meets Henry family and Alexie Forrester

1963   Travels to Africa and meets Louis Leakey at Olduvai Gorge
        Hires a guide and travels to Zaire (Congo), where she sees mountain gorillas
        for the first time

1966   Meets with Leakey in Louisville and has her appendix removed to prove her
        resolve to him
        Travels to Congo with Leakey's blessing
        Captured by Congolese rebels
        Escapes to Uganda

1967   Meets Rosamond Carr
        Meets Frank Crigler
        Establishes Karisoke Research Station in Parc des Volcans, Rwanda

1968   Meets Bob Campbell of National Geographic Magazine

1969   Coco and Pucker arrive at Karisoke
        Forced to relinquish Coco and Pucker to zoo officials

1970   First recorded human contact with a gorilla, Peanuts
        Moves to England to complete doctorate at Cambridge University

1974   Awarded Ph.D in Zoology

1977   Meets and hires Amy Vedder and Bill Weber (V-W's) in Chicago
        Ambassador Frank and Betty Crigler arrive in Kigali
        Digit murdered by poachers on or around December 31, 1977

1978   Baby gorilla Mweza retrieved from Congo
        Mweza dies of infection and wounds
        Captures Batwa poacher Kanyarugano
        Digit Fund established
        Uncle Bert murdered by poachers
        Digit Fund rebuffed by the International Union for the Conservation of
        Nature
        Cindy's (dog) food contaminated by sumu
        Poacher Sebahutu, killer of Digit, captured in village

1979   Dian instates anti-poaching patrols
        Problems with V-W's intensify
        Sebahutu released
        Poacher Munyarukiko dies
        AWLF takes Digit Fund money and establishes the Mountain Gorilla
        Project, led by the Belgian national, Pierre von der Becke
        Bill Weber attacked by gorilla

1980   Dian resigns directorship of Karisoke and accepts an adjunct professorship at
        Cornell University, Ithaca, N.Y.
        Pet monkey, Kima, dies at camp in Dian's absence; she brings dog, Cindy,
        back to States with her
        Baby gorilla, Bonne Année (Charlie), is returned to the wild
        Robinson McIlvaine resigns as Secretary/Treasurer of Digit Fund
        IPPL takes over Digit Fund on temporary basis

1981   Karisoke is robbed, and hole is cut into wall of Dian's cabin

1982   Beloved dog, Cindy, dies in October

1983   Gorillas in the Mist published
        Researcher throws Dian's gun away in the forest (Walther PPK)
        Dian returns to Karisoke in June
        Emotional reunion with gorillas of Group Five

1984   Dian delivers Batwa baby at annual Christmas party. Baby is named Karisoke.

1985   Sebahutu captured again and released
        Nunkie dies
        Parrots poisoned
        Poacher Yavani Hategeka captured
        Visa renewed for two years
        Christmas party postponed until New Years Eve to accommodate visitors
        Murdered on December 26
        Dian buried in gorilla graveyard, alongside of Digit

1986   Gorillas in the Mist filmed at Karisoke

1990's Genocidal wars force closure of camp
        Forest reclaims Karisoke

Acknowledgments

I owe my biggest debt of gratitude to the spirit of Dian Fossey. She has been at my side throughout this process and has kept me honest as I tried desperately to find her voice.

The great Canadian author, Farley Mowat, graciously opened his archives to me when I told him that Dian Fossey was being vilified on the lecture circuit. Thankfully, Fossey's words are protected in the collection at McMaster University.

Rosamond Carr knew and loved Dian as only a friend could and allowed me to enter a world of treasured memories. I can never thank her enough.

Mrs. Carr's niece and co-author, Ann Howard Halsey, brought me to Mugongo where I stretched out on the floor of Dian's room and counted the beams in the ceiling. I wanted to see what Dian saw before she fell asleep at night.

Former United States Ambassador to Rwanda, Frank Crigler, heard Dian's voice in the early drafts of the manuscript and took the time to tell me so. As Dian's friend and confidant, he agreed with my own and Canadian author Farley Mowat's assessment of the true state of affairs in the "viper's nest" that was Karisoke.

Freya Manfred did the impossible with Dian's complicated narrative. Freya made the story whole.

Dr. Shirley McGreal helped immensely as I tried to sort out what happened to the original Digit Fund. I agree heartily with Dian Fossey's statement that there should be "more Shirley McGreal's in the world."

The staff members at the William Ready Division of Archives and Research Collections at McMaster University Library are congenial, helpful, and true guardians of Dian Fossey's legacy. Thank you, especially, to Renu Barrett, Adele Petrovic, Kathy Garay, Dr. Carl Spadoni, and Margaret Foley.

Dr. James King, Farley Mowat's biographer, took the time to have lunch with me at McMaster University and encouraged the pursuit of my "crazy idea."

Others have been near in spirit—constant friends and companions through creative times and again in hours when the mind feels empty: Al Cibuzar, Dr. Kathy Blake, Pam Perry, Anita Travica, Martha Brown, Sandy Carlson, Denise DeClue, Cheryl Debes, Sharon Nix, Nancy Smith, Pam Pruitt, Karin Baltzell,

PhD, Laura Rosecrance, Marjorie Nolan, Donna Meyer, Ken Perry, Deb Poole, and Charley Poole. I cannot thank them enough.

Thank you, Dr. Sian Evans, for introducing me to the owl monkeys and King. The owl monkeys see everything.

My husband, Brett, and daughter, Sarah, were understanding and allowed Dian and Digit to move in with us for over two years.

I must thank the new friends I have made in Rwanda, especially the new generation of guides and trackers at ORTPN, who now understand more than anyone what Nyiramacyibili wanted for Rwanda and the gorillas. Kivu Sun—thank you for your gracious hospitality.

Finally, there is my friend from far away who listens to my worries about the uncharted ocean and who will forever be my link to it all.

Preface

It was important to have this work reflect Dian Fossey's story as she wants it told. I use the present tense with good reason, and the reader will gain an understanding of this as Dian's story unfolds. In March of 2005, I returned from a pilgrimage to Dian's beloved research camp, Karisoke, which is located high in the saddle region between Mounts Karisimbi and Visoke in Rwanda. I can report that she and the gorillas are very much in evidence there. The beautifully twisted branches of ancient Hagenia trees are silent sentinels and witnesses to the life, love, and dedication that defined Dian Fossey's life.

For organizational purposes, Chapters One through Eleven include discussions between Dian and the gorillas as they, together, examine the implications of their brief time on earth. These imaginary discussions are drawn from Dian's writings and are referenced as endnotes when archival or research material is available. Any text that is italicized reflects a verbatim transcript from these materials. Chapters Twelve through Nineteen are a chronological recreation of the last years of Dian Fossey's life and draw heavily upon archival materials. I would suggest that the reader refer to *Woman in the Mists,* by Farley Mowat, as a companion reader. Mowat wrote what I consider to be the definitive biography, while this manuscript brings Dian's voice to the forefront and is written in the first person for that reason.

I would caution students of history to not rely upon this text as a historical document. However, it may be used as a starting point for research, since all numbered attributions made to Dian Fossey are based upon the historical record and can be located by referencing the endnotes. Any other "comments" made by Dian Fossey after her death flow from the author's imagination.

African traditions allow the belief that the dead are not dead. Indeed, they live on in spiritual form and protect their families that remain on earth. After visiting Karisoke in remote Rwanda, I believe that the spirit of Dian Fossey stands watch over her beloved gorillas. If one listens carefully, her voice is still whispering in African breezes that murmur in the leaves of ancient Hagenia trees.

Author's Introduction

I went to Rwanda to see Dian Fossey's gorillas and to visit her grave. It was imperative that I climb the muddy trail to Karisoke and see it all for myself. Dian Fossey got me into all of this. Her photo is smiling down at me, mockingly, from the place on the wall where I taped it over two years ago. Her left eyebrow is raised, a smile is plumping her cheeks, and I can almost hear her challenging me to even TRY to get it all down as well as she did.

"I spent eighteen years alone on the mountain," she is saying. "You were there for two weeks. Big deal."

She is definitely mocking me.

I want to argue with her and blast her insensitivity. "You have ruined my life, I cry to her. You have consumed me, I have fallen in love with your ghost and your gorillas, and now you mock me!"

When I taped Dian Fossey's photo next to the window that looks out upon the rising moon, I was inviting her ghost to provide inspiration for me. I have tried to find meaning and continuity in the always contradictory stories of her life that have surfaced in recent years. As I struggle now with my feelings about it all, the light of the full moon flickers across her photo just as it did on winter evenings over two years ago when I sat up night after night, fueled by coffee, sometimes staring at her face for hours, trying to find the right words to describe her legacy; trying to find the language that would allow her to, somehow, speak through me.

It is all but impossible to put words, thoughts, and emotions on paper regarding the mountain gorillas I visited in Rwanda's Virunga Mountains. Now I struggle to find my own voice and describe my brief encounter with the gorillas. How can you describe the light of a soul that shines through the eyes of a being so much like the human form, yet possesses a countenance that is far beyond the human experience? Fossey lived with them for eighteen years. I had little time to observe them, absorb their essence, and experience their world. I had a decision to make. Should I spend every minute taking photographs, the very act of which creates distance? I knew the lens observes, records, and captures the moment, but does not participate. A compromise was reached within the contradictory aspects of my own psyche, and I decided to shoot as many frames as fast as possible, not worrying about composition or bothersome technical details. That allowed precious minutes to center myself, breathe and become the watcher. In the end, I was never able to fully enter their world. I think that right was reserved for Dian Fossey alone.

"Now, you understand," her photo seems to say.

How much time has passed since I began this effort? In my mind I have been wandering with the gorillas, but there are still no definitive words about them on the paper. The moon is halfway across the sky, and the shadows have moved once again. It is hours since I began, and still no sentences appear. What are the gorillas doing now? It is mid-morning in their mountain home. Have they left the comfort of their night nests? Is mom picking celery, and are the twins tucked safely within her great arms? How many pounds of gallium vines has the silverback devoured by now? Are they moving, or content to linger near the nests? Is it raining, or is the sun breaking through the morning mists? Now I begin to remember. I wanted to linger near the nests. The trees, scenery, and even the rarified air felt familiar. It was as if I had come home, the one who never had any desire to travel to Africa—of all places! Home. Home with the mountain gorillas. Impossible. Was it some kind of primeval recognition, or genetic memories combined with the ancient mitochondria of pre-human ancestors? No, it was their eyes, burning with an ancient, universal light. As the ancient Buddhist saying goes, "…trust it, and merge with it." It is my own true nature. It is home, and it is forbidden.

Forbidden thoughts and unattainable desires are the gifts the gorillas gave to me. It is these things that propel the mind to consider reckless and impossible impulses as a real possibility. It is the power of the gorillas. Their presence is so compelling that one is willing to sacrifice all to be near them. Is this the definition of love, or madness? The silverback walked up to me, close enough that I could smell his breath. I dared not look into his eyes, but I had a compelling urge to follow as he turned away, one step from brushing up against me. I remember all of this as if looking through a tunnel. I am a ghost glancing back into the tomb. Every hour the memory is more difficult to access, but I must not; I cannot forget.

"Come with me to my mountain," she says.

"I want to, but I am afraid," I say.

"Coward."

She has thrown down the gauntlet. It is within my power to follow her, and it is the beginning of my own descent into madness and indescribable beauty. I know now why Dian Fossey lived with the gorillas, defended them, and died for them. I know if asked, I would sacrifice myself for her memory and for them.

—November 8, 2005

Prologue

"At least she can go back to where she was happiest, and that's the way it should be for all of us."[1]

My casket was covered with Gallium vines, yellow lilies, thistles, and a single red rose. I believe Rosamond Carr was responsible for the rose, but I am dead, not omniscient, and since I did not really observe who placed it there, I am not certain. The funereal arrangement of African flora was unusual but beautiful in its simplicity. My biographers have since insisted that the thistle was a representation of the gorillas' favorite food, but I suspected at the time it had a more sinister symbolism.

Digit crawled out of his mound to stand with me as I watched the somber faces. Rosamond couldn't find a Catholic priest willing to slog up the mountain, so the eulogy was delivered by the reluctant Reverend Elton Wallace. He gave a first-rate sermon, even though he was shaken that I was being buried with the gorillas. I was very appreciative of the ceremony, but I categorically did not agree with the Reverend's last statement that managed to link me with the Christ:

> "She will lie now among those with whom she lived, and among whom she died. And if you think that the distance the Christ had to come to take the likeness of man is not so great as that from man to gorilla, then you don't know men—or gorillas—or God."[2]

I, for one, got closer to the gorillas than God did to man. Theologians will have a fit that I am saying this, but what I do know is that God abandoned mankind, and I never, never, abandoned my gorillas. There were those who wanted to force me away from Karisoke, of course, and those who knew who murdered me blended into the group gathered at my grave. Their faces are in the photographs of the funeral if you want to go to the libraries and see for yourself.

People have said that I did not have any friends, but I know for certain that Rosamond Carr was one of those who loved me. My life did not always allow

1

time for recognition of the steadfast love that Rosamond held for me. As she stared at my wooden coffin, I tried to tell her that she shouldn't have made the three-mile climb up the slippery trails to Karisoke. She was seventy-three, and it was far too difficult a climb for someone her age. Of course she couldn't hear me, but I think she felt my whisper, because she kept brushing her silver hair away from her ear as the Reverend Wallace prayed. Some of my enemies had the audacity to stand beside Rosamond at my grave, hiding their satisfaction behind sober faces. Their righteousness was energized with the assertion that Dian Fossey got what she deserved. The witch of the Virungas was finally vanquished by her own sumu.[3]

The duty officer from the American Embassy in Kigali managed to get her Toyota up the rutted path. It wouldn't have killed her to give Rosamond a lift. I suppose the official was still disgusted that she was forced to trek up the mountain to identify my body after the murderer slashed my face with the machete. It was her bad luck to be on duty over the Christmas holiday, but she was a smart cookie to notice the hairs I was clutching in my fists. The investigator at the scene said that the hairs were European and not African. Too bad that the FBI and French labs could not agree on the analysis.

The dead gorillas, Macho, Uncle Bert, Kweli, and Nunkie were romping through the group, and Uncle Bert actually jumped up and down on my plywood coffin for a bit. The Reverend was thrown off track in the final throes of his eulogy when some of the thistles fell into the hole in the ground. Uncle Bert scrambled down after them while his baby, Kweli, started hooting and chest pounding. Macho was poking and prodding at my former student, Amy Vedder, and seemed perplexed that she gave no response.

Rosamond said that after the rope began to tighten around my casket, she couldn't take it anymore and left the grave, walking unsteadily toward the meadow near my locked cabin. As she was standing there, wiping the tears from her eyes, she saw the big old bushbuck that I used to watch from my window. She said she was surprised that he had come so near.[4] If Rosamond had been able to see through the veil separating the living from the dead, she would have glimpsed me beside the old creature as I waved farewell to her.

Before I died, I never realized that gorillas dream just as humans do. Death has allowed Digit and I to visit one another's dreams and communicate in a manner that has enabled both of us to come to terms with our violent deaths. I am no longer alone in my nightmares, since Digit is forever and steadfastly present, often cradling me as I tremble in the aftermath of old memories. Digit alone understands that my violent death will continue to defile my dreams until I either accept my fate or find the hand of God in my existence. We have spent the twenty years since my death walking the paths of Karisoke with the other gorillas. Kweli and Macho enjoy rattling the Hagenia tree adjacent to my grave. This spooks tourists and researchers alike, but it is good fun for the gorillas, so I do not ask them to stop.

Digit often asks me to remember the speech I gave about the thistle plant during one of the Leakey Foundation tours. He has become a kind of counselor for me in the afterlife, mirroring my emotions just as I attempted to compassionately understand the gorillas' experiences in my research. Going back to those days is not easy with a fragmented spirit, and I often resist, but Digit in his wise way gently takes my hand just as he did while we were both alive. When I am calm in spirit, I hear my own words echoing through the mists.

"The thistle plant is one neither you nor I would care to touch, but in fact, it forms an important staple in the gorilla diet. With all its pricks and spines the gorillas' hands seem impervious to the same."[5]

Digit seems pleased as I recite the words long ago lost to the entity called human memory, which is so often a distortion of events reorganized to suit individual perceptions. During one of our "conversations," he lumbered off on his knuckles, and then stopped to pick and strip a stalk of wild celery to share with me while my damaged memory recalled the parables shared with my old friend, Father Raymond.[6] Digit was listening to what amounted to a parable! The Parable of the Thistles! As monstrous a plant as it is, the thistle plays an essential role in the gorillas' feeding routine. The adults learn to deftly peel the leaf from the central stem, and the young learn the hard way, and with some apprehension, to employ considerable caution as they strip the plant. The gorillas assign no judgment to the thistle plant. Digit told me that as far as the gorillas are concerned, the thistle plant is neither here nor there. They don't really think of it in any way except as a source of nourishment, preferring different parts of the plant in different seasons. The young learn to be cautious as casually as they learn to climb a bamboo plant.

"So, what is the moral of the tale, old man?" I asked.

Now understand that Digit does not "speak" in a way that you might understand. Our thoughts flow freely, and during those brief moments of clarity, I can feel the injured pathways of interrupted memories, thoughts, and feelings leading me toward an understanding of my life—an understanding that thus far has been elusive.

Digit "replied" that morality is a human concept. Evil men and organized theocracies created the concept in order to provide the gray, ambiguous areas that permit everything ranging from thoughtlessness to atrocity. A God did not invent morality, he said, humankind did.

"Then there is a God?"

Digit went back to his celery stalk and said that if it made me feel better there could be, although the gorillas had been looking for a sign for millions of years and had found none. For a while they thought that man was God until the poachers starting severing the silverbacks' hands for ashtrays. Even though I am very angry about this and want vengeance, Digit does not think it is in my best interest to continue haunting the dreams of my enemies and suggests that I stop immediately.

I tell him I don't see any difference between an innocent haunting and the gorillas scaring the tourists gathered in my graveyard, but he replies that the gorillas don't do it out of vengeance. They just like playing there.

I know now that every experience and decision, road taken, or not, have determined my destiny. Just as the mountain gorillas have evolved in the shadows of Mount Visoke and throughout the Virungas for millions of years, so have the billions of moments that shaped my life brought me here to this moment of reflection and mental evolution. Perhaps my death has allowed me to "live" and reflect in a manner that corporeal existence did not.

Digit recommended that I tell my story in my own words. There are many who go to the lectures, hear the lies about me, and do not believe them. They are hungry for the truth, but not knowing where to find proof, they are afraid to defend me. Digit says I have the ability to end the lies once and for all and to heal my spirit at the same time. The only way to accomplish this is to go back to the beginning and reveal truths that have been long-buried by fear, ambition, and greed. Twenty years have passed since my murder, but if you look you will find me. I am still here. I am not hidden, but I am broken. I want to be put back together. I want to be whole in spirit. I am not a fragment in a movie or novel. I want to reclaim my existence from the researchers, scientists, foundations, biographers, screenwriters and novelists who have used my memory and reassembled my life to suit their own needs.

1

The Family Group

My father's heart was my birthright, and I lost it when I was six years old. I was trying to explain this to Digit as we sprawled in the grassy glade just to the south of my old cabin and the gorilla graveyard that contains both of our tombs. The rest of the group had left us alone for the afternoon in favor of a romp in the rolling bamboo hills along the slopes of Mount Visoke.

I rested my head in the old silverback's lap, just as I did on the day many years ago when he made his first contact by putting his arm around my shoulder, patting my head, and snuggling next to me in the wet jungle foliage. During our first close encounter I was trying to get a photograph of the injuries he sustained while acting as a sentry for his family group. The neck wound he received as a result of the violent encounter with another gorilla group had become severely infected, and I wanted to get a better look at it.

Digit was wondering what this memory of our first encounter had to do with the memories I had of my absent father, since the gorillas have no concept of parental abandonment. I told him that during the first ten years of my study I felt I was an intruder into the gorilla world. For the first few years, Digit's family group would flee when they saw me. This was a common response with all of the groups. I was a complete outsider, someone not to be trusted with access to gorilla society.

Digit replied that he was sorry and so were all of the gorillas, but the reaction was understandable considering that they had only met poachers and hunters before I came along. At the turn of the twentieth century, a white hunter penetrated the seclusion of the Virungas. The gorillas did not realize the meaning of this attention and ran into the meadows to greet the hunter. As they gathered closer to the man, he raised his rifle and murdered the lead silverback. Shrieking and crying, the remnants of the group vanished into the mists.

"So, tell me about your father," he said, picking up a thistle plant and carefully stripping the leaves to get to the heart of the plant.

Even though Digit was the first gorilla to completely accept me in the wild, and I trusted him wholly and absolutely, his question hit a nerve. I felt the painful slash of the panga across my face as vividly as if I were experiencing my murder for the first time. So, I angrily left the comfort of his lap and started back to my cabin. Digit made no move to follow and released that terrible musty odor the gorillas exude when they are frightened or agitated. The scent is a mixture of sweat, urine, and fresh manure. I instinctively scanned the woodland fringes of the research center for the source of Digit's fear and apprehension, but of course there was nothing that could harm us now. We were already buried in the mounds next to my cabin.

Then, I realized with complete clarity and understanding that Digit was using the ancient means of gorilla communication with me. He was "vocalizing" my own fears through the release of the odor of fear, thereby reflecting my anxieties as a warning to me. I could take the opportunity to face these anxieties while he was there to protect me from my memories, just as he had protected his family from poachers during the years of our first encounters. Or, I could skulk off to my mound and rattle the Hagenia and Hypericum trees while scaring a few tourists. I took the path of comfort and returned to Digit's side to continue the kind of free mental association that he was encouraging in me. My father was the first person who came to mind.

The archivists have a wonderful picture of George Fossey, resplendent in his naval uniform. He is swaggering towards the camera, and he appears confident and happy. This photo is often included in the collections about me, but what no one knows is that it was not any particular image of my father which I remembered—not as a three-year-old child, and not as a grown woman. I was most comforted by the SMELL of him, part spice and part liquor, which transcended any fears or apprehensions I experienced as a result of my parents' divorce. In fact, in later years, the smell of alcohol so reminded me of him that I am certain the experience led to my own on-again, off-again, affair with the bottle. This addiction was conceived in the sorrow I felt when his name was not allowed to be mentioned after my mother married Richard Price. In a way, you could say that my father's memory was murdered.

The books and articles written about me make a great deal of the fact that my goldfish died when I was a child, and I was not allowed to get another. It is true that I wailed and wept and even mentioned this event in my diaries, but it wasn't the goldfish that I missed. I missed the opportunity to have intimate contact with something that depended upon me for love and nourishment. The goldfish rewarded me with recognition and excitement as I approached his aquatic globe with morsels of food every morning and evening. That he loved me, I was certain.

Now, when you give your heart to an animal, be it a rat, a goose, a rabbit, a horse, a cat, a monkey or a dog, some day, usually before you yourself die, that beloved animal is going to die. I don't know if there is any way you can prepare yourself for the eventual severance.[7] I was a parent, protector, and kin to that goldfish, just as I became parent and protector to the gorilla groups in my care as a scientist and active conservationist. I think early childhood experiences led to my theory about active conservation and the care and preservation of my gorillas. Unfortunately my deep convictions about animal sentience and the importance of behavioral studies caused the scientific community to attach the dreaded label of anthropomorphism to my work. The consequences of our professional and personal disagreements would ultimately bend the fabric of my universe.

It is also true that Richard Price did not allow me to eat meals with the family until I was ten years old. This did not wound me half as much as the denial of my real father's existence within my family group. I rather enjoyed the solitary meals with our housekeeper, since I did not have much to say to the adults in my family group in any case. My mother and Richard Price paid for horseback riding lessons that sustained me through adolescence and gave me the first opportunity to develop trust with a large animal. Equine and primate communications are quite different, though. Having evolved as an animal of prey, the horse is not capable of the complete surrender to humans that I have experienced in my gorilla families.

Digit continued to listen and began to "groom" my hair as I looked into his eyes. I could see my own reflection in his pupils and for the first time did not feel ugly. Throughout my life I had felt too tall at over six feet, wanting to be blonde instead of brunette, and considering myself to be hopelessly ugly.

Digit snorted at this revelation and discontinued grooming me. He reminded me that gorillas differ in countenance as much as humans do, but no value is assigned to this variation because gorillas regard human characterizations of beauty as extraneous. Stature and respect within the community and family group depend upon strength, intelligence, and loyalty to the family structure—as well as the ability to hold the group together in the face of danger, whether from within or without the population. Digit reminded me of the time Bob Campbell from *National Geographic* was photographing me with Group Eight[8] and was concerned about my bedraggled appearance. The gorillas were in close proximity, especially the young blackback, Peanuts,[9] but Campbell was complaining the whole time about how untidy I looked. He said that the audience for the magazine did not want pictures of a tired hag; they wanted a glamorous Dian Fossey. During this encounter, Peanuts reached out and actually touched me, which was the first time physical contact was ever recorded between a gorilla and a human. I was ecstatic. At that time glamour was the least of my worries, since I would soon undergo a botched abortion, an unfortunate and heart-breaking consequence of my romance with Campbell. In addition, my teeth were decaying due to a poor diet and lack of proper dental care. *National Geographic* had been late with my research grant, so I had been unable to return to the States. As my teeth fell out, I had taken to preserving the gold fillings in specimen bags, hoping that a dentist somewhere would find the creativity to re-utilize them. I had so many abscesses that I was forced to lance my jaw with a certain macabre regularity. Peanuts gave me a gift of acceptance that for the moment made me forget the pain, suffering, and psychic abuse that filled my existence.

Digit shook his head and growled at this recollection. He said he remembered it well and that the gorillas were perplexed that Campbell, whom they knew had impregnated me, was not more solicitous. As the silverback of the human group to which I belonged, and as my mate, Campbell had failed in his evolutionary duty to his family group because he failed to protect his line. Within the gorilla group, a male will kill the infant of a female if her mate is absent or neglectful. This will immediately bring on another estrus and the newly dominant male will impregnate her again to ensure that his genes and not those of the failed male will continue. The deposed male will suffer humiliation and immediate loss of stature within the group, and other relationships will be strained as well, until all is sorted out.

I realized that the gorillas were performing for me as a silent way of offering comfort and support. The gorillas understood more than any of my friends, colleagues, benefactors, and admirers that some members of the human race had failed me. I had been deeply hurt and abandoned by almost every man in my life. If the gorillas could have vocalized in a manner that was comprehensible to me when I was alive, they would have invited me to join their own family unit. Many researchers and academics will deny it, but the truth remains that although mankind may ultimately supplant the gorilla and erase the last of them from the Virungas, gorilla social organization is superior to human society in the most fundamental of ways. These realizations deepened my anxiety, and memories surfaced that were far too painful to revisit. I left Digit to his meal of wild celery and thistle and took a long walk past the camp stream and into my favorite meadow. Mount Visoke formed a magnificent backdrop as I found a comfortable spot near the stream and allowed the melody of rushing waters to drown out all unpleasant thoughts.

The skies had been somewhat overcast and gloomy during my period of solitary reflection, but the sun had finally broken through when I spotted Digit nearby, grubbing for worms and beetles in a decaying Hagenia tree. He kept about his project until I vocalized a soft grunt, and then he knuckle-walked his four hundred pound bulk silently through the grasses and vines, approaching me as I lay face down upon the ground. It was this impassive, vulnerable position that had gained me access to the gorillas during the first years of my study.

Digit did not vocalize or even attempt to groom me. Instead, he gave me a familiar pat on the head and took off down the trail toward the bamboo forests. He was moving quickly when suddenly he stopped, spun, and sat to face me. He crossed his huge arms and stared at me. I felt disconcerted by this behavior until I realized he was recreating the photograph on the posters for the tourism campaign begun by the Rwandan park conservator. Bob Campbell had originally taken the photo for *National Geographic*. I was furious at the time that Digit's magnificent image had been purloined by the park conservator to attract people to the Virungas. This was the last thing the gorillas needed.

"Digit, what are you saying?" I complained.

"What do *you* think I am saying, *Nyiramacyibili?*"[10]

This was extraordinary! Digit was vocalizing in English and Kinyarwandan! There was certainly no doubt that I was hearing him speak.

"Why are you calling me by that name, Digit?"

"It was what you wanted to be called after you were put into the earth," he said. "The woman who lives alone on the mountain." Digit rolled over onto his back and invited me to play the belly scratching game we invented for the photographers.

Nyiramacyibili. I still love the sound of it. The Africans gave me that name and I was always very proud of it. To me, it signified my deep connections with not only the gorillas but the African continent as well.

"Digit, some of my biographers have gotten it all wrong and say that my marker is misspelled[11] and that the play on words describes me as a small woman who runs fast. It is humiliating to be described in that manner, since I have always been sensitive about my physical appearance."

"Why does this concern you?"

"I wanted a reference that tied me to the Africans and the gorillas forever. I was the woman who lived alone on the mountain and proud of it. My friends made a beautiful marker, and I rather like to admire it at times."

"Some humans prefer the story that your tribute is a mockery. Why? If it is false, why do humans want to repeat this?"

"Maybe my enemies still feel the need to establish power over me. I honestly don't know. I do know that Rosamond was determined to give my grave a proper marker. She was appalled that my grave had been left unattended and concerned that the gravesite was completely overgrown."[12]

"Your friends did not want you to be alone in your death. When they wrote your name, it gave them some comfort that you would be remembered."

"I was very happy with the words they wrote. It says that 'no one loved gorillas more, so rest in peace dear friend, eternally protected in this sacred ground, for you are home where you belong.'"

Digit rolled over on his elbows and stared me straight in the eyes.

"Do you feel at home here, or do you still feel alone, Nyiramacyibili?"

In life I was certainly alone. My passionate desire to protect the gorillas had fueled professional jealousies, political ambitions, and powerful debates within academic and international circles. Even the deep love of my friends could not save me from the lies and innuendoes that still lurk around my grave, for I had enemies who were sick-minded enough to make fun of my tombstone.

Suddenly, I experienced, rather than remembered, the moments after my murder. I was floating above my body, which was lying on the floor of my old cabin. My left arm was flung across my chest. My right arm was under the bed, and my head was under the bookcase. I was wearing long johns that were tucked into my socks and a warm pullover pajama top that was soaked with my blood. It reminded me of the ratty old sweatshirt I wore when I was nursing Coco and Pucker back to health just two years into the beginning of my time on the mountain. The covers were partially pulled from the mattress, but the vase of wildflowers I had picked was untouched and still exuded the sweet scents of the meadow. But it was the memory of my life in the cabin that made me see that the afterlife holds not only dreams but also tears. The impossible recollection of the beauty of it all made me weep. The devotion of my beloved pets, the love of my friends, the affection of the Africans, the quiet beauty of the forest and, of course the trust of the gorillas, were gifts at once rare, unexpected and undeniably treasured.

My face was wet with tears evoked by these exquisite memories when I felt the comforting arm of Digit once again about my shoulders in his familiar gesture. His huge face peered into mine, and I was just about to smile at his hopelessly odd heart-shaped nose when two black furry balls came barreling out of the woods. My beloved Coco and Pucker! Coco scrambled up and over my back, wrapping fuzzy arms around my neck in a simian version of piggyback. It was not really a reunion; it was as if no time had passed. They were robust, healthy, and wanting to play, play, play. Coco held tightly to my shoulders, and Pucker romped behind as the four of us wandered through the grassy glade. I had last seen Coco and Pucker when I cried goodbye to them before the authorities forced me to nail them into the crates for their journey to the Cologne zoo.

Two years into my study of gorillas the corrupt park conservator was bribed by a collector for the Cologne zoo to ensure the safe passage of two baby gorillas. Ten adult gorillas were slaughtered so that the babies could be captured. Malnourished, and with limbs infected as a consequence of the wire snares used to restrain them, the babies were near death when the official came to me and demanded that I save them. I resolved to try, although it appeared to be hopeless. I rounded up antibiotics, ointments and formula, asked my African staff to create a jungle environment within the walls of my cabin, and set about building nesting boxes for the two. I determined that they must be siblings because of the similar webbings on their feet. Surprisingly, Coco and Pucker Poo insisted on cuddling with me as they would have in their true parents' nests. Every morning I awoke covered in gorilla dung and slobber. My cook quit in a huff, saying that he was a cook for Europeans, not animals. The rest of my staff was in open rebellion at my constant demands that they fetch suitable food from the mountainside and assist with the dung clean up in the morning. I soon realized that I was being afforded the perfect opportunity to learn about gorilla grooming practices, vocalizations, and family life. Thanks to Coco and Pucker I came to understand the gorillas' need for love and affection and the desire of young gorillas to constantly play. In three months my study was greatly advanced, and I became part of a family unit, since the young gorillas looked to me as any child would look to its mother.

I feel that Coco and Pucker might well have died while in my care if it had it not been for the ministrations and constant love of my dog, Cindy. She gave herself totally to them, and despite their fear of dogs, as they knew them only from poachers, Cindy brought them to life. Coco, especially, took delight in riding Cindy piggyback style and chasing her in endless circles until they both collapsed dizzily in an exhausted heap of tawny and black-haired bodies.[13] During this time of rehabilitation, I wrote excitedly to Louis Leakey, and he arranged to have *National Geographic* sponsor Bob Campbell's first trip to Karisoke. Campbell filmed and photographed Coco and Pucker, which led to a cover story[14] and enormous publicity for my research. This exposure greatly enhanced my reputation and stature within the budding worldwide environmentalist community. But when Rwandan authorities forcibly took the babies from me, the entire series of events ended in tragedy. All along I had been under the impression that I would be allowed to return the babies to the wild, but this was not to be. In my recorded speeches about this event you can hear me saying that my parting from Coco and Pucker was "maudlin."[15] In reality, it was a dagger to my heart. The bitter bile that rose to my throat as I nailed shut the cover of the crate holding my trusting charges remained with me for the rest of my life, forever fueling my desire to protect the gorillas from any further human encroachment. Coco and Pucker died in captivity eight years later, within days of each other. The official necropsy reports indicated that both died of infections and shock,[16] but I knew that they had died of broken hearts. I came to believe passionately that the rights of the animal must always supersede human interests. I believe this principle extends even to the methods and observational techniques of the scientific observer.[17]

I was beginning to understand that I was never truly alone on the mountain. I had my gorilla family. I turned to express this thought to Digit when, suddenly, Coco began vocalizing excitedly, and my old dog Cindy came bounding across the meadow. I knelt down and took her big old head in my hands as she eagerly slobbered all over my face, lapping at the tears that streamed down my cheeks. She nourished me once again with her ever-wagging stump and her continuous gifts of joy, love and total unselfishness.[18]

"How did you ever find them, Digit? And, why?"

"They never left you, but you could not see. I show you this because you are ready now, and because you are our family, *Nyiramacyibili*."

2

Forming Bonds

While Digit's extraordinary gift—bringing Coco and Pucker to greet me—brought me great happiness, I soon found myself once again anxious that my violent death would leave me forever without a sense of association and union with my earthly accomplishments. Bits of energy and even my DNA permeated the soil and surroundings at Karisoke. My blood-soaked mattress remained unattended for years after my murder, and the floorboards absorbed what remained of the fluids that once flowed through my veins.[19] By revisiting the scene of my death, I find that with an act of straightforward will I can transcend time and space to revisit any memory I choose. I can examine the fragile emotional bonds of my previous existence with great detachment.

I will begin by attempting to organize a continuum of my life, using the same techniques I employed while organizing my data on the "family trees" of the gorilla groups I studied. This early data, or map, was crucial to my understanding of genealogy and group movement. During my life I was always very good at the "soft" sciences of biology, psychology, and social studies, while the hard sciences escaped me and led to my abbreviated stint in veterinary school. My eventual work with handicapped children was a consequence of these earlier academic failures. Not many people know that I did not excel in my sophomore year at the University of California at Davis where I was enrolled as a preveterinary student. Chemistry and physics were my undoing. This apparent failure as a hard scientist preoccupied portions of my life and led to great insecurity when I was later challenged by formally trained primatologists who wanted to usurp Karisoke. I was mocked continually regarding my behavioral studies by scientists who would rather count the number of insects crawling on a bamboo stalk than spend time sitting with the gorillas and observing their social structures. For students in search of the almighty doctorate, it was all about the collection of data, which in turn leads to reams of charts, diagrams and spreadsheets.

That is not to say that the hard sciences did not have a valued place in my career. I completed volumes of reports on the acoustics of gorilla vocalizations, necropsy examinations, parasitology, birth and death rates, and social interactions. I published all of it and earned my own doctorate from Cambridge as well. However, despite all of my work, I was still viewed as an amateur by a growing number of primatologists. Ironically, my habituation of the gorillas and discovery of their intricate social organizations made all subsequent scientific work with the mountain gorilla possible.

One day I wandered through the meadow adjacent to the old cabin site and saw with some pleasure that the calla lilies I had planted long before my death had multiplied around the perimeter. The bulbs were a gift from Rosamond Carr, who ran a flower plantation at the base of the mountain. The beauty of the blooms made me long for her company, so I decided to visit the orphanage she now runs in Gisenyi for children victimized by the wars that raged in Rwanda. Her old plantation, Mugongo, was overrun, looted and destroyed during the wars. Rosamond is still energetic, focused and dedicated at ninety-three. She did not know I was "visiting" when I overheard her tell a writer that the stories about me being a hermit were a "complete fabrication." Every few years there seems to be renewed interest in the circumstances of my life and death, since my murder has officially remained unsolved. There is a well-worn path to Rosamond's door, although she has expressed some apprehension that her reminiscences about me have been distorted. She worries about this, and I wish I could reassure her that it seems to be my fate both in life and death to be misunderstood.

The reporter was asking the requisite questions about my tendencies to be what others perceived as a loner. Rosamond was going to great lengths to explain to the writer that I was often the life of the party at the American Embassy. This was true. I found great enjoyment with my friends there, Ambassador Frank Crigler, his wife, Bettie, and their children. Rosamond's friendship was a gift, solace, and inspiration for me to continue my work, even though she did not approve of my ideas about active conservation. I was happy to hear her relate these things, and grateful that she held me within her memory in that manner, since it is, after all, memory which forms the framework of existence. I knew that my early relationships with my father and mother were broken soon after they were formed, but Rosamond could not possibly know that these damaged attachments would intensify my internal sense of isolation after Digit's death.

My mother, Kitty Fossey Price, unwittingly helped to form my negative self-image. She was a beautiful model, well known in San Francisco social circles. While she never overtly criticized my appearance, she seemed excessively fretful about my height, since at a very young age I was taller than both my mother and stepfather—over six feet tall at the age of fourteen. I was taken to a succession of doctors who reassured my mother that I was just tall, but in the mid-1940's height was not in fashion for young girls, and my mother's apprehension was contagious. I soon began to overanalyze all aspects of my appearance and refused all compliments, since in my heart I believed that I was in some way freakish. My sorority sisters tried to reassure me that my bone structure was a beautiful contrast to my height, but the seeds of self-revulsion were already sown. In addition, I could never decipher my mother's internal feelings towards me. I would hope that she loved me in the well-worn cliché of her "own way." In my later years, I always made time in my schedule to visit with her in California, although I did not look forward to visits with my stepfather, Richard Price.

My mother maintained, even after my death, that I adored my stepfather, but this is simply not true. In many ways Richard Price acted as a dominant silverback does when he steals a mate. His refusal to acknowledge me with either affection or interest killed a portion of my spirit as deftly as a male gorilla murders a new mate's offspring who does not carry his genetic code. I observed this several times in my research, most notably when Nunkie, an aged silverback, took three females from Group Four, killing an infant in the process. This knowledge of gorilla behavior distressed me greatly because it shattered the image I had formed of them as gentle, non-aggressive creatures. In the same way, I now realize that I was a compromised and conflicted child. The conflicting aspects of my own personality have caused much consternation among my friends and much fodder for the machinations of my enemies.

After my college difficulties with science, it became obvious that I must entertain the possibility of a career that was more oriented towards the liberal arts. I graduated with a degree in occupational therapy and was fortunate to secure a job at the Kosair Children's Hospital in Louisville, Kentucky. Here I became good friends with Mary Henry and was introduced to the entire Henry clan. Gaynee Henry, the matriarch of the group, fascinated me to the extent that I was more than happy to consider myself an adopted member of what I viewed as an extraordinary extended family. In one of my articles for *National Geographic* I described an amoeba-like map that charted the movements and family interactions of the gorilla groups as they roamed the slopes and saddle between Mount Visoke and Mount Karisimbi.[20] My association with the Henrys was the beginning of my life map, as it were, and the seeds of new associations had been sown and sprouted. I was alone and searching for the family group that would nourish me, protect me, and ensure my survival. The Henrys were that group. They were bold, rambunctious and unlike any family I had ever known. Their home life consisted of a circus-like atmosphere of festive gatherings, fascinating conversation, and typical Irish revelry. Gaynee was never one to stand on pretense, even though the family was part of Louisville "high" society.

In the world of the gorilla, transfers between family groups were the result of simple population dynamics. Understanding the *reasons* for gorilla movement has always been a major goal of mine, one that I expressed at many times in my writings and lectures. Gorillas would never struggle seriously over food, but they fight, sometimes to the death, in order to maintain the cohesion of the group. I think that I recognized this trait in Gaynee Henry, and I longed to be part of her protective mantle. The observations I made of her role as family matriarch carried over in subtle ways when I was studying my gorillas. I was her adopted daughter and she proudly claimed me as her own. When I finally received the go ahead from Louis Leakey to begin my studies of the mountain gorilla in Africa, it was the seventy-seven year old Gaynee who insisted that she, and she alone, would accompany me on my final cross country drive to California. The old Saab's cooling system broke down somewhere in the Great Plains, and we had to keep the heater on to prevent the radiator from boiling over. We had a wonderful time and laughed our way across the countryside.[21] Gaynee was my closest friend and cohort during my time in Louisville. She was everything to me that my own mother had not been. She introduced me to Catholicism through the renegade Irish monk, Father Raymond. Father Raymond provided the attention of a man who viewed me as an equal intellect. He challenged my beliefs and perceptions to the extent that, in order to seal my relationship with him and the Henrys, I converted to Catholicism. My conversion was a kind of spiritual marriage and commitment to those who had introduced me to a new worldview. I will be whoever you want Dian Fossey to be.

As I thought about my own transfer from family group to family group, I missed Gaynee and the rest of the clan and began to long for Digit. How could I continue this journey through my memories without him? I recalled having the same overwhelming feeling of sadness, fear, and isolation when Ian Redmond ran down the mountain and told me of Digit's murder. Ian noted at the time that he was surprised at my quiet response to the news. My devastation was apparent, but some sort of steely resolve took over as I immediately began writing letters to every conservation group and political organization I could think of, expressing my outrage at what had happened to my beloved Digit. Ian could not see that I was suffering a kind of internal death—bereavement brought on by complete despair that my best friend was gone and my life's work was bearing no fruit whatsoever. I also harbored the secret fear that it was the poachers' hatred of me that resulted in Digit being singled out as a target. I once confided this fear to Amy Vedder, a student researcher who appeared at Karisoke shortly before Digit's death. I had no way of knowing at the time that she would soon begin a political campaign to discredit me and my work in her attempt to gain control of Karisoke for a group that wanted to exploit the gorillas for tourism. Vedder was one of many enemies who would compete viciously for access to my gorilla groups, and her concerted effort at character assassination continues even after my death.[22] My immediate family is dead, and there is no one left willing to defend me.

There is a photo of me in one of the collections that speaks volumes about my fascination and association with the Henry family. I am sitting on a floral tufted chair in the living room of the Henry household. It was dubbed the "Henry Hotel" because of the constant flow of Louisville society, friends, and confidants of the family that filtered in and out. Mary's poodle has an expression of ecstasy on its face as I am busy scratching away at its chest, trying to look elegant and sophisticated, while balancing a lit cigarette in my right hand.

As I focus upon that moment, the clarity of the memory becomes reality. I taste the cigarette and feel the warm breath of Mary's dog on my hand. The smoke was already beginning to eat away at my lung tissue, an antecedent of the lung disease that would later plague my years on Mount Visoke, and the dog was providing a kind of grounding for me as I straddled the worlds of the living and the dead. I was never comfortable in social situations. I could put up a good front, but the part of me that felt freakish was constantly on guard. If the dog accepted me, I hoped that the others in the room would do the same. I remember now, that at that particular moment in my past existence, I had felt a peculiar "out of body" experience. This occurred from time to time throughout my life and it was quite frightening.

How I longed to be accepted into that family! As I view my former "self," I find myself yearning to comfort the young woman who was feeling too tall, too ugly, too uneducated, and too unsophisticated to fit in. The young woman in the linen dress was terrified of rejection and was compensating with a show of sophisticated bravado. If only one could learn to become a mother to one's self! As I watch the scene, it is obvious that the Henry family adores me, but I don't think I ever truly believed the extent of their devotion. In my own eyes I would always be defective. But I gained an important skill in those early years. By imitating the mannerisms, accepting the mores, and adopting the social affectations of the Henry "group," I was able to achieve complete acceptance within their world. I would unwittingly use this adaptation technique on the fog-ridden slopes of the Virungas in order to gain the trust and acceptance of my gorilla groups. I gained entrée into Digit's family by comforting the patriarch silverback, Uncle Bert, with imitation. If Bert scratched, I scratched. If the group peeled celery stalks, I copied the behavior. If the group vocalized, I vocalized. What was lauded as my superior scientific instinct in the movies and newsreels made about me in the early years of my studies was really learned behavior on my part. A component of my survival mechanism was the ability to imitate those from whom I craved acceptance. In scientific circles, it became known as "habituation." Jane Goodall had used the process in her work with the chimpanzees. To me, it was nothing more than common sense. I had used it, unconsciously, as a protective social technique throughout my life.

By the time I became involved with my research in Africa, I had developed a persona that would keep my student researchers at a comfortable distance, while at the same time allowing the force of my personality to enthrall them. Getting drunk with them was often the perfect way to introduce the reckless side of Fossey. In inebriated moments, I would carry on that Father Raymond had been my lover, but that is irrelevant except to the male biographers who have an unfortunate fixation upon my sex life. I always maintained that sex and love were not the same thing and managed to keep that compartmentalization. My sole purpose during these rantings and ravings was to shock people. I also used this technique on the lecture circuit to enhance my eccentric image. My lecture audiences loved it when I used the term "round the bend" to describe what the rest of us at Karisoke called "going bushy." I told the story of one exceptional day when it seemed everyone at camp was at one another's throats. I was angry at the men for smoking up the house with their fires and gave them hell all day long. I was so upset that I fired the tracker Semitoa for being late with the morning fire. We were all mad at each other for the remainder of the day, and I finally relieved my stress by yodeling[23] far into the night. I wanted to guarantee that I would not be placed on a pedestal because of my scientific work. I wanted to expose my faults on my own terms, before anyone could discover my flaws through scrutiny. The simple and direct explanation is that I was manipulative.

Gaynee's daughter, Mary Henry[24], remained my friend and champion until my death. She has since steadfastly refuted charges brought by my safari leader and others that I had become some sort of a sexual predator in the wilds of Africa. In fact I brought my first suitor, Alexie Forrester, to win Gaynee's approval. Alexie was a rugged plantation heir and perfectly fit the description of the type of man I should marry in Louisville society. Most significantly, he was taller than I.

Since Alexie and Mary Henry were the catalysts that instigated my love affair with Africa, it is ironic that my obsession with Africa proved to be the force that would ultimately break my fragile bonds with the human group that I had labored for so long to join. I left the Gaynee family and broke off my engagement with Alexie in order to pursue the romance of Africa.

I wanted badly to go to Africa after hearing Mary's exciting accounts of the romance of the place, and I mortgaged my salary in order to raise the funds. After I met Louis Leakey at Olduvai Gorge, and miraculously managed to sprain my ankle so that in later years he would have a dramatic reference point with which to remember me, he become my benefactor, my mentor, and my intimate companion. He provided the opportunity for me to begin my life's journey in earnest, and I again formed another intimate bond that I would be forced to break. He was a warm and vital personality, immersed in his own work, aware of the minutes passing, and his boundless curiosity, enthusiasm, and eventual support made my long-term study possible. Louis's intrinsic quest for knowledge served as a constant stimulus for my research. Also, we held in common a basic optimism that everything would work out one way or the other. I believe he was a different type of man to everyone who came to know him: argumentative and perhaps even impetuous to some of his colleagues, stubborn with his family, tender with young children, and affable and personable with young people seeking to follow in his footsteps.[25]

So at the age of 32, with Leakey's help and encouragement, I fulfilled my destiny and established the research camp at Karisoke, deep in the forests of the mist-shrouded Virunga Mountains. I was an adult woman who had freed herself from the bonds of an impending engagement to pursue what had been a lifelong dream. I entered this phase of my life with several foundation grants and the determination to learn more about the mysterious giant apes that inhabited the mountain forests. What I did not know at the time was that I was seriously lacking in the emotional skills necessary to navigate a foreign culture. I had not had the benefit of family bonding that would imbue my psyche with the skills necessary to navigate the emotional and political landscape that lay before me. The rock-solid foundation of unconditional mother love and approval from a father figure was a chasm in my emotional terrain. Any acceptance I had gained at this juncture in my life had been earned with grim determination on my part. Also, I had never been exposed to the labyrinth of seething jealousies and cutthroat competition that existed in scientific and academic circles. In many ways I was more vulnerable than the gorillas I was determined to protect. The mud that sucked at my boots as I hiked the final 3,000 feet to my base camp was a trap that even the gorillas avoided. At least they had the benefit of cohesive social structures and deep family bonds that would support them in times of stress, uncertainty, and danger. I was about to become ensnared in a literal fight to the death, without even a rudimentary foundation of family or social support. I was truly a lone representative of my species, about to be welcomed with open arms by *Gorilla beringei beringei*. I would become the first human to be completely accepted within their society, the first to bond with them, and the only one to die while protecting them.

3

Breaking Bonds

"Naoom, naoom, naoom."[26]

I had been sitting in the fork of an ancient *Pygeum Africanum* tree and vocalizing belching sounds in an attempt to locate Digit. The fruit of this oak-like tree is a favorite delicacy of the mountain gorilla. It looks like an oversized cherry and is an irresistible staple of their diet.

I was becoming quite melancholy in my lonely perch, since I had been reflecting on how the loss of a leader will destroy the structure of a mountain gorilla group. Group Four was my most closely observed group, but in my time on earth I had observed 220 gorillas in thirty-five groups of five to twenty members each. I had watched with horror as poaching, hunting, and collection expeditions for European zoos decimated the leadership structures of the gorillas' social units. Other family structures also suffered as the surviving members struggled to form new alliances with the remaining individuals. Even my beloved Digit had sacrificed himself so the silverback Uncle Bert and the rest of his group could flee to safety. Digit's heroic stand resulted in the amputation of his limbs, the severing of his head, and a partial evisceration of his internal organs. I could barely allow myself to think of his anguish, his pain, and the total comprehension he suffered knowing what humans were doing to him.[27] Poachers killed Uncle Bert not long afterward, and this contributed to the complete disintegration of Group Four. In the chaos that followed, the silverback Nunkie claimed Simba as his mate and killed the infant, Mwelu, who was probably Digit's only child.

From my tree-house vantage point in the saddle area between Mount Visoke and Mount Karisimbi, a great portion of the Parc des Volcans was visible. I had seen many births and too many deaths in the magnificent vista that stretched before me, and wondered again why my own death was not providing any respite from the anguish I endured after the murders of Digit and Uncle Bert. My journey to examine my early life, and the resulting resolution and understanding of family bonding, had come at great emotional expense.

Suddenly I heard a thumping, and Digit strutted into view, flinging vegetation to and fro in a great display designed to get my attention. He had what I call "the fun and games" expression on his face. He used this look with me when he wanted to prolong contact. Digit directed my attention to a rock outcropping that formed a ledge at the base of my tree. I realized he had carefully arranged drawings and photographs that I had collected of the gorillas during my studies. It was an amazing sight. The names attached to each of these lovely faces had been included in the "family tree" charts I had painstakingly composed for my research reports to my benefactors: Louis Leakey, *National Geographic*, and the Wilkie Brothers Foundation. I hadn't seen or thought of the portraits in years. Looking at them now, I could hardly believe that I had drawn them in such delicate detail.

"Wherever did you find these, Digit?"

He appeared to ignore me at first, and with a great show of concentration, arranged each of the drawings and photographs so that the organization clearly showed the interrelationships of the family groups. Then, he again flashed his "fun and games" smile as he took special care with the drawings of himself and Uncle Bert. If I could assign a human emotion to Digit, I would say that he was "proud" of his connection to the silverback patriarch.

The portraits brought back memories of the individuals I had come to know so well. Uncle Bert was the dominant adult silverback in Group Four. Digit had wandered into the protective circle of Bert's care when he was four or five years old, and he and the other immature members of the group were the recipients of Bert's seemingly infinite abilities to create new forms of play. I was the first human, I believe, with whom the gorillas displayed this ability to play, and I think it was their way of indicating my acceptance into gorilla society. I particularly recall the sight of Uncle Bert tickling the abdomen of a younger member of the group with a flower. Emboldened by these instances of frivolity within the group, I decided to try an experiment, and produced a mirror that enthralled Simba and the other youngsters. They were curious and I was overjoyed at their response. Curiously, though, Bert and Digit watched for a while and then knuckle-walked past me as if they were bored beyond belief. Perhaps Digit had reached a more mature state whereby he took on the responsibilities of the "rear guard" of the group. This duty entailed patrolling the fringes and alerting the group to danger when necessary.

This was in contrast to Digit's younger years, when he would prop himself up on his forearms and sniff the hand mirror I would carry with me into the field. He would purse his lips; cock his head and sigh; staring at his reflection while reaching around the mirror in search of the gorilla who was standing before him. I decided at the time that it would be presumptive of me to believe that he recognized himself.[28]

I realized that I now had the perfect opportunity to quiz Digit about his behavior with respect to the mirror incident. His attitude had always perplexed me, since previously he had been very interested in the tools and clothing I used and seldom missed an opportunity to examine my possessions. He was fascinated with all manner of field equipment including thermoses, gloves, notebooks, and cameras. Often he would take my glove and examine it as if it represented an artifact of tremendous interest. After playing with these objects, Digit would carefully return all of them to the rightful owner, almost as if he did not like the clutter of it all littering the forest floor.

Digit was sitting back on his haunches, inspecting his arrangement of my drawings and enjoying a few morsels of fruit, when I questioned him about the mirror.

"Naoom," he belched in contentment. I couldn't tell if it was because of my question, the fruit, or his satisfaction with his artistic arrangement of my sketches. "First tell me why you drew these pictures of us, *Nyiramacyibili.*"

"I wanted to record your nose prints. Each of you has a distinct set of wrinkles that shape your nostrils." I included them in my field notes and also used them as artwork to decorate the shelves of my cabin. "So, tell me, why weren't you and Uncle Bert interested in the mirror?"

"What do you see when you look into the mirror, *Nyiramacyibili?*"

I bristled a bit at this question. I sensed that there was a right or wrong answer, and I did not want to fail the test.

He read my mind.

"There is no answer I expect from you. WHY do you use a mirror? Is it a necessary tool in human society?"

Was a mirror necessary? Did I need it for myself, or did I need it to ensure that others found me acceptable? Bob Campbell had been upset when my discolored teeth showed in the footage for *National Geographic*. In one scene, I had gone to the village to get supplies and, while I am smiling at some of the natives, my decaying teeth are very evident.[29] In the remaining close-ups I am smiling with my lips pursed. I never did like that footage because it gave the erroneous impression that I was being smug or self-serving. The truth is I was ashamed and embarrassed about the way I looked.

I was annoyed with Digit at this point, but he had found a piece of wild celery and was giving it his undivided attention.

"Aristotle and Pliny," Digit belched.[30]

What did Digit know about Aristotle and Pliny? What did I know for that matter? I thought I had truly gone bushy.

Since Digit had returned his concentration to the celery, I decided to climb down from my perch and establish a closer contact with him. By the time I slid down to the rocky ledge, he had rolled over onto his back and was flashing his huge canines in an all out yawn. I snuggled into his bulk as he began to snore and racked my brain for any vestiges of Aristotle.

The ancient historian, Pliny, had written that the explorer Hanno visited remote regions of Africa almost 550 years before the birth of Christ. Hanno's expedition set out from the port of Carthage and encountered hairy creatures that walked like men and threw stones at the explorers. History has since recorded that these were probably encounters with chimpanzees, but who knows for certain? The strange creatures were named "gorillai" in the historic descriptions of the encounter.[31] Did the gorillas retain some ancient memory of the early visits of mankind to their realm?

I also recalled a text from one of my psychology courses in which Aristotle set forth a theory that has come to be known as "face-reading."[32] This theory states, that to the observer, a person appears to take on the essential characteristics of whatever animal he or she most closely resembles. If you have the countenance of a hound, for example, you would be considered trustworthy, but prone to sleepiness. In another class I learned that the face of a human child holds millions of years of evolutionary characteristics, and that this beautiful, young, innocent, face inspires love in human society. The profile of any young mammal is fashioned by evolution to provoke feelings of parental care, concern, and even love.

During my tenure with the Henry family in Louisville, I rented a cottage that was set a quarter mile or so back into the woods. I adored the privacy it afforded and the opportunities it provided to observe what little wildlife remained in that area. I also developed quite a reputation with the local populace as a sympathetic rehabilitator of orphaned pets and wildlife. All manner of creatures found their way to my doorstep, and I happily took them in. I especially remember an orphaned woodland rabbit that a pack of hounds had dislodged from its nest. Its blunt profile was remarkably similar to that of a human infant, and I would sit for hours, nursing it from a toy baby bottle, gazing at the outline of its fuzzy head.

I left Digit's side quietly, not wanting to wake him, and walked over to the sketches he had arranged on the lava rock ledge. Looking at the gallery of familiar faces, some killed by poachers, some still alive in the Rwandan forest more than twenty years after my death, I realized that I had captured more than just the ana-tomical differences in their facial structures. Oh, the scientist in me dutifully recorded the wrinkles, swirls, and hair differences that established each individ-ual's unique physical qualities. But something else stood out that I had never noticed before. In my careful detailed work on their eyes, I had somehow cap-tured the spirit of each member of my gorilla family. These portraits, which had adorned the shelves and walls of my cabin for many years, were more than a sci-entist's rogue gallery of study subjects. They had kept me company in my solitary existence as much as any human family's collection of grandmothers, fathers, aunts, uncles, and cousins might have. When I was murdered, their eyes peered down—a silent witness to what happened that night.

Digit grumbled and rolled over in his day nest, while I crept back to his side and watched him sleep.

I knew why he showed no lasting interest in the mirror. He had no natural curiosity about the physical characteristics of his own face. Watching gorillas interact in grooming rituals, one notices the amount of time they take with the face and head of the grooming partner. It is the *condition* of the *other* that elicits care and concern. Grooming is social, but it is also nourishing. Young primates groom their mothers, and vice-versa, as a way of learning and bonding, but it is also a symbiotic relationship that helps to condition the fur by removing food and debris. This is especially important in a climate that is constantly damp and where it rains over fifty per cent of the time. Young gorillas cling to their moth-ers' bodies during the first year of life for warmth and pick bits of discarded food from the fur as an introduction to their natural food supply. Thus, the close-knit gorillas have no evolutionary stake in the physical characteristics of other mem-bers beyond the individual traits that indicate status and health. Recognition of one's status within the group lessens anxiety, and knowledge of the condition of another gorilla's fur indicates the overall health and well being of that individual. Silverbacks establish their status by chest pounding, vocalizations, and displays: such as leaf and log throwing, swinging, and stomping. Beauty as a sole measure of status is a conceit born in the eyes of human beholders.

The mirror provided nothing for me but a reaffirmation of my self-loathing. The reflective glass could not groom me, offer comfort, or fix the teeth that were rotting out of my skull. The person that millions of years of evolution brought closest to me, a member of my own species, and my intimate companion, Bob Campbell, offered no reliable comfort. His best response to my pitiful condition was a complaint that I was not living up to the standards of beauty he was used to seeing on American and British television.[33]

I snuggled back into Digit's nest and picked a piece of leaf debris from his back. Surprisingly, my new mental clarity regarding my sorrowful, dysfunctional relationship with a member of my own species was not distressing. On the contrary, I felt emboldened and ready for the first time to examine an incident that haunted me more than most any other. Sharing the nest with Digit produced a safety net that allowed me to journey to a place in my past that I had assiduously avoided for the twenty years since my death. There are two states of being in the afterlife, much as there are in the before life. One is characterized by a heavy, electrically grounded "body," and the other is accessed with a force of will or desire that is similar to what the practitioner of yoga would call a "meditative state." I chose this latter state to examine the death of Mweza, a baby gorilla, since I felt it would be too dangerous to attempt to scrutinize the tragedy without a detached vantage point—one that would offer protection from one of the worst memories of my lifetime.

The months before the momentous and unnecessary death of the little gorilla were a cauldron of tragedies, betrayals, and anxieties that would lead to my mental and physical deterioration. I had been ten years on the mountain and at times very ill. The pain was so great at times that I was certain I had cancer. My advancing emphysema made extensive forays into the bush all but impossible. I had broken my ribs and other small bones so often that doctors subsequently told me I was suffering from osteoporosis brought on by a poor diet and advancing age. I only had one true phobia in life, and I would often scream like a baptized baby when forced to scramble over steep slopes as I climbed in and out of ravines in my search for the gorillas. When faced with a slope that even a two year old could jump across, I was reduced to a shivering weakness.[34] One day, I was trying to outrun a charging buffalo and fell into a deep drainage ditch, fracturing my fibula in the process. I used whatever materials I had at hand, including tape and a splint, to repair the damage. However, my orthopedic surgical skills were quite lacking, and I later had to have the leg broken again and set at a hospital in Germany.[35]

My diet at Karisoke consisted mainly of bananas, local tubers, and whatever "care" packages I could elicit from friends in the States. An occasional tin of meat would be used to enhance pots of vegetables or rice that I would brew. Digit has informed me that on many occasions the gorillas would offer me food because they intuitively knew that my diet was barely enough to keep me healthy. My hair did not look shiny to them, and my increasing lack of flexibility, endurance, strength, and mental acuity was of great concern to them. Just as they would attend to ailing members of their group, so, too, the gorillas offered me delicacies that gave me vitality and provided the elements missing from my diet. At the time, I thought the offers of wild celery and thistle plant were merely a socialization technique. Little did I know that the gorillas were trying to heal me.

I met Amy Vedder and Bill Weber, or as I liked to call them, the "V-W couple,"[36] in 1977, while I was on a speaking tour in Chicago. I had utilized this trip as a means to visit doctors and dentists in an effort to get a bodily tune-up and repair my broken bones. We decided to meet at a restaurant so that I could go over their application to conduct a census of the gorilla population. They had no formal training in primatology, but had been Peace Corps teachers in Africa, and were fluent in Swahili and French, which I was not. Although I was, as always, reluctant to bring new people to Karisoke, they seemed sincere, and with my deteriorating physical condition it was becoming more and more difficult to trek the mountainsides conducting population counts. Their fluency in the local languages would also be valuable. I decided to invite them, but had I the prescience of Vedder's later mocking description of our dinner conversation; I probably would have reconsidered my initial evaluations.

In her book, *In the Kingdom of Gorillas*, Vedder cruelly reported that my fish entree went uneaten while I ravenously consumed at least a dozen pats of butter, and then emptied the contents of the sugar bowl into my purse.[37] She added this incident to a list of eccentricities she compiled to discredit and defame me. Vedder had no way of knowing that my social anxieties sometimes made it difficult for me to eat in front of others, or that my cravings got the better of me when I saw the heaping piles of butter pats and a bowl of sugar cubes on the table. Pure fat and simple carbohydrates were totally lacking in my diet. Much as my gorillas would do, I took advantage of a food source that was seldom available to me. While I was willing to provide Vedder and Weber access to my sanctuary, they were already busy sowing the seeds of betrayal. Instead of offering me sustenance, they banished me to the fringes of polite human society, unable to recognize both my physical and spiritual starvation as my beloved gorillas had. Another tentative human bond of trust was broken in its infancy!

In fairness to all of us, pressure had been building long before the V-W's arrival at Karisoke. In the span of two years, poachers had killed thirteen members of my beloved gorilla family, and I found my emotional state was spiraling into feelings of hatred, desperation, and most damagingly, despair and paranoia. The culmination of these dark feelings came with the murders of Digit and Uncle Bert, which in turn led to the social disintegration of my much-loved Group Four. I felt my existence no longer had purpose; my life's work had been a failure; and, most damning, I believed that I had no personal self-worth. The fact that I had predicted the slaughter much earlier didn't make me feel any better. In my first published article for *National Geographic Magazine*, barely three years into my work, I had expressed the fear that, unless human trespassers were controlled, I doubted that my forest friends would survive. I blamed lack of cooperation between conservation groups and political authorities for what was about to unfold,[38] and my grim prediction would come to fruition with Digit's murder.

After Digit's murder, which took place shortly before the arrival of the V-W's, I was truly alone on the mountain. I had no human family or group to absorb the hellish loneliness that washed over me. In my observations of gorilla behaviors, it was clear that close family bonding was the mortar that supported social structures in the face of tragedy and broken bonds such as the death of a family member. My family was Group Four, and with the murder of Digit my life was on a parallel track with them. Thus, I felt that I was running in terror for my life. I ran straight to the comfort that my generation had grown up with in polite social circles, alcohol. However, I was no longer drinking to mask my social dysfunctions as I had with the Henry family. I was trying to erase all feeling from my consciousness. My body had been ill for several years, and it was now ruled by an unhealthy mind.[39]

Barely three months after Amy Vedder and Bill Weber arrived at Karisoke, the death of Mweza permanently destroyed what remained of our professional and personal relationships. Things became so strained that Amy returned, unopened, a gift I had delivered to her in my feeble attempt to gain admittance to her inner circle and atone for my social inadequacies.[40] After her rejection, I found myself once again stretching for acceptance and using bravado and anger as my impenetrable shield.

The tragedy commenced when I learned a baby gorilla was being held for sale in the Congo.

Mweza is Swahili for "can do."[41] We first heard he was being held for sale when my network of informants reported that a young gorilla had been caught in a poacher's snare. The park staff at Rumangabo was holding Mweza at the main headquarters of the Congo's Parc National des Virunga. My network indicated that it was very possible that the baby gorilla had originated on the Rwandan side of the park border. Although it was dangerous and foolhardy for me to cross the border, I was not going to stand by and abandon the captive gorilla, especially since I was still angry about Digit's recent murder. Vedder and Weber had the appropriate documents, so we made our way back down to the parking area, 3,000 feet below Karisoke, and took my battered blue VW bus across the border to Congo with the help of an assistant Conservator from Congo, who shall be known only as "Faustin."[42]

Mweza had a gangrenous foot due to the loss of blood supply from the poacher's snare, and he[43] had been malnourished by a diet of formula for the seven weeks the park staff held him. His cheeks were sunken, and his fur was matted and covered by a foul, greenish-yellow diarrhea. I began to negotiate for his release to my care. The park officials seemed more than eager to accept this arrangement, but they stated that they needed the permission of none other than the Congolese President, Joseph Désiŕe Mobutu, the self-proclaimed "King of Zaire." Bill Weber was very helpful in the translation of this request, and two days later Mobutu granted permission for Mweza to be transported to Rwanda and Karisoke. When Faustin warned us that driving would be impossible because of the border crossings and the inability to communicate the President's instructions regarding the baby to remote outposts, the V-W couple agreed to make the sixteen-hour hike across the mountain range carrying Mweza in a sling on their backs. Armed guards would complete the procession, and I would meet them back at Karisoke. I had decided to leave the baby with the couple, since it would be dangerous for me to remain while political unrest was brewing in the Congo, and I quickly drove back to the Rwandan side of the park. The horrific memories of my earlier incarceration at the hands of the Congolese were still very fresh in my mind, and I had no desire to stay there alone and risk spending additional time in a wooden cage.

As I waited in my cabin for their return, my anger mounted at the thought of helpless little Mweza. Mweza's plight brought long-hidden emotions roiling to the surface because I knew firsthand what it felt like to be imprisoned in a cage. Also, from past experiences with other captive young gorillas, and judging by his condition, I thought it very likely that he would die.

"What do you think Mweza wished for, Dian?" Digit whispered.

"Life."

"Mweza was ready to die, Nyiramacyibili."

"Don't all living creatures cling to life?"

"Mweza's parents were killed by the poachers. He was being carried away from all of the sights, sounds, smells, and foods that he knew while clinging to his mother's back."

"But you were a lone gorilla before you joined with Bert's group. You didn't want to die."

"I had a strong life force within me and had not fulfilled my destiny. Mweza was destined to die in your care."

And die with all of us he did. Whether we accomplished anything is doubtful, and what truly haunts me is that my anger may have contributed to his suffering in the end. Several days of seeming recovery were followed by a steady decline, and Mweza looked far worse a week after Vedder and Weber successfully brought him back to camp. After spending several hours with Mweza in my cabin, I found that I could not endure the spectacle of yet another death, and refused to bond with the baby. My gut instinct told me he was doomed, so I gave Mweza back to Vedder and Weber with instructions on how to administer antibiotics and other medicines. I also tried to arrange for a leper pediatrician[44] I knew to come to Karisoke to amputate the gangrenous foot, but it would be three days or more before she could make the journey. I was becoming more and more depressed about the chances of any miracle keeping him alive.

During this period, I wrote a letter describing Mweza's condition to Russell Mitteremeier, head of the Primate Group of the New York Zoological Society. I described Mweza's condition in gruesome detail, noting he was emaciated, dehydrated, and producing blood-filled diarrhea. He also had oozing sores and was covered with lice and fleas. I was certain that what would kill him would be his stump of a left foot, a testament to the poacher's snare. His little foot was gangrenous, hot, swollen, and bound to his body by a wire snare deeply imbedded in the lower leg. In addition, his toes were flexed up into the rotten skin on the sole of a foot that really had no shape whatsoever.[45] My graphic description to Mitteremeier was meant to shock. I wanted word to get out about the horrific consequences of the poacher's snares. I had been fighting this practice with little success during my tenure on the mountain.

One evening, Vedder sent word to my cabin that Mweza was having difficulty breathing. I had been in a foul mood, fueled by drinking, and not long after I reached Amy and Bill's cabin, Amy and I began to fight. I grabbed the vial of antibiotics and tried to pour it down poor Mweza's throat. His gag reflex was weak or nonexistent, and he choked. When I left he was breathing, however he died that night, and Amy has remained convinced that I directly contributed to Mweza's death. The reassurances of the doctor who performed Mweza's necropsy did nothing to soothe my guilt. He said that Mweza had an advanced pneumonia and was unsalvageable.[46] When an infant loses the gag reflex it is a sign that death is near. His gangrenous foot had caused a massive system-wide infection. There was no saving him. No matter. The self-hatred and recriminations were more than I could bear.

"Oh, Digit, I must know! Did I kill him?"

Digit put a comforting arm around my shoulder.

"Dian, we are on the road to death from the moment we are born. Physical bonds are in an eternal state of disintegration. In spiritual terms, Mweza began to die when he was captured by the poachers. He lived a short while in order to teach your human group."

"But he suffered so much, and maybe I made it worse."

"Think, Nyiramacyibili. Use your mind that is so compassionate with the gorillas. Look at yourself with empathy."

"Help me, Digit."

"Mweza's fate was already determined by the actions of the poachers. Your human group contributed to its own suffering by turning on one another. No one assumed the position of leader in your group to offer reassurance. Each one of you was terrified to face the death of the baby for different reasons. You were incapable of acting calmly because of the breakdown of your emotions, and the other humans were frightened of you because of your erratic behavior."

Digit was right. The stage had been set at our first encounter in the Chicago restaurant. We would fail as a group unit since we were all suspicious, rather than supportive. We had not learned to put the interests of the gorillas ahead of our petty differences. Each side was "well meaning" in that over-used human sense of the word, but the road to hell is often paved with good intentions.

"Oh Digit, can you ever forgive me?"

"There is no need for the gorillas to forgive, Dian. We accept our existence without questioning."

"But he suffered too much!"

"He was cared for with loving tenderness when his mother carried him across the chasm to this side. The gorillas who had gone before protected Mweza. He tried to rally to make you feel better but was willing and eager to join the others. It was time for him to leave you."

"Describe for me how the gorillas view death."

"You had no time to observe, because you were always directing your staff to remove the bodies for your research."

This was certainly true. Whether a gorilla had been killed by poachers, or had died in its sleep in its night nest, we would always remove the body and carry it back to camp on a leaf-strewn litter for a complete necropsy.

"I have seen members of your group come back repeatedly to sniff the location or nest where a group member died. Is this your form of grieving, Digit?"

"Dear Nyiramacyibili. We have wanted to show you. You have not observed the most surprising part. Why would we grieve? Things unfold as they should as far as the gorillas are concerned. We *sing*[47] over the body."

Digit took my hand and lifted me with strength and grace, indicating that I should climb upon his back. Together we bounded through the forest, across the grasslands and back to Karisoke. Along the way, he thrilled me with great leaps through the branches of the Hagenia trees, which were dripping with moss, vines, and succulents.

As we approached the camp at dusk, an astonishing whisper drifted across the treetops and remained suspended in the mist-laden air. The whisper swelled into an opus of harmonic purity that seemed to flow from the gates of heaven itself. I had been willing for so long to give hell its due, but the sound I heard could only have come from the throats of celestial beings. The resonance was so pure in its quality, that I held my hands over my ears, unable to assimilate the holiness of it all. I buried my face in Digit's fur, afraid to look.

Unexpectedly, the arms of the great silverback, Uncle Bert, tenderly pried me from my sanctuary. Bert carried me in his arms as a parent would carry an infant to the source of the sounds.

I opened my eyes to see all of the residents of the gorilla graveyard harmonizing over the grave of Dr. Dian Fossey.

4

Bonds of Happiness

My encounter with the gorilla choir opened a floodgate of new memories regarding my earthly existence in the Virungas that required serious examination on my part. The extraordinary experiences that Digit had shared with me in the afterlife provided a necessary foundation for this undertaking, for the journey would be difficult and spiritually dangerous. However, Digit and the others assured me that they would form the "rear guard" for my journey and would not allow my spirit to be further harmed or broken.

My work with the mountain gorilla began on the slopes of Mount Mikeno in the Congo.[48] I was happier there than I had ever been in my life, feeling that I finally had solid direction and purpose. Unfortunately, within six months, I was forced to flee to Rwanda because of political strife in the Congolese province. In my public writings, I gloss over this period as being but an inconvenient interruption of my work. The truth of the situation, and what I chose to reveal only in my diaries and in emotional confessions uttered during the later years of my life, is that I was brutalized and held captive in a wooden cage for several days by Congolese militia. My captors urinated on me, raped me, and displayed me in the town square, bragging that they were holding me for the local general.[49] My spirit was robbed of its dignity, and seeds were sown for my hatred of Africans who were capable of torturing me and the gorillas I had come to study, learned to love, and pledged to save.

There are close friends of mine who will maintain to this day that I was not raped, but "only" psychologically abused by my captors. If I am to regain a sense of self-worth, it is also important that I admit to my rape at the hands of Congolese soldiers during this time. I told the photographer, Alan Root, and several others about the rape, but Alan was reluctant to give this information to my biographer, considering himself a "gentleman" who should respect my privacy on the matter.[50] I don't know why I was afraid to include this information in my book, *Gorillas in the Mist*. Perhaps I was fearful of the unwanted attention it would bring, and I did not want to face the shame of it all. It is somewhat like the feelings experienced by the abused child who believes that the abuse is to some extent deserved, or it would not happen. Besides, my mother was alive at that time, and the truth would have been more than she could bear.

Shortly after these devastating events, the son and two companions of one of my expatriate benefactors, Alyette de Munck, took a wrong turn in their Land Rover and were captured, tortured, killed, and thrown into a river by the Congolese military.[51] My dear friend, Rosamond Carr, broke the news to me and related in later interviews that she thought I had "gone berserk" at the report.[52] I remember standing in Rosamond's gardens, throwing fistfuls of thousand franc notes into the air and screaming for anyone to venture into the Congo to avenge the murders. She was so angry at me for my tirade that she asked me to leave the next morning.[53] Whether I had truly "gone berserk" or not, the agitation, revulsion, and depression that these events stirred in me only added to my determination to return to the gorilla population. Seeing my obsession to resume the fight to save my gorillas, and as a way of facing her own grief, the murdered boy's mother, Alyette, became my benefactress and vowed to help me rebuild my camp in a new location. Thus, Karisoke was born.

To the dismay of both Rosamond and Alyette, I would sometimes use racist and derogatory language in describing the African members of my staff after these events. Thankfully, as I aged, I no longer directed racist remarks toward my African staff. "Wogs" was a common insult, used by the British colonialists, and worked its way into my vocabulary. Although I understood the offensive nature of this word, and tried to muzzle my speech; it became as common as any profanity that ingrains itself into one's language patterns and cannot be excised, even with an act of will. Foolishly, I publicly defended my use of this term, saying that it arose because of my frustrations with what I considered to be the "lazy" nature of my African workers. The true reasons were buried deep in my damaged psyche. Alan Root, for one, realized that I had put much love into Africa and received little in return except humiliation. As a result, I sometimes spoke badly of some Africans. I remember breaking into tears when I told Alan of my rape and torture, although tearful displays were not a common occurrence in my life.[54] The fact that some Africans had mistreated me was an inescapable truth. When I used insulting and racist terms in anger, I was allowing my frightening memories to fuel my outbursts.

There were many instances when I was grateful to my African friends and staff, and I did not hesitate to rave about them in my regular correspondences to friends residing in the States. I wrote to my mother, during the final years of my life, that the Africans were the "backbone of Karisoke."[55] I also asked my mother to please write back and direct the term "Jambo"[56] to Kanyarugano[57] and Basil, my houseboys, who would be totally thrilled to see their names in writing from an American they had never met.[58] My enemies have continued to accuse me of being a colonialist who had racist attitudes toward the Africans. To extrapolate blatant racism from my admittedly insensitive use of language is another example of my enemies using instances of negative actions on my part to construct a faulty impression of my true personality, motivations, and feelings. It has been a hard-earned spiritual lesson on my part. Our actions do define us. Good or bad, they will indeed follow us through eternity.

Nine months before my murder, I wrote a long letter to my friend, Jeffrey Short, who resided in Chicago.[59] I was elated that the park guards, my African staff members, and even their extended families were helping me to record the original place names of all of the hills, valleys, rivers, and streams in the Virungas. These locales had never been mapped, and their histories resided only in oral traditions. It was a labor of love on my part to translate over 300 names from the local Kinyarwandan[60] language into French, Swahili, and English. My goal was to create an inexpensive booklet that would be published by the University of Butare in Rwanda. Jeffrey wrote back that it was an interesting project, but the animals must be preserved or all the work would be for naught.[61] He need not have issued this admonition, since I was still well aware of the threats that poaching and tourism presented to the gorillas.

That I considered myself to be the gorillas' protector, allowed me to assume, with impunity, certain postures and engage in activities that would not be acceptable in polite academic circles. Although my detractors described my behavior as antisocial, and I agree that I was often unsociable and certainly unfriendly, I can only say that I was deeply wounded by how I was treated during my first months in Africa. When I tried to balance feelings of grandiosity with what I considered to be a justified paranoia, my mood swings became increasingly worse. I chose to carry a gun and was not afraid to fire a warning shot over the heads of fleeing poachers or intruding tourists. I did not take direct aim at them as some have accused me of doing. A gun with an empty clip was found next to my body after I was murdered. If I had not been blindsided in my sleep, perhaps I would not have hesitated to mortally wound my attackers. My story might have ended differently if the clip had been in my gun before I retired for the night. Of course, these events became fodder for the Fossey myths that have endured for twenty years after my death.

In my day-to-day dealings with the poachers that attempted to overrun the Parc des Volcans, I preferred to utilize a more culturally sensitive and intelligent deterrent than gunplay. But, there was no question that I declared all out war on the poachers and the Tutsi cattle grazers. I earned my nickname, the "Witch of the Virungas," with grit, determination, and a certain amount of self-effacing humor in dangerous situations. Since witchcraft was a staple of the Batwa pygmy culture that conducted the bulk of the poaching and smuggling across the Congolese-Rwandan border, I was never satisfied with the textbook approaches to field study and conservation. Only an active approach to saving the mountain gorilla would bear any fruit, and thus my theory of "active conservation" was born. My arsenal of deterrents included Halloween masks, smoke bombs, tear gas, firecrackers, and any other artifact of modern society that would appear to give me superhuman powers in the eyes of the pygmy poachers. I have never understood why accounts of my "sorcery" by white biographers have assumed such a negative tone. Although I was quite serious in my displays of witchcraft, there was a theatricality about it all that I found quite humorous. I was using African traditions to my own advantage.

In one instance, a large group of fifteen or more poachers and their dogs chased a water buffalo into the middle of Group Five. Absolutely infuriated, and emboldened by my rage, I donned a Halloween mask and armed myself with a water pistol, camera, and tear gas canister, and took off into the brush screaming like a banshee. My display of sorcery, hysteria, and fury scattered the poachers to the four winds and greatly enhanced my reputation. Undaunted, the poachers exacted their revenge by kidnapping my dog, Cindy, one of the many pets I kept at Karisoke. I immediately upped the ante by taking eight Tutsi cattle as hostage, and my workers spread the word that I would kill one cow a day until Cindy was returned. I also painted an obscenity on the side of one of the cows. I admit to this now, because I am not afraid to face the childish side of my nature. Needless to say, the dispute was solved without a single shot being fired, and Cindy was home with me by nightfall. And so it went, day after day, and year after year. It would have been an amusing diversion, except that the stakes remained high for the mountain gorilla. Even my good friend, Ambassador Frank Crigler, expressed genuine concern at both my mental state and the effects some of my poaching deterrents were having on international relations.

I see now that my behavior was not in my best interest given the violence, threats of civil war, smuggling, and other unsavory activities that were a staple of African life at that historical juncture. Human life was hardly valued more than that of the gorillas, yet I persisted in placing myself in high profile positions that would invite retaliation. My stature as a sorceress probably worked to my advantage, since I was not harmed during those early years. Perhaps there was a deeper reason for my recklessness. A psychologist might say that my reaction to my father's suicide may have been the catalyst for my reclusive and reckless behavior. I certainly felt abandoned and orphaned when he died. His death was surely the result of despair, since in all of his letters to me, he expressed a melancholy attitude about our separation and his life in general. Although, he also said his new wife was taking good care of him during his long periods of ill health.[62] I have no idea whether he continued to drink to excess, but I do know that he loved to hear about my adventures in the wilderness and was very proud whenever my exploits were featured in the newspapers in San Rafael, California. I think he would have loved the Virungas, as wild places always fascinated him, and I believe that I inherited his passion for the outdoors.

I first learned of my father's death when Bob Campbell was visiting Karisoke during the summer of 1968, barely a year into my studies. *National Geographic* had sent Campbell to get a feel for my work and to plan a photographic shoot that would eventually culminate in a movie and illustrations for articles in the magazine. It was largely through Bob's work that I became known globally as the "gorilla lady." Bob became a sympathetic sounding board when I was overcome with the news of my father's suicide—news that arrived by telegram from my stepmother, Kathryn. His quiet nature made him a compassionate listener as I shared with him the contents of a letter that I had carried with me since 1959. In this letter, my father revealed that he had been following my career, as well as my academic successes and failures, and expressed his love of animals and the outdoors. Most importantly to me, my father repeatedly referred to me as his "beautiful" daughter and expressed an anxious desire to see me. In no uncertain terms, he begged me to write to him, and he closed his letters with "All my Love, Your Dad, George Fossey."[63] The man I never really knew "knew" me, even though we had no real personal adult contact. He was the ghost of a father, not a genuine father in the true sense of the word, but still so very important and precious to me.

While I was ruminating about my father, Digit and the others retreated to their protective positions, but I summoned Digit with a question bark vocalization of "wraagh!" Gorillas often use this sound in situations of mild alarm or curiosity,[64] and I knew it would get his attention. It worked, and Digit appeared. He sat, Buddha-like, and peeled a thistle plant, but did not offer to share his meal with me. This was unusual and I found it a bit off-putting.

There was a long silence. I finally asked, "Did my father want to die like Mweza?"

"Mweza did not *want* to die. He accepted what had happened and wished to join his murdered parents."

"If my father did not want to die, why did he take his life?"

"I don't know. Gorillas don't know suicide. What do you think, Nyiramacyibili?"

"Why do you sometimes call me by that name and sometimes 'Dian'?"

"From time to time it makes you feel better to be alone. Remember, you insisted that it be on your tombstone. Do you think your father wanted to be alone?" Digit offered some of the thistle plant to me, but I wasn't hungry and was still feeling too perturbed with him to be pleasant.

"I don't know. Does death mean being alone? I am dead now and I am certainly not alone. All I had of my father were his letters, and he seemed happy enough not to go so far as to kill himself. Even so, he was often sad."

"Humans expect to be happy."

"Why shouldn't we? Isn't that what life is all about?"

"For the gorillas, existing is enough. Happiness is not a concept we consider. Please describe happiness to me."

"It means having everything you want out of life."

"Do most humans experience happiness before they die?"

I had to admit to myself that I didn't think I knew anyone who had attained happiness. Colleagues, my parents, friends, acquaintances, fellow researchers, and my students all seemed to be in search of various goals that, once attained, would provide happiness. I could not say that anyone ever confided to me that they had achieved this state. Maybe our very humanness and awareness of our inability to achieve a perfect existence contributed to our feelings of inadequacy and despair. "I don't think humans are ever truly happy."

"Then why is it so important to you? If the goal is impossible, why continue grasping for it? Can you not be content in your existence?"

"We are surrounded by wars, crimes, greed and injustice. How can we be content?"

"And why do humans undertake these negative activities?"

Why have wars ruled human history? Why did the Batwa poach wildlife and snare gorillas? Why do professional jealousies fuel competitions that slow research? Why does loneliness lead to despair? I had come full circle trying to follow Digit. "Because we want to be happy, and someone or something is always standing in the way of achieving that goal of perfection. That makes us angry.

Being unhappy makes humans so angry that we sometimes turn the anger on ourselves."

"So, humans behave in a negative manner and contribute to the unhappiness of the group." Digit began to grub in the earth, as if signaling the end of the conversation.

I was beginning to understand why the gorillas had no concept of unhappiness. Their entire existence as a species depended upon group cooperation and support for the individual. If the individual did not thrive, the group would fail. Obviously, I was contributing to my failure to achieve happiness in the worlds I now straddled.

What of my father? Was he responsible for the misery that led to his suicide, or was it a culmination of bad luck, failure at love with my mother, and chance? What demons forced my father to run from me at such an early age? Why did he wait until I was over thirty years old before he decided to contact me? If I was as beautiful as he said, why did he abandon me? Richard Price and my mother certainly made it clear that I was no classic beauty. All through my early life, I assumed my father probably considered me "a burly girl from California," as I was described in a newsreel, and worried that my physical countenance was so repulsive that maybe he couldn't bear to gaze upon me. But then, so many years later, he wrote that I was his beautiful girl. Would my father's unconditional love in my early years have guaranteed my happiness?

I now had far more questions than answers and felt like retreating into the forest. At the same time, I was aware that the protective phalanx of the gorilla group was moving closer to Digit and me. They formed a circle, and sat quietly with a reverent attention directed at Digit. Digit sat impassively. "Dian, why do you want to disappear into the mists?"

"Because I cannot think clearly; there is no hope; and because I have failed all of you by dying."

"Like your father failed you?"

For a moment I felt the machete slash into my brain again. Light and heat flashed into my consciousness.

"Yes!" I cried.

The gorillas began to croon softly.

"My dear Dian. You sacrificed your life for us. Why do you continue to hold this sadness close to your heart? You are free now."

I did sacrifice my life. In spite of my human failings, my mental and physical illnesses, and my incompetence at intimate relationships, I had out-done every researcher that went before me. I put the plight of the gorillas on the world stage, regardless of my despondence that they were doomed anyway. I fought on in my own crazy manner, lost some major battles, but did not lose the war—even in death. I became the world's authority on the mountain gorilla and had a movie made about me as well, starring one of the world's most popular actresses.[65]

Digit's simple statement that I was now free was the catalyst that began the slow process of healing my broken spirit. When I saw more clearly why I was born, I began to feel more hope. If I could learn to accept the fact that in spite of my death my destiny had been fulfilled, I might finally rest in peace and join the gorilla chorus. Because my personal quest for happiness was forever bound to the fate of the mountain gorilla and my hope for their successful future, my journey was—in a sense—just beginning.

5

Bonds of Fate

The circle of gorillas crooned softly, settling into their nests as darkness enveloped the mountain, but I was restless and spent the night roaming the grasslands around Karisoke. The camp as I knew it was gone. Only the graveyard remained. Even though the gorillas were at rest, I did not feel alone, since other wild creatures kept me company until the sliver of the new moon faded with the faint light of dawn. Elephants and water buffalo rumbled down to the stream, and the shiny eyes of the hyrax peered from the tall grasses. I felt very comfortable in the arms of the night, perhaps because it was a comfort that was hard won. I went down the mountain, through the lava tunnel, and followed the trail made of gray lava pebbles, mud, and boulders to the base of Visoke. Passing the car park and the old rondavel cabins I continued on to Ruhengeri, where I finally found the house I was searching for. While perched on the tin roof, I tried not to wake the sleeping researcher inside. It was her fate to take over my position at Karisoke in a political climate much more charged with racial and civil tensions than existed during my tenure. She had been unable to enter the Parc des Volcans due to civil unrest that lingered in the aftermath of the tragic genocidal wars. Placed on permanent standby, she was nonetheless ready to make a last-minute excursion into the park if conditions permitted.[66]

I found it uncanny how much this researcher resembles me with her tall build, long dark hair and a steely determination in her eyes that I particularly like. She seems very capable, though, and stronger in body and spirit than I was. I wish I could read her mind and peer into her soul. I wonder if she has been swept into the politics that proved to be my undoing. She sees to it that the field staff and poaching patrols are doing their jobs well. It is truly miraculous that the decade of civil war we have witnessed from our vantage point in the after-life has not done more to harm the gorillas. I believe that Digit and Bert have remained as the rear guard for their worldly family through these terrible years, but I still have worries. Are the proponents of Rwandan tourism still hiding behind the mantle of conservation? Does behavioral research have any real meaning after the gorillas have become completely habituated owing to constant human intervention and observation? Will the interests of the gorilla and human populations of Rwanda continue to clash so violently that neither will have a future?

While on one of my previous forays into the researcher's home, I was able to read one of her reports. I noted that in spite of tour operations running expeditions into gorilla territory, and ten years of military activity in the parks, the gorilla population had grown to 324 individuals.[67] The researcher sadly noted the death of 17 of our gorilla friends, but she was as proud as I would have been that only one, the silverback Mrithi, came from the Rwandan side where Karisoke is located. Mrithi was the unfortunate casualty of military gunfire. I wanted to tell her that Mrithi was thriving now, having fulfilled his destiny by becoming part of the researcher's consciousness, just as Digit had become forever part of mine. She will be very surprised and happy, when her earthly destiny is complete, to find Mrithi and his friends ready to guide her to the other side, should she need assistance.

I recognized the tensions inherent in the collision of gorilla and human habitat when I wrote *Gorillas in the Mist*. Both gorillas and man live in an ecosystem barely able to sustain their competing needs. The Parc National des Volcans, which is the gorillas protected home, also contains the most fertile topsoil in Rwanda. Struggles over control of land fueled a genocide that resulted in the mass slaughter of both Hutu and Tutsi families. When I began my studies, there were over 780 human inhabitants per square mile in the fertile valleys and slopes of the Virungas. While I recognized the roots of competition for the volcanic soil, I also feared that encroachment upon the terrain might eventually be responsible for the mountain gorilla becoming one of the seven or so other rare species both discovered and extinct within the same century.[68] I understood the Malthusian conundrum,[69] but the focus of my studies was on the most endangered of the species, the mountain gorilla.

I have been unfairly criticized for caring more about gorillas than the impoverished populace of Rwanda. In fact, ethnic unrest has plagued central Africa since the seventeenth century, when the nobility, military commanders, and cattle herders were Tutsi, and the remaining population consisted of farmers of Hutu heritage. The resulting competition for land has been the driving force behind ethnic conflicts that repeat with regularity. To place the blame upon the gorillas for millions of dead, dying, or starving people, is nothing more than a smokescreen for, and diversion from, competing international political interests and colonial influences that have encouraged unrest for hundreds of years The resulting hellish conclusion was the murder of 800,000 Tutsis at the hands of militant Hutus in the genocide of 1994.

My replacement's report duly and sadly noted that the Interahamwe[70] genocide squads murdered one of my favorite trackers from my initial years at Karisoke, Nshogoza Fidele. He was my chief woodcutter and, although he had a quiet and reserved personality, he always wanted to take pride in his job. I have seen Nshogoza from time to time silently refilling the kindling basket of the new director. The director thinks she has been conserving fuel and has no idea of the ghostly assistance she is receiving. True to form, Nshogoza does not interact with me, but he has given a quirky little nod in my direction, so I believe that he knows that I am here.

This new director, tragically, also lost one of her good friends and trackers to rebel squads during the period in which the Interahamwe took over the volcanoes. She titled her report, "A Tribute to Mathias Mpiranya and the Trackers of Karisoke," declaring Mathias always the "strongest and the bravest."[71] I tried to leave a sign for her that I was pleased with her reports, but I am not certain she ever noticed the items that were "rearranged" in her quarters. Always the practical one, I feel she had no time for ruminations regarding supernatural goings-on.

I was especially heartened when she confirmed that one of the most serious threats to the gorilla population is the transmission of human parasites and disease. When I was alive, I would tear through the park in a rage upon discovering human feces and tampons littering the brush in the gorilla habitat. My diaries recount my anger at one researcher in particular who would defecate on purpose in the vicinity of the gorillas and then gauge their reaction. My inevitable ranting and raving created additional anxiety in the camp, and this added to the list of quirks and eccentricities that were sent down to the American Ambassador to prove I was unfit to manage Karisoke. Meanwhile, I was baffled as to why no one took my logical concerns about pollution seriously. As "eco-tourism" deposits more and more human waste in the gorillas' pristine environment, the risk to gorilla health increases. I was gratified to see that my new counterpart had a veterinary team in place to monitor this situation.

I have tried as much as possible to stay out of this new director's home, even though it reminds me of my old cabin. I confess to occasionally rummaging through her papers out of sheer curiosity and I wonder if she ever writes about me in her diary. One day I was examining some old gorilla bones that looked familiar when she walked into the house. The veil between the two worlds is heavy, but sometimes a burst of energy moves it ever so slightly. She once looked straight in my direction, causing me to flee the room since I had no desire to frighten or harass her. During my hasty departure I forgot to close the desk drawer and dropped the bones to the floor. Fortunately the window was open and she went to close it, no doubt assigning my breezy exodus to a gust of wind. I have tried ever since to respect her boundaries and have asked the gorillas to refrain from playing on the roof as they did in the early days. The sounds disturb her sleep.

Life at the Karisoke Research Center is still very difficult. Even though it is located 100 miles from the equator, the altitude accounts for very chilly nights that dip often into the thirty-degree range. The rain forest environment, thick canopy and shadows cast by the crater rims make for little sunshine and plenty of fog, rain, and mist. Some who come to live there find it quite difficult to adapt, and the climate does nothing to help strained personal relationships brought on by the stress of such unforgiving living conditions. I remember a couple in their twenties who came to do research after I had been living on the mountain for almost twelve years. I was nearly fifty years old, very ill, and I did not have the strength to fetch my own firewood, so my camp staff brought me baskets of kindling every evening from dead Hagenia trees. The couple complained that no one was bringing them wood, but I did not want to burden my African staff with yet another errand when my demands upon them were constant enough. This perceived lack of concern on my part caused great tension in the camp. For my part, I thought they were able-bodied enough to get their own wood. Of course, another letter was duly sent to the Ambassador noting the "mean-spirited" nature of Dian Fossey.

When I first arrived at Karisoke, I longed for human companionship and could not bring myself to listen to the short-wave radio that Louis Leakey had given me to help pass the solitary nights. The crackling sounds increased my sense of isolation and intensified my feelings of loneliness. Even trying to read my scientific journals created a kind of panic in me, magnifying the sensation of distance from friends and colleagues. The nights were like black gauze, punctuated by star glow and moonlight, and muted by the ever-present mists and fogs. The California surf and the woodlands of Kentucky were an ocean and continent away, and I longed for familiar sights, sounds, and smells. Even if I briefly entertained notions of leaving, the vast physical distances from my beginnings felt insurmountable. Both logically and emotionally, I had every reason to abandon my study. So far Africa had offered me imprisonment, torture, and the gruesome deaths of the sons of one of my closest friends. If it were not for the almost mystical enchantment I found in the company of the gorillas, I might have returned to America, married Alexie Forrester, and established a conventional existence for myself. Instead of an abortion, I might have had a family. Instead of death at fifty-three years of age, I might still be alive. I might have found peace of mind and soul, and I might have found love. I might have been bored instead of murdered. I also might have missed the greatest learning opportunity ever presented to a human being—the gift of the mountain gorillas.

From the shelter of my tent in the early years, and before my tin cabin was completed, I could hear the grunts of the duikers, the rustlings of the jungle rats, the whimper of the rabbit-like tree hyrax, and a multitude of screams and whistles that continued throughout the night. A host of eyes, yellow, red and green would peer at me from the grasses and the limbs of the Hypericum trees. The forest looked like an army of giants with arms and legs akimbo, ready to march on the camp. Sometimes the buffalo would feed very close to my tent as I sat hidden in the shadows of my makeshift porch. In time, my appreciation of the beauty of the night supplanted my loneliness. Sinister thoughts no longer ruled the night, and I came to value the moonlit beauty of Mount Karisimbi, which rose nearly fifteen thousand feet into the star-lit heavens. Gradually the night became my friend, and Karisoke my paradise. Love became an abstraction, destiny a non sequitur. If I were to fulfill my dreams to study the mountain gorilla, I had to master the day-to-day challenges and demands of life in an alien, primitive culture. I had no inkling that my final resting place would be forty feet from my cabin, or that my destiny and legacy would involve much more than a wooden box that was two inches too short for my body, buried in a gorilla graveyard on the slopes of a dormant volcano in remote Africa.

Besides adjusting to the isolated place where I lived, I had to try to reach some kind of accommodation with my African staff. My first challenge was my cook, who did a fantastic job but was very unpleasant to be around. Sadly, I found that the only way that I could get him to treat me with any respect was to treat him with disrespect. I never completely understood this aspect of the African culture. Contrary to the gossip about me in white diplomatic circles, I did not enjoy treating my staff in this manner. It increased my feelings of loneliness and isolation to assume such an angry affect.

I found myself in the same position with the park guards. If I gave them an inch they would take the proverbial mile. Because I had to assume a domineering facade, by the time I acquired enough rudimentary Swahili to communicate, no one was particularly interested in socializing with me. I felt I was a failure. If I'd had the opportunity to communicate with the researchers who had gone before me in other parts of Africa, I would have known that they experienced many of the same sorts of difficulties, born of major cultural differences. Many of them fled to civilization, but I elected to stay. But perhaps "elected" is the wrong word.

I did not weigh the pros and cons, as it was obvious that the cons far outweighed any personal rewards. I was, simply, *driven* to learn more about the gorillas. It was almost as if I really had no choice in the matter, and perhaps that is the definition of fate. I wanted to understand the society of the mountain gorilla come hell or high water. Seeing them, smelling them, feeling their touch, and sensing their warm breath on my neck was a lure more powerful than anything I had ever experienced. I would sacrifice love and endure hell in order to remain close to them.

Dawn was breaking in the eastern sky when Digit scrambled up the side of the house to join me. I was surprised that he had followed me so far from the mountain. The separation between worlds must have been absent in the early hours, because the researcher was drawn out onto the porch and aimed a dim flashlight at our ethereal presence. Satisfied that we were not there, she returned to the confines of her shelter.

Digit reached over and patted me on the hand, his exquisite, perfect fingernails looking so much like my own. He picked a few remains of Hagenia leaves from my braided hair. "Nyiramacyibili, do you remember why you named my child Mwelu?"

A deep sigh escaped from the core of my being. After agonizing over the V-W's involvement with baby Mweza's death, I was not quite ready to go over this mental territory again. The death of one baby was far too many.

"It is Swahili for 'a touch of brightness and light'."

"I know what it means. WHY did you give her that name?"

"It had a hopeful connotation. It would bring her good luck."

This little bit of Digit was given the name originally chosen for Debre Hamburger, an American girl who was scheduled to study with me, until breast cancer claimed her life at an unexpected and early age. Africans gave her the name, Mwelu, when she was working as an archeological research assistant in another part of Africa. She had been determined to come to Karisoke in spite of the deadly diagnosis. Instead, she died. I eventually hired a plane to spread her ashes over the Virungas, as that was what she wanted, even though her wish for a little more time on earth was not granted.[72]

"But, how could a name help my child escape the guns and snares of the poachers?"

I considered this for a moment. All of the names that I gave to the gorillas had a particular significance for me: Digit because of his deformed finger, Uncle Bert after a kindly old uncle of mine. "It is a common practice of humans to give names with significance. The meaning of her name carried strength."

"Naoom. Tell me about those you called Uncle Bert and Simba."

"Digit, you know who they are. Uncle Bert was the dominant silverback in your group and Simba was your mate."

"But tell me why the naming was important to you, Nyiramacyibili."

As I sat back to recall the events that shaped Simba's early years, Digit rolled onto his back and gave a yawn. I had the sense that the telling of the story was comforting to both of us in some small way; much as a parent reads a bedtime story to a child, and somehow both are soothed.

Simba, whose name means "Lion" in Swahili, was orphaned at the age of three when poachers killed her mother. When I named her, perhaps I wanted her to learn to be as ferocious as a lion in order to ensure her survival. At the age of three, a young gorilla is learning to be autonomous through play activities with other youngsters, but at the same time the mother's back is the perfect playground for the baby. I can only speculate that the violence of her mother's death contributed to Simba's suddenly morose, withdrawn state. I truly believe that Uncle Bert's intervention at this point helped Simba to survive. He protected her from all of the animals and from the rough play of the adolescent gorillas. He spent more time grooming her than a mother typically would and allowed her to share his night nest. This was unusual behavior for an adult silverback, but I liked to imagine that he was living up to his namesake, my kindhearted old Uncle Bert Chapin. Slowly, Simba responded to Bert's ministrations and began to play again. Her temperament remained restrained, however, and she appeared mildly depressed and reserved. She learned to throw temper tantrums when the other young got too rough with her. These tantrums brought Uncle Bert to her side immediately, scattering the perpetrators to the depths of the foliage. By the time Simba had matured, Digit had joined the group and eventually took her for his mate when he reached silverback status. Mwelu was born shortly after Digit was murdered. This thought was disturbing and broke my concentration.

"Digit, you never saw your child, Mwelu, come into the world."

"Mwelu was destined to join me shortly after being born. We are together now."

"Nunkie eventually claimed Simba as his mate and murdered Mwelu in order to ensure the continuation of his line over yours."

"Nunkie did his duty. Simba had no one to protect her. It was necessary that she not be abandoned again. Her spirit would be forever broken if this happened again."

"But your lifeline was broken by the death of Mwelu."

"My destiny with the group was fulfilled. We were all there to teach you, Nyiramacyibili."

Teach me. What could all of this tragedy teach me? "I don't see any reasonable lesson coming out of this, Digit."

"You have called yourself an orphan many times. Did anyone take care of you? Did any human play with you or respond to your cries for help?"

"I have been alone for as long as I can remember, Digit."

"What about Uncle Bert? You used empathy to assign his human qualities and his name to our silverback. Why did you do this?"

"My Uncle Bert was kind to me when I was young and included me in his will. The small amount of money he left me eventually went to the maintenance of Karisoke. Your groups lived my family ideal. Your silverback, Bert, took care of the helpless members. No one was ever orphaned. None of you were alone."

"Naoom. But, you were separate from your species. We understood this. The gorillas had been separate from humans since the beginning of time. Our only contact with your human group members over thousands of years was distressing and violent. Your humans stole our babies, took our forests, and set painful traps for the duiker that would sever our limbs. Eventually they set traps for the adults in order to take our body parts so that men could decorate their nests with our limbs and heads. Then the awareness of you spread through the forests."

"I don't understand."

"Our group consciousness told us that you were a wounded orphan. It was essential that you be accepted into our groups. We recognized you immediately as the one who would describe our struggle to the humans who were destroying our forests. Only a human who had experienced life as an orphan, and who had longed for the safety of a group, would be able to tell the outside world about us in a way that would be comprehensible. We knew it was our duty to teach you, but we could not interfere with your destiny any more than we could influence our own. We only know acceptance of our fate. Life unfolds as it will. We recognized the sacrifice you made to join us. You will never be alone again. You made an ironic choice in your name, Nyiramacyibili."

I had never *wished* to be alone. I spent most of my life searching for a human bond that would sustain me, but I was unlucky in love. Although my choice of a long career at Karisoke made attainment of a loving relationship all but impossible, I almost achieved love with Bob Campbell. I should have known when it came time to make the choice to return to civilization and his family, that there would be no contest. Whenever I made overtures to unattached men, camp gossip called me "predatory." And when a Rwandan doctor wanted to marry me, the price exacted would have been exile from my beloved gorillas.

Clearly, fate played a hand in my life, but so did choice. I felt constricted by the machinations of civilized society. Here, in the jungle, I could rule my world. Witch, friend, lover, maniac, or beloved gorilla lady—I was all of these; my identity was dependent upon the eye of the human beholder. The gorillas were the only entities that accepted me completely, as "Dian," openly and lovingly. I was probably not destined to live in human society.

I still wonder whether there is a godlike being fashioned in the image of mankind. Indeed, I have seen no evidence of such a being in the time and space that I now inhabit. I am not without faith, however. I sense a universal benevolence that has pity and generates great feelings of well-being once one is able to come to terms with the meaning of one's existence. The gorillas are my guides in this endeavor, and I believe that with their help I will come to a greater understanding of all earthly life and how it conjoins with universal purpose and fate.

We left the researcher alone with her dreams and climbed carefully down from the roof as the sun rose over the mountain peaks. With Digit's hand clasped firmly over my own, I thought about all of these things as we returned to Karisoke in mutual silence.

6

Bonds of Love

"Digit, do the gorillas have memories of ancient times?"

This simple question produced a sudden and unexpected display from Digit. One moment he was rooting around for celery stalks, and the next he was giving high-pitched vocalizations that sounded like a baby screaming. He snapped a limb from a Hagenia tree and beat the brush furiously before settling down and fixing his brown eyes upon my own.

"Naoom. Before the time of man there was a great sea of gorillas that stretched from sun to sun. After eons of harmony, man evolved from our life's blood, eventually separated from us, and went his own way. Mankind wanted to stand tall and abandon the nests in the trees. Generations of gorillas were born and died and man forgot about us. Then man tired of looking forward and began to look back to the nests and trees from which he came. When he returned to his nest he found us and was frightened because we reminded him of things that he thought were better forgotten."

"What did man forget, Digit?"

"Mankind forgot how to live peacefully. Even though the gorillas have great physical power, we govern a society that does not wage war. This dichotomy is fear-provoking, and fear begets violence. Man was terrified when he saw how much we were alike in countenance, so he decided to kill us. He could gaze upon our lifeless heads and bodies with a sense of superiority and feel safe. Soon, the sea of gorillas became a trickling stream. The first white hunter who came to the Virungas killed members of my grandfather's family."

Digit's recollections of ancient gorilla history were in some ways a reflection of the conversations I had once had with Louis Leakey, the man who sponsored my initial foray into the Virungas. This was an exhilarating "conversation," because I felt that, in a profound way, Digit was embodying Leakey.

"Digit, what hunter killed your grandfather's family?"

"The hunter is buried in the meadow, but something or someone scattered his bones. The gorillas tried to put the bones back into the tomb, but many are missing."

In this reference to the meadow, Digit was obviously describing Carl Akeley's camp at Kabara in the Congo. Akeley was considered to be one of the world's most notorious white hunters. With funding that Louis Leakey secured for me in 1967, I set up my first observation post at that same cabin before I was ousted and imprisoned by the Congolese. I wondered if Digit's display indicated displeasure with me for utilizing the cabin. Several of Akeley's mountain gorilla specimens can be seen in the Hall of the Great Apes at the American Museum of Natural History in New York. I had seen them many times myself. It was deeply distressing to think that they were Digit's family, yet fascinating to hear Digit relate that the gorillas bore Akeley no ill will. It seems as if they tended Akeley's grave by protecting his bones.

"Did you know that Akeley regretted his massacre of the gorillas in his later years and fought to preserve your home here?"

"His regret did not erase the blood that was spilled here. But the brutality was ordained by fate. To some extent it was our blood that brought you here."

Louis Leakey recruited me to study the gorillas because he believed that by studying gorilla society we might gain a window into our human past. My observations would, hopefully, support the hypothesis of an evolutionary link suggested by the ancient hominid skulls he had unearthed. When I first encountered Louis's archeological dig at Olduvai Gorge in Tanzania and sprained my ankle, the die was cast. I was maneuvering to get a picture of the oldest fossil beds on our planet, when I slipped and injured myself. The pain was so severe that I nearly vomited, and my guide had to half-carry me back to Leakey's tent. Louis and his wife, Mary, tenderly ministered to my injury, and my misfortune gave Louis the opportunity to size me up and encourage me to continue my safari in search of the gorillas.

In my diaries, I described my first encounters with the gorillas as "magical," and I soon saw that a better understanding of gorilla behavior and social structure was vital. In my hubris, I thought that it was because of my openness and tenacity that I was totally accepted into gorilla society. I had no idea that the gorillas were waiting with open arms for a sympathetic *consciousness* to enter their domain. In many ways, they were like the autistic children I had worked with. I only had to come to an understanding of their world in order to be accepted.

I was a woman of great passion, and Africa became my forbidden night journey. Under the cover of the Dark Continent, I could experience and embrace all that civilized society in Louisville had denied me. My romantic life, or lack thereof, has been a source of endless consternation and fantasy to my biographers. After my death, my friends related that they considered me somewhat asexual, and that they had never seen me undertake a serious romance other than my failed engagement to Alexie Forrester. They were correct in their observations, but this was before I had been brutalized by the Congolese and witnessed other atrocities. In the face of evil, I would become reckless with my body, and morality was the first casualty of my loss of innocence. Biographers mention three men with whom I became involved. There were others for whom I was more of a mother figure, and one whom I still consider to be my friend. I was not a chameleon, nor was I a witch or whore; I had always maintained that sex and love were separate entities. Love and sex, as human concepts, do not exist in gorilla society; gorillas rely upon a regard for the well-being of the individual. The best word I can use to describe what gorillas might feel about love is a kind of universal altruism that ensures a feeling of safety within the group.

Louis Leakey and I would become lovers for a short time while on safari in Kenya. He had come to my rescue after the trauma of losing Coco and Pucker to the Cologne Zoo, and his presence at this troubling time was reassuring and comforting. To my dismay, he fell in love with me and the feeling was not mutual, although I did succumb to the console and understanding of a man I respected. The deep, mysterious, and romantic African safari nights we shared had a lot to do with my abandon. Good food, wine, hot baths, and clean sheets at night were luxuries I had not experienced in many months. I am sure now that my longing to be desired created an aura of seduction, and it was Louis's misfortune to be lured into my night nest, only to be abandoned as others would abandon me. I found his amorous attentions embarrassing and tried not to encourage him, since he was sixty-seven years old, and married. My letters to him were factual, while his were filled with endearments and professions of love. Louis purchased a ruby ring for me, and it was only after he became very ill that I agreed to accept it as a gesture of friendship, because it was Louis who gave me the gorillas, my hopes, and my salvation. By defending the gorillas, I was defending my right to exist, and this undertaking gave me a feeling of great strength even in the face of much physical frailty. Unfortunately for Louis, it also gave me the fortitude, in the end, to reject a passion that had evolved into a state of romantic love.[73] The fact that Louis would love me was his own dark destiny.

The gorillas gave me an opportunity to love and be loved without fear of abandonment or retribution. This pure love was unfettered by expectation, societal conventions, or sexuality. Some have viewed my involvements with men as predatory. Even gorilla society does not include the concept of the lone female. A male will claim any female of breeding age. One would think that "civilized" society would extend the right to choose a lone existence to the female, especially one who is too tall, too outspoken, too plain, and too "burly" to conform to societal standards of femininity. I have no regrets that I embraced emotional excitement whenever it was obtainable. My only regret is that Louis carried a torch for me until his death, and Mary Leakey suspected what had happened, forever straining our relationship.

Digit was listening to my thoughts with his arms folded, while staring at a duiker that had wandered close to our location.

"Digit, why did you present such a fearsome display, earlier?"

"Must I have a reason?"

"It just seemed out of character."

"Character. What do you mean by character?"

"Digit, you can empathize with my thoughts. Why are you ignoring me?"

"I was feeling your uncertainty, Nyiramacyibili. It is the nature of the silverback to display violence, thereby creating order and confidence. You asked if I remembered when the gorillas and man were one, and I explained that we were fashioned from the same forces of creation. Man chose to take a different form from us and fled. You were the first to want to come back. We wanted you to stay and not leave the nest."

In fact, there was only one human lover whom I did not want to leave my nest. Ironically, it was Louis Leakey who arranged to have Bob Campbell come to Karisoke to film my interactions with Coco and Pucker for *National Geographic*. Alan Root was originally scheduled to be the cameraman on the project, but he became seriously ill after being bitten by a viper. It took a while for me to trust Bob, but once his photos of Coco and Pucker made the cover of *National Geographic*, the attention brought worldwide acclaim to both of us and new sources of funding. As I got to know him better, I appreciated the fact that Bob was quiet by nature, and his temperament fit well with mine. He spent months at a time with me in the mountains and learned to track the gorillas as well as any of my staff. I was able to train him in the operations at the camp so that he could take over when I took my annual trip to the States for medical check-ups and lecture duties.

Over time, we established an intimacy that flowed from the deepest soul of Africa. I was well aware that he had a wife and family, but I had come to hope that he would be willing to abandon that existence in order to join our efforts into one grand life journey. A part of me realized that I would forever be the lone woman on the mountain, and that he was incapable of a lasting commitment to me. The movie that was made of my life makes a great deal of our relationship, which was tempestuous as well as tender. One can roll the reels and search for meaning beyond that of a passionate relationship born of loneliness and despair, but you will not find it. What we shared cannot be explained, or categorized, and certainly not captured on film.

I was trying desperately to find some sort of resolution regarding my relationship with Bob, when I discovered I was pregnant. Undergoing an abortion was difficult, if not impossible, for a woman in Rwanda, so I was forced to seek the help of a Belgian doctor who lived across the Congolese border. There, medical professionals were not bound by the moral stance of Rwandan Catholicism. I did not tell Bob, who was out doing field work with the gorillas and about to leave to visit his wife in Nairobi. The abortionist met me in Gisenyi and performed the operation, which was botched, and I nearly hemorrhaged to death before I confessed what happened. This abortion probably left me sterile. Bob brought me to the hospital in Ruhengeri and postponed the visit to his wife until I was in Rosamond's capable hands at Mugongo, where I recuperated.

One thing few people understand is that Bob's ambition meshed perfectly with my heartbreak. Most of the time we both took what was necessary from the other in order to keep the vestiges of a relationship alive. Since my death, he has found it necessary to claim some of my successes as his own.[74] He is still angry with me because I did not give him much credit when I wrote *Gorillas in the Mist*, and he is not the first person to call my research into question after my death. I have no way of defending myself except through what remains of my writings. If he honestly feels that my habituation techniques were fabrications, he could have called them into question when I was alive, or even after my death when he was hired as a consultant by the movie producers.

I don't believe that I sacrificed an opportunity for children and a family as my enemies have suggested. First of all, the opportunity never existed because I had no income other than the small grants I received from foundations and *National Geographic*. These grants were barely enough to keep the camp supplied with food and salaries for the anti-poaching patrols. In these difficult circumstances, I was uncertain every year whether or not any monies would be forthcoming. Secondly, Bob was already someone's husband, and my brief moments of true elation were with my gorillas. Bob captured one of those moments beautifully on film when my beloved Digit took a notebook and pencil from my hand. Perhaps that is Bob's best contribution to my memory. Dian Fossey was not destined to be a Scottish housewife with a brood of children in tow. She will forever be the gorilla lady, who was most content, if not happiest, with her gorilla friends.

"Digit, sometimes I wonder if it was immoral of me to terminate my pregnancies."

"You are destined to always struggle with actions taken and not taken, Nyiramacyibili."

"Did I murder my children? Was my death retribution?"

"Those who condemn your legacy are the ones guilty of murder."

"But I was afraid; my actions were cowardly."

"When you learn to have compassion for yourself, inspiration and understanding will follow."

I had not yet been able to reach this state of compassion. Love, understanding, and intuition remained elusive. Whether lack of human love or its profound entanglements were the source of my emotional bondage, I was not yet certain.

Digit broke my concentration by suddenly pounding me on the back, which is a gorilla signal that it is time to play. He grunted and indicated that I should follow him to the opening in the trees where they made the movie about me. He was standing in the exact spot where one of his group members acted as his stand-in.

"The movie people were foolish when they tried to show the first time we met, Nyiramacyibili. I was busy encouraging the other gorillas to cooperate with the actors and not frighten them, but I was angry when the film crew drugged the baby chimpanzees and made them look like the gorillas,[75] Coco and Pucker. I thought about ruining the footage, but since the damage was already done to the babies, I allowed things to continue."

If you look closely at the footage, you can see branches rustling in the background when there was not a whisper of a breeze in the air. That was Digit, "directing" what was left of his family, since he wanted the world to see the gorillas as they truly were with me in life. This may be unbelievable to some, but others who have visited Karisoke in the years since my death have attested to the fact that there is an unusual feel to the place. The film's production crew said that they savored many magical moments as the gorillas ate, played with their babies, and entertained themselves in close proximity with the motion picture cameras.[76] Sigourney Weaver, the lead actress, said that getting acquainted with the gorillas who had been in my research groups was easier than anyone had expected. She said that she had been taught never to look them directly in the eyes, but she disregarded this rule because she "just could not help it." Weaver went on to recall that she thought she was "meeting an old friend"[77] when she interacted with one of the individuals in my study group. She should not have expected otherwise. Her physical stature and presence is much like my own, and the gorillas were more than willing to cooperate and revel in their memories of me.

Digit and I stood in the brush for a long time, both of us lost in memories of better times. What I am beginning to understand from Digit's patient tutelage is that my instruction is in its infancy.

7

Children of Antiquity

Revisiting the motives for my abortion required a time of spiritual renewal. I spent a long time roaming meadows and trails in the Virungas after my conversations with Digit. I was not yet ready to come to terms with my earthly actions, but I was able, temporarily, to distance myself both in dimension and time from the consequences. The mountain forests and soothing mists were akin to a blanket of compassion.

The Virungas offer a perfect setting for a spiritual retreat from violent thoughts and self-recrimination. The eight volcanoes form the crest of the spine of Africa and have inspired legends from the dawn of antiquity. King Solomon's mines were rumored to be located here, as well as the source of the Nile River. I once remarked that the setting was as close to God as one could hope to be. I am not sure that I ever really believed in God's existence, but some part of me always wished or hoped for the reassurance a supreme being could provide. I wonder if I will find God when I have finished exploring my surroundings.

One can fully understand how the gorillas evolved their peaceful existence here. There are over one hundred edible plants, although curiously, the stinging nettle is one of their favorites. The steep terrain, coupled with the cool rainy climate, has kept competition for resources down. Lack of pooled water is never a problem since the gorillas rarely drink, getting most of their hydration from their plant intake. In fact, gorillas seem to avoid water, rarely sleeping near water or fording a stream. They lead an idyllic existence when not threatened, sleeping in until well after sunrise, and napping in the late morning to early afternoon.

The active volcanoes are a linkage to the birth of the planet and the forces that forged the commencement of time. I learned early on that the gorillas do not range there. Magma churns and reshapes the surface of the planet as it is forced by pressure and ancient waters to reach the surface in the two remaining active volcanoes. I often watched the glow of the active peaks from my cabin. The red and orange flames would filter through the mists and cause me to wonder about

God, or at least some divine presence that ruled over earthly matters. My Catholic catechism never prepared me for the profound experience of living in an environment that was so close to the forces of creation. Almost mockingly, the late November 1971 rumblings of Mount Nyiragongo formed a terrible crimson backdrop after my first abortion[78] and kept me up all night. The volcano's name means, literally, "mother of Gongo." Gongo is one of the most revered spirits of the region, and local legends associate the volcano's lava bed as a source of atonement for past sins and wrongdoings. Danish vulcanologists described a feeling akin to viewing the depths of Dante's Inferno within Nyiragongo's crater, and the wrath of mother Gongo was not lost upon me.

In happier times, I would have a stunning view of the mist-shrouded summit of beautiful Mount Karisimbi. Its Kinyarwandan name means "white shell," and it is the highest of the eight Virungan volcanoes that form the eastern side of the Great Rift Valley. It is just to the north of Lake Kivu, which empties into the Ruzizi River, which then flows to the great Lake Tanganyika. Kivu and her flowage would all too soon gain a horrific association as the place where the bodies of thousands of victims of the Rwandan genocide would be abandoned to the forces of antiquity.

Karisimbi's crater shelters a pristine alpine lake that was formed by ancient volcanic forces. It rests in a serene state, contrasting sharply with the restless Nyiragongo. The waters are ice cold if you are in the earthly realm and marvelous if one is unencumbered by the physical body. I can swim with abandon now, afterwards stretching out upon the lava rocks and reveling in the sun's energy. It is difficult to impart sensation as experienced in the afterlife. My energy level rises or falls depending upon the amount of light that resides in my aura. I exist in a state of pure energy now, and with the passage of earthly time I find it more and more difficult to reconnect with corporeal memories in a concrete way.

I find it ironic and remarkable that I was able to construct pioneering studies of gorilla family structures and bonding while being unable to experience familial cohesion and safety in my own life. My research has shown that the female of the gorilla species is dependent upon the protection of the silverback if she is to successfully raise her young. Individual, as well as group health and well-being, are totally reliant upon a predictable social structure. I especially remember the nulliparous[79] female, aptly named "Bravado." Nulliparous females would usually attach to a lone silverback or to a smaller group structure because, in the world of the gorilla, status is everything. Association with the oldest and most established silverback ensures a secure social standing. I was amazed that Bravado had somehow muscled her way into a dominant group of older females who were

Beethoven's established mates. This left her isolated from her birth group, which was protected by the silverback, Uncle Bert. Bert was, in many ways, much less experienced than Beethoven. A ravine separated the two groups. Though it was only about 100 feet wide, it clearly marked the perimeter of each group's range.

One day, Uncle Bert decided to initiate a huge display of hootseries, chest beating, and branch breaking—which immediately piqued the interest of Bravado. She was drawn to her old group and brought some of the younger members of her new group across the ravine, where they immediately began playing with some of the members of Uncle Bert's group. This foray initiated several instances of strutting by Uncle Bert, followed by admonitions by Beethoven. The two silverbacks would face off on the ridge, until Bert eventually would back down. Through it all, Bravado continued to be the catalyst and instigator of the confrontations, while Beethoven seemed totally perplexed at the lack of protocol involved in the encounters. Beethoven was absolutely capable of inflicting serious injuries to the younger and less experienced Bert, but chose not to do so, substituting ritualized intimidation displays.

Bravado finally returned home, ending the specter of a bloody confrontation. Eleven months later she gave girth to a male infant I named Curry, who had been sired by Beethoven. I hoped that the birth would secure Bravado's status within the group, but she became very reclusive and worried about interaction between the infant and older members of the group. It wasn't until the baby was nine months old that Bravado relaxed a bit and allowed the youngster to interact with Beethoven's other offspring.

As if in fulfillment of Bravado's worries, an unexpected and terrible event happened when a lone silverback attacked and killed Curry, and Beethoven and the older females were bloodied in the encounter. Afterwards, Bravado's behavior changed radically, but not in the way I expected. Instead of grieving, she became very playful, almost as if a great burden had been lifted from her. She wrestled and played with juveniles and seemed to be thoroughly enjoying her new freedom. I learned later that this was common for first time mothers. I concluded that this type of behavior might provide the means whereby a female strengthens and renews social bonds with other females in the group after infanticide. On the other hand, it could have also reflected a mother's sudden ability to move about with abandon after so many months of having to feed and care for the infant while still trying to follow group movements.[80]

I wish that I had been able to experience this kind of predictable and reassuring social bonding within my own human groups, but it is interesting that female gorillas do not ordinarily form bonds with other females, except in family lineages. In fact, the female gorilla is much more prone to squabbling than the male. I was also not one who bonded very easily. My friends have reflected that I would usually wait for others to make the first move when trying to establish a friendship. I realize that many of the female researchers who came to Karisoke during my tenure were prone to diverse forms of competition. My research became the "food" they were willing to fight for. Inflicting damage upon my reputation became their favorite weapon. One student,[81] who became a competitor, remarked after my death that a "clean whack" with a machete was my comeuppance. She has since reviewed many of my findings and written her own textbook. This does not bother me as much as the personal betrayal she offered as payment for my acceptance. In philosophical terms, I am not surprised, since this kind of ruthless competition is common in academia, but it has tragic consequences nonetheless. Besides the students who betrayed me, there are many other primatologists who have compromised my life's work and corrupted its meaning. They have disseminated it for academic consumption with only their own names attached. So much time has passed since my murder, perhaps no one will notice or care. My research is my abducted child.

These recriminating thoughts made me feel very lonely, so I made my way down the mountain trails in search of Digit. I found him sitting on the lava outcrop where he had previously arranged my gallery of gorilla portraits. He balanced a sketchpad in his huge hands, and he labored over a drawing, adroitly holding a piece of charcoal between the deformed fingers that prompted his name.

"Hmmm, hmmm." Digit was grumbling in the "close-call" vocalization that the male uses to gather females into the group. In human terms it sounds like an obese male clearing his throat or humming. If one had to define the effect of the sound, I would say that Digit seemed inordinately pleased with himself. I half expected him to hide the sketch from my view as I approached for a closer look, but he kept at the task without a glance in my direction.

I reclaimed my perch in the Pygeum tree, which was now barren of fruit, and peered at Digit's drawing from above. I started to chuckle when I saw the subject of his artistic endeavors, and the sound of my human vocalization sent him into frenzy. Before I could catch my breath, he had thrown down the pad, all the while hooting and chest beating. Vegetation was flying in all directions, but then, just as suddenly, he settled down and resumed sketching. For the first time in our association, Digit had exhibited a "bluff charge" for my benefit. Clearly he did not appreciate my reaction to his artwork.

"I think I have captured your likeness, Nyiramacyibili."

Indeed he had, but I was not certain that I was enamored of the results. Digit's charcoal rendering approximated a photograph taken of me in the year before I was murdered. My face is very full, and my hair is parted down the middle with gray roots showing. Crows feet and baggy eyelids dominate, and my smile looks rather smug. I had put on a considerable amount of weight after three years in the States lecturing, writing, and fulfilling duties as a faculty member at Cornell University. There was something else about the portrait that I found troubling, but I could not put my finger on it.

Digit grumbled another "hmmm" as he tore his sketch neatly down the middle.

I recoiled at the result, it being too similar to the effects of the machete blow to my skull. Digit was left holding two parts of "me" in his massive, yet gentle hands. "Aristotle said that the whole is more than the sum of its parts," Digit said.

"Aristotle again?"

"Tell me what you see in the drawing." Digit climbed the tree and handed the ragged halves of my face to me. As I studied the right and left sides, Digit busied himself by bending branches and fashioning a tree nest big enough for the two of us to share. Try as I might, I did not understand what Digit wanted me to comprehend. "Separate the eyes, one from the other. Look with your heart, Nyiramacyibili."

Abruptly, the images appeared as pieces of a puzzle that do not quite join together. The edges appeared to be a good fit, but something was a bit off, and I had to search for the correct part. I only had two pieces of "me" to work with, and the incompatibility of the two sides of my face was suddenly quite striking. My right side looked quite a bit younger than the left. My right eye seemed brighter, with almost a happy glint in the iris. The bags underneath this eye looked like the product of a jolly expression rather than fatigue. I appeared relaxed, young, carefree, and cheerful. The left was another story. My eye looked troubled, almost angry, and there was a general world-weariness in the shadows formed by my plump cheeks. With an eyebrow arched in a defiant gesture, I appeared both physically and mentally exhausted.

Was my physical self the sum of these two persons? I looked both beautiful and frightening. What was the truth of the "me" that walked the earth? Had my experiences shaped my countenance, or had the multifaceted aspects of my personality determined my experiences? Am I defined by this image? If the eyes are the windows to the soul, how can beauty and emptiness coexist there? I was once again flooded with questions, which begged an answer that was not forthcoming.

I found myself sobbing as hard as I did the day that Peanuts, the young black-back from Group Eight, reached out to touch my upturned hand in my early days at Karisoke. I cried at that moment because I thought he had recognized the decency and compassion in me, trusting me enough to do something no gorilla had ever done before. I had been accepted at last, and the tears that ran down my cheeks were born of relief and gratitude.

"Oh Digit, how can a single soul harbor both personalities? Who am I to you?"

"You are our friend, Nyiramacyibili."

"How does being a friend relate to my question, Digit?"

"What is a friend but a single soul dwelling in two bodies, Nyiramacyibili?"[82]

If only I could become a friend to myself, perhaps I could see the decency that Digit and my human friends saw within me. Digit had told me the truth, and I recognized it as such. With a thankful heart, I snuggled next to him in our tree nest and cherished the moment. As I reveled in the blessings and grace that flowed through my being, Digit sang softly until welcome sleep overtook me. I dreamed peacefully of ancient voices whispering in the African night and children playing on the mountain slopes.

8

Faces of Death

Woe, woe, alas! Earth, Mother Earth!

—Cassandra[83]

There is an African legend that declares, "The souls of the good will spend their eternity on the summit of Karisimbi."[84] Whether I am destined to remain in the company of the gorillas in this paradise will be determined by my success or failure as I come to terms with the contradictory aspects of my life. The idea of putting the pieces of my face together to access the opposing facets of my personality opened a new avenue of exploration to me. I had unconsciously used a similar technique over the years in my assessments of gorilla personalities. A detailed photographic record exists of the changes in Digit's countenance as his duties and rank within Group Four changed throughout the years. There is a well-known photo taken of Digit when he was a young blackback. He is chewing on a stick and shows no apprehension about the proximity of the camera. He is seemingly relaxed and confident. The image is so charming that the Rwandan Office of Tourism used it as part of a promotion to lure paying visitors to Kigali.

"Come meet him in Rwanda!"

The caption on the poster was an open invitation for human encroachment into the realm of the gorilla. I was furious when I saw the promotion, since it was in direct contradiction to my feelings about respect for the gorilla's mountain habitat and my theory of active conservation. In *Gorillas in the Mist*, I wrote quite clearly, with much conviction and moral indignation, that "the rights of the animal supercede human rights."[85] This sentiment was met with much opposition in a country where there was barely enough cultivatable land to support the local population. The terraced plots of the farmers were marching up the mountain, and at times I had found gorillas resting within sight and sound of the local

Bahutu village; there being no discernable buffer zone between gorilla and human habitat.

I believe the publication of that poster was Digit's death sentence. Government officials in Ruhengeri Province were coming to the belated realization that encouraging gorilla tourism would increase local coffers more than the illegal trade in gorilla body parts. After Digit's murder in 1977, I received an official letter from Dismas Nsabimana, the Director of the Rwandan Office of Tourism and National Parks (ORTPN), in which he "deplored" the act of poaching that caused Digit's death, but chastised me for preventing tourists from seeing the gorillas. He sounded almost apoplectic that I did not recognize the authority of the ORTPN.[86]

I encountered a similar situation in 1980. I had just returned to Rwanda after completing study and lecture duties in the States. By this time, Francois Benda-Lema, for whom I had little or no respect whatsoever, had replaced Dismas, who was fired shortly after he did an about-face and authorized a significant donation to my anti-poacher patrols. I suspected that Benda-Lema was spearheading an orchestrated effort to keep me out of Rwanda, and my suspicions were verified when four phone calls to his office went unreturned. When I finally reached him at home, he hung up when he recognized my voice.[87]

I would eventually expose the fact that tourism monies were going to road improvements for the local officials' private properties as well as new vehicles and homes for those in political power. In addition, Mutarootkwa, the Zairoise Tutsi who worked on the poacher patrols during this time, reported that coffee smuggling from Zaire into Rwanda had increased tremendously during my absence.[88] As I struggle to come to terms with my extreme actions regarding these events, I question whether my continual exposition of corrupt political practices, including poaching of gorilla body parts by those involved in gold smuggling, resulted in retaliation aimed at my gorilla study groups.

Two years after the publication of the Digit poster, there was an upheaval in the social structure of Group Four predicated by the death of Old Goat due to natural causes. Her body was found tucked within the hollow of an ancient Hagenia tree and nearly obscured by vines. She was the group's dominant female and shared sentry duties with Digit. Digit had reached sexual maturity as a silverback by this time and was forced by her death to assume sole sentry duties. He remained with the group because mating opportunities were still available to him, but the photos taken of him during this period showed a haunted, piercing look in his eyes.[89] In addition, the corners of his mouth are turned down, his body language is very formal, and one would have to say, uneasy. In one of the last photos taken of Digit and me in 1976, I am kneeling next to him and imitating a feeding gesture. His body language is one of tolerance, but he is clearly leaning away from me, not particularly interested in what I am doing, and it looks as if there is a tremendous weight on his shoulders. The final photo I took of Digit was just before Christmas in 1977. He was on sentry duty, situated away from the main group and surrounded by lush jungle vegetation. A photo of the Christ in the Garden of Gethsemane would not be as provoking. One can see fear, apprehension, and ultimate acceptance in Digit's earthly countenance. Whether he was aware of his impending fate, or not, I have no idea. When I ask Digit about these changes, he prefers to turn the discussion back to my spiritual journey and continues to remain accepting of his role in the evolution of Group Four.

Creationists and scientists alike continue to damn me for my anthropomorphic approach to gorillas, which has risen to the stature of a mortal sin in the dual worlds of fundamentalist religions and "proper" scientific endeavors. Even my death did not end the constant character assassinations. My work, personality, morality, and even my sanity is still being dissected and questioned in what Ian Redmond once called "the gutter press."[90] Nearly twenty years after my death, my former student, Amy Vedder, has written a book that denies the truth of my legacy. I dread that my life and research will be dismissed by opportunists and hijacked by purloiners of my legacy. I willingly faced the dangers inherent in my research in Rwanda; civil war and social unrest was unfolding throughout the region. It is still hard to accept that I was also subjected to constant attacks from members of the scientific community who felt I had gone too far in my close association with the gorillas.

I am afraid that the opportunity will soon be lost for the human race to understand the profound implications of its origins. The gorillas are our cousins. To look upon the gorillas is enough to realize the connection. But for a simple shift in the arrangement of DNA patterns, it could well be the gorillas, chimpanzees, or orangutans standing in our place. By dismissing them and all other members of the animal kingdom as lesser beings, we have guaranteed the ascendancy of the human race at the expense of all of the other creatures with which we share this planet. The cook boy, Manual, expressed this sentiment perfectly upon his first contact with a gorilla when he said, "Surely God, these are our kin."[91]

While I was alive, I saved many of my camp notes as well as all of my personal correspondence. I'm not sure why I saved the notes, as they were at times very hurtful. I recall that Amy Vedder returned a Christmas present I had prepared for her and enclosed a cruel note, because she felt I had used an abusive term to describe her.[92] The gift had been meant as an olive branch on my part, and it hurt to be rejected, especially during the Christmas season. On another occasion, many years later, David Watts sent me a note saying that he had been "pretty cooperative" maintaining Karisoke during one of my long absences. He concluded that I could "goddamned well re-assume (sic) all YOUR responsibilities for it now."[93] This was yet another instance in which a relationship had soured. My initial years with Watts were filled with hope that he might be an individual who would understand my approach to the gorillas. Indeed, he was very instrumental in saving one of the gorilla groups in the early days.

David Watt's note was symptomatic of the general animosity that developed between me and the hard core scientific researchers. Watts and I had just engaged in a serious disagreement about what I considered to be his overpayment of African staff at Karisoke during my absence. Contrary to what my enemies have implied about sloppy bookkeeping on my part, I kept precise records on expenditures at the camp. By 1980, I was funding many of the poacher patrols from the inheritance I received from my real Uncle Bert, but the money would not last forever. My abrasive stance in defense of the gorillas, and my allotment of funding to anti-poaching patrols rather than tourism, alienated my co-workers to the extent that they no longer treated me with any shred of respect. It was as if I were beneath them, somehow. I had become one with the gorillas. The Mountain Gorilla Project was relentless in its efforts to force me off the mountain because of my efforts to stop tourist interaction with the study groups. But who, after all, has the moral authority to sacrifice one species for another? One can make the argument that mankind has succeeded all too well on the face of the earth. Not only loss of habitat, but also disease transmitted by humans has decimated certain gorilla populations. Digit and I have watched helplessly as the lowland gorillas have contracted the Ebola virus. This was one of my greatest fears as I fought desperately with conservation groups that wanted to use the habituated groups as tourist traps. But my warnings had all the effect of Cassandra during the Trojan War, as everyone rushed to kill the messenger.[94] If only I were truly gifted with prophecy and physical beauty as the lovely daughter of the King of Troy was, perhaps I could have saved all of the gorillas, if not myself. Unfortunately, the public fascination with my eccentricities has become bigger in death than my contributions to gorilla conservation were in life. I fear that this is, perhaps, my biggest failing, although Digit does not see it as such. In my continuing studies with him, he assures me that there is a bigger picture that will be revealed. I can only expect that this is true, because I trust Digit.

These reflections once again increased my anxieties to the point that I felt my lungs constricting as I struggled down the slope in search of Digit. As I clutched at the vegetation for support, I felt the stinging nettles and thistles piercing my flesh as plainly as if I were still alive. The gorillas were exhibiting their usual behavior, waiting for the lagging or sick member of the group. Just as they would shorten their day ranges to accommodate a wounded or ill comrade, so, too, were they patiently waiting for me to recover from the psychic ills I'd been burdened with in this new life. I found Digit waiting for me in the lava tube that serves as a passageway between the bamboo forests of the lower slope of Mount Visoke and the dense, silent forest that is the home of the mountain gorilla. Although it is only thirty feet in length, the tunnel held great significance for me in the early years at Karisoke. In 1967, Alyette DeMunck and I led a procession of supply-laden Bahutu porters to the utopian saddle region that would eventually house the camp. This flat plain is located midway between Mount Visoke and Mount Karisimbi.

The solid tunnel of lava forms a dramatic entrance into the world of the gorillas. Within it, you are still shaking off the noises of the populated cultivation below, and upon emerging you enter the silent world of fog-laden Hagenias whose trunks are securely bedded down in tall, lush vegetation. The trail is more defined than in the village, for it was kept open by elephants and buffaloes commuting to and from the upper slopes.[95] The tunnel also served as a passageway for the animals from the tilled fields of pyrethrum to the mountain wilderness. In my early study days, once you arrived at the opening to the forest, the sights and sounds of civilization faded completely away, and one was filled with a sense of wonder and magic, as if traveling a million years back in time.

Lava tunnels are created in volcanic hot spots. As liquid lava flows down the side of the volcano, the upper layers cool while the lower layers form conduits beneath the surface. This geological feature is unique to volcanic regions—a link to the beginnings of time when magma first formed in the earth's core. Twenty years after my death, the tunnel is still here, but the bamboo forest has been replaced with a parking lot for the benefit of the tourists. The genocidal wars of the past years have destroyed many of the structures, but the government is in the process of rebuilding them. In fact, the structures have been rebuilt a number of times during the conflicts of the past decade. My campsite is no longer in existence, the canopy and forest having reclaimed all but the graveyard. Only two rondavels remain in the parking area, and rotten wooden pilings define the outline of my cabin.

I noticed that Digit had assembled a crew of gorillas from the graveyard. They were busily returning the crumbling walls of the lava tube to an approximation of its condition when I first encountered it with Mrs. DeMunck. For eons, great processions of elephants had used this passageway as a means to traverse the slopes of Visoke and enter the food-rich bamboo forests below. In more modern times, the great herds used this route to make many a night's journey to the pyrethrum fields below. Rosamond Carr used to say that there must have been a seminal moment in human history when an individual elephant discovered the delicacy of the pyrethrum root and rumbled the information to the greater herds across Africa. From that day forward, there was no keeping the herds from the vast fields of daisy-like flowers.

The plantation owners did not greet the elephants' intrusion passively. Rosamond's ex-husband, Kenneth Carr, shot a bull elephant that led a small herd into the fields at Mugongo plantation. It initially appeared that the shot was not effective, as the bull remained standing, and several females surrounded him so that another shot was not a possibility. As it turned out, the females formed their protective phalanx to support the mortally wounded bull. When they could bear his weight no longer, they retreated to the forests and the enormous bull fell to the earth.[96]

Centuries of rough hides brushing against the lava walls had left a texture not unlike that of a fresco painting. The floor of the tube had an undulating surface, a testament to thousands upon thousands of elephant feet shuffling along throughout the years. Batwa poachers gradually murdered the great herds of elephants for the ivory trade, and mosses grew over the walls—obliterating the evidence of the gentle giants that once roamed the slopes. I saw this change in my lifetime and it saddened me greatly.

"Naoom, naoom," Digit belched his greeting.

He had rocked back on his haunches and was scratching his forehead while he examined his work on the wall. The other gorillas took this as a sign that it was time for a rest break and stopped their work long enough to great me with murmurs, grunts, pokes, and prods. Macho, Digit's child, Mwelu, and Simba were among the group. There were others whom I did not recognize from my earthly days, but that was to be expected, since the extermination of the gorillas did not stop with my death. Only one gorilla, a silverback, who did not have any family ties to the group, did not stop working. He was energetically removing moss from the wall in an agitated manner.

Digit once again growled a response to my questions before I could vocalize them. "He was cooked and half-eaten by Hutu militiamen during the last genocidal war because the men were hungry and could not get any other bushmeat. Although he has completed his journey through death, he has not told us his name since his spirit is still damaged. Assigning tasks to him seems to help," Digit added.

I moved to a position where I could look over the shoulder of the spiritually damaged silverback. Michelangelo himself could not have approached this endeavor with more care and artistic genius. The once moss-covered surface had taken on an exquisite transparency, with a vibrant color and detail that could only be rivaled by the Sistine Chapel. My sense of awe, inspired by the silverback's efforts, was enhanced by what was revealed. My earthly eyes had seen only the scrapes and swirls produced when the tough elephant hides scraped along the tunnel walls. Now, I was permitted to look deeper, and what was revealed was a diorama of the historical evolution of mankind, including the gorillas and the other wildlife that inhabit this unique ecosystem. The vegetation zones of Visoke were arrayed in stunning detail. Alpine meadows flowed into bamboo forests; herbaceous zones blended seamlessly into grassland and saddle. Tutsi, Batwa, and Hutu were depicted in villages that surrounded, but did not encroach upon, the animal habitat. The painting reminded me of dreams I once had in which gorillas and mankind found a happy medium in the tiny ecosystem they share.

"Is this what was, or what could be, Digit?"

"What was, is, Nyiramacyibili."

I was completely disheartened by Digit's answer. I had hoped that the visiting silverback's efforts would somehow have the power to alter time and history, but Digit reminded me that the events of history are static, forever unalterable. A crushing sadness enveloped me, and I sank to my knees on the tunnel floor. If the rapid destruction of the forests continues as the landscape is further transformed to accommodate the exponential growth of the human African population, the annihilation of the mountain gorilla is guaranteed. If civil war were to return to the region, millions more of the central African population will disappear, and the lowland gorillas will again be murdered for bushmeat. The gorillas' fate is directly tied to that of the African human populace. The outlook for both species is bleak, but the gorillas would certainly be the first to succumb in the struggle for survival.

When I was alive, I was a champion of what I termed "active conservation," a concept which allowed for the proper payment and equipment of the African villagers so that they would be encouraged to guard against poaching. This method provided personal incentives for individual Africans to take pride in their heritage. Since my death, sociological studies have emerged that theoretically tie environmental scarcity to violent conflict and genocidal wars in Rwanda.[97] But, even though Rwanda has received more conservation foreign aid than any African country, most of that money has gone into the private coffers of corrupt officials. This "theoretical conservation" is embraced by African government officials, foreign aid organizations, and propaganda machines struggling to win the hearts and minds of the African populace. It is hidden behind the political motives of various aid organizations that espouse community outreach but serve more sinister masters. While proclaiming to protect the gorillas and the Africans, these organizations are in actuality protecting access to precious metals and other natural resources as well as secret military and mining installations in the heart of darkest Africa. Developed nations, in particular, have a vested interest in maintaining a western bias in the populations. Gold, diamonds, and coltan, a mineral used in the manufacture of computer chips for the telecommunications industry, are prizes far more valuable than the gorillas. It greatly saddens me that some organizations use the impoverishment of the African people as a cover to encourage mining in the mountain gorilla habitat. Increasing numbers of sightseers to the Parc des Volcans also bring in money, but at a disproportionate cost to the gorillas and other animals that inhabit the volcanic slopes of the Virungas.

In the months before my murder, The Fauna and Flora Preservation Society published a flyer that looked at the income generated by the tourism campaign in the Parc des Volcans. Twelve months before my death, the total income for the park was roughly 156,000 francs. Half of that was eaten up in operating costs.[98] I have to wonder if the disruption caused to the gorillas was worth the profit. The immediate needs of the several hundred remaining mountain gorillas are not being met by the practices of theoretical conservation. The gorillas and other park animals have no time to wait.[99]

Digit interrupted my ruminations as he knuckle-walked over to me and put his face level with my own, gazing deep into my eyes. He made no effort to touch me or give me one of his reassuring pats on the head, though I deeply wished he would. "Nyiramacyibili, despair is born from past deeds and actions. We are quite pleased with our friend's diorama. Look deeper and you will see anticipation for what is possible."

I strained mightily to follow Digit's direction. While beautiful in scope and execution, all that was visible to me was a utopian vista of humankind and gorilla, existing side by side with no disease, war, or corruption to upset nature's delicate balance. The realization that this was a delusion, never to be realized, caused familiar angers and frustrations to well up within me. I wanted to don the old Halloween masks and terrorize poachers and interlopers. If only I were young—alive with the grace and agility to scale the steep slopes, burn huts, confiscate snares, and kidnap cattle and poachers alike! I would once again instill the fear of the "witch of the Virungas" in anyone who would dare to harm my gorillas—or the other wildlife that lives here!

Tears poured down the machete scar that divided my face as I completely collapsed on the smooth rock floor. The undulations of the ancient elephant tracks pressed into the bones of my knees and arms. I wept for the gorillas. I wept for love lost and love never realized. I wept because of fear. I wept for the time when the sunlight that filtered through the mists of the Virungas gently caressed the land that bore our mothers. I wept for my unborn children and the unborn of all of the gorillas who had fallen, mighty warriors slain in countless battles while defending their rights and the rights of their unborn. I wept also for the children of the Rwandan genocide.

The damaged silverback joined my lament. The only other time I had seen a gorilla cry was when Coco looked out of my cabin window at the mountains after she had been taken from her group by the German poachers. Her wail was not at all unlike that of a human infant, and remains seared in my memory.[100] I felt that the damaged silverback and I were pilgrims on the same journey. Our path was traveled only by those beyond all earthly redemption. We were both alone, both abandoned by hope, although at least I had a name—Nyiramacyibili. Would there be no one remaining to remember our struggle?

The nameless silverback was consumed with sobs and I reached over with my nettle-scarred hand to wipe the tears from the great face. As my dirt-stained fingers gently brushed the moisture from his eyes, an enormous scar became visible through the matted fur around his nose. It was the diagonal scar of a panga blade and it matched my own deformity both in symmetry and form.

9

Death and Dreams[101]

The anguish I experienced after my encounter with the silverback in the confines of the lava tube induced a restless, dream-filled slumber. I was vaguely aware of Digit carrying me to one of Rosamond's pyrethrum fields and gently depositing my sleeping form amongst the daisy-like blooms. Battle-weary soldiers from the First World War who fought in the African campaigns had sought rest and refuge in very similar fields. The soldiers discovered a unique property of the plant, in that it possessed potent insecticidal properties, killing the lice that inhabited their bodies, hair, and clothing. Pyrethrum would become a cash crop for the African planters and a highly sought-after export. Unfortunately, the wildlife that depended upon natural flora paid the consequences, since the planters' cultivation of the fertile volcanic soil sacrificed both space and food sources.

My dreams were wild and disjointed, filled with vague sounds, conversations and whispers, until the sensation of the panga blade crashing into the back of my skull caused me to gasp for breath. I struggled into a sitting position, and with each desperate gasp for air I felt my lungs constricting, which made me breathe even faster. My heart was pumping so fast that the beats became erratic as the chambers in the organ fell out of synch with a normal rhythm. I felt dizzy, and a grey veil obscured my vision. I had wrestled with this kind of panic attack during life and often used liquor or valium to quell the anxieties I experienced during my solitary existence at Karisoke. I found myself instinctively reaching for my 9mm Walther PPK/S—the gun that I had in my possession when Digit was murdered and dismembered. I experienced a similar nocturnal attack after we'd spent nearly a week in an unproductive search for Digit's head and hands. I'd been sick and restless all night long and awoke coughing blood and suffering from severe aching and chills.[102] I am certain now that these attacks were a premonition of what was to become my ultimate fate. Strangely, during this period of searching for Digit's remains, the patrols encountered a lone silverback of unknown origins; he was new to the Rwandan side of the mountain.

The term "waking the dead" had more than a symbolic meaning for me during this new and terrifying episode. Thankfully, my fears and exhaustion were forgotten when I heard the shrieks and hoots of the lone silverback nearby. Fossey the researcher re-emerged, and I set off in pursuit of this elusive interloper, much as I would have in the days when I was alive in the bush. Soon my head cleared, my breathing and pulse rate returned to normal, and I was back in my element: strong, confident, and slogging through the muddy soil. Before long, I caught up with the spirit of the damaged silverback in a cloud of mist that was descending upon the tilled field from the lower slopes of the mountains. Upon closer inspection, I saw that the mist was emanating from the opening of the lava tunnel. I approached, and immediately encountered a ferocious bluff charge from the silverback. As was my custom when I was alive, I met the charge by standing my ground, but I must admit his explosive screams and fierce charge reawakened repressed memories of the stark terror I felt at the first bluff charge I experienced in my early days at Karisoke. I wrote at the time that the only thing that kept me from running was the death grip I had on the surrounding vegetation. In death and in life, there is nowhere to run when you are being charged by a huge gorilla. I had no alternative but to face him. His immediate response to my attitude was not unexpected, as I had experienced similar behavior in my earthly studies. He stood down from his charge and cocked his head at me. I vocalized the familiar "naoom" belch, but my new acquaintance was not in the mood for pleasantries, and responded with a "hoot" series and much chest pounding. I assumed a submissive position on my stomach for several minutes and listened to a succession of "hoo-hoo-hoo," and "pock, pock, pock," before the silverback began to pig grunt and settled into a more relaxed posture. The grunts indicated that the he was attempting to communicate, while remaining wary of my presence.

I remained prostrate until the silverback's anxieties abated, and he knuckle-walked to my position, settling his hulking frame incongruously into the frail flowers. I held my position out of deference to the species-specific form of communication the gorilla was using. Finally, he tentatively reached out and prodded my back, but in the split instance before he touched me I telepathically heard him "say" MGAHINGA GORILLA. My first thought was that he was telling me his name, while my interpretation of his telepathic communication had mangled the syntax. The silverback prodded me again, urgently, and I heard once again, MGAHINGA GORILLA.

I took this opportunity to rise to a sitting position and face the silverback. The brown eyes, which gazed into my own from either side of the deep machete scar on his face, did little to soothe my own anxiety or shed any discernable light upon our communication difficulties. We were not speaking the same language. Yet it was obvious that the Mgahinga Gorilla was desperately trying to communicate with me, and that I was deficient in the skills necessary to bridge the gap. Suddenly the panga scar on the gorilla's face ruptured, and blood began pouring down upon the surrounding flowers and across the volcanic soil. As I gazed in horror at the pattern it was making upon the flower bed, the significance and symbolism of the images created by his life's blood opened the blocked communication pathways. The history of the gorilla's existence and the anguish of his life were revealed with a clarity that was stunning in its horror, and similar to my own experiences on earth.

Rivulets of the silverback's blood coalesced into a map of the Virungas and the countries that border their blue-shrouded volcanic peaks. The Parc National des Volcans straddles the African continental divide and shares boundaries with Rwanda, the Democratic Republic of the Congo and Uganda. Twenty million years of evolution produced the mountain gorilla species, of which perhaps slightly more than seven hundred individuals remain. The damaged silverback was one of many gorillas to whom artificial political boundaries had no meaning. He had roamed freely throughout the Virungan forests from the Ugandan side of the mountains. I now understood the meaning of what I initially interpreted as his name. "Mgahinga is the name of the park in Uganda you inhabited with your group."

Mgahinga, as I would name the silverback, "replied" by breaking a pyrethrum stem and sniffing it. He resisted my attempt to examine the bloody wound on his face and batted my hand away. I was faced with a dilemma because this was not one of my habituated gorillas, and we had fewer connections upon which to build a means of establishing physical contact. So, I resorted to the telepathic modes that Digit was fond of using with me. As Mgahinga Gorilla continued to examine the blossoms, I hoped I would find a way to learn more about his life and untimely death. This gorilla had spent most of his life on the Ugandan side of the mountains. Occasionally, he explored the mountain passes and entered Rwanda, but he entered the Parc des Volcans permanently on the day he fearfully fled Uganda. I realized, abruptly, that our meeting in the lava tube was not our first encounter. We had met when we were both alive in the terrible days after Digit's death. "Were you the lone silverback we glimpsed in Group Four's territory after Digit's death?"

"Naoom, Nyiramacyibili."

Finally, he was willing to communicate. For this I was grateful, but what he was about to reveal would take all of my remaining spiritual and intellectual power to assimilate. I did not know that, ten years after my death, a German primatologist by the name of Klaus Jurgen-Sucker had assumed my mantle at a research station similar to Karisoke on the Ugandan side of the Virungas. This area is known as Mgahinga. Mgahinga Gorilla had befriended Sucker in much the same manner as Digit had allowed me to enter his world. Jurgen-Sucker was as fervent as I had been in his attempts to keep tourists and "conservation" programs from raping the environment and the indigenous population. The Mountain Gorilla Project and other forces had tried without success to oust me from Karisoke. Jurgen-Sucker managed to "out Fossey Fossey" in his endeavors to protect his gorillas from encroachment, just as Mary Leakey once predicted that I would "out Schaller Schaller."[103] With the arrival of a USAID/CARE organization that wished to install an irrigation system in the heart of gorilla terrain, Jurgen-Sucker was fired from his position by Uganda National Parks and transferred to another park. Shortly before Jurgen-Sucker was scheduled to leave, he was found hanged in his cabin, with his feet touching the floor, and his lunch half-eaten. The official report was that he committed suicide, but his friends suspected foul play and conspiracy on a par with the circumstances surrounding my murder.[104] In a timeline fraught with reverse symmetry, the researcher in this case would be murdered before the gorilla. After Jurgen-Sucker's murder, Mgahinga Gorilla fled permanently to the Rwandan side of the Virungas, unable to assimilate the loss incurred by the murder of his human friend and protector. As a lone silverback, his only comfort flowed from the friendship and ministrations of Jurgen-Sucker.

Because the silverback had lived a life much like my own, he gradually came to understand that that my empathy with the tragic aspects of his existence was complete. That he was ultimately killed and eaten by hungry militiamen during the genocidal wars had profound implications for me. I had spent many years in the study of Catholicism, until I was forced by my own intellect to reject a god who would allow the innocent son and nephews of my good friend, Alyette, to be killed and tortured by Congolese militiamen. The fact that men could murder with impunity, and then consume the flesh of gorilla and human alike, was a concept that went far beyond any answers that god or man could possibly provide to me. Humankind seems intent upon devouring all that will nourish the flesh and fill the empty coffers of individuals, governments, and corporations that have the means to destroy the last vestiges of wildness left on earth. I am afraid there will soon no longer be safe haven for man or beast.

Mgahinga Gorilla broke a stalk of wild celery and timidly laid it near my boot. This gentle gesture was exactly how Digit first approached me when he was still a shy young blackback. He would often proffer offerings of succulent vegetation and then run bashfully to a hidden spot in the brush to watch my reaction. As I took the offering and returned a contented "belch" vocalization, Mgahinga Gorilla suddenly raised to his full height and chest-beat a fierce staccato that echoed through the hills and mountain saddle. He screamed, "hoo, hoo, hoo," initializing a long call sequence that left no doubt he was communicating with the deceased gorilla groups within range of his display. There were many times during my earthly studies when I felt I had been listening to a foreign language with no translation available. The gorillas have a complex social structure, and vocalizations are a primary component, indicating status, purpose, and threat—as well as reassurance. Mgahinga was a lone silverback, but he was announcing his intent to properly join the fringes of local gorilla society in the afterworld. He had finally accepted that he and his beloved friends were dead, but he could choose to roam the misty slopes of the Virungas with his own kind. I was watching the miraculous transformation of a beaten, defeated, and bloodied individual into a being who was assuming his former splendor as one of the oldest and most magnificent gorillas I had ever seen. His wound was healing before my eyes, and his black and silver hair glistened with droplets of mist. Brown eyes had a hint of fiery red in them as he strutted back and forth, intermittingly rising again to his full height. A terrible and frightening beauty now defined his countenance.

I understood now why Digit had left us alone as I dreamed in the field of flowers. Digit was a formidable silverback, and his presence would have inhibited Mgahinga gorilla from finding his voice and his power. Gorilla etiquette would demand that Digit's status not permit me to commune in close proximity with another elder without one or the other being forced into capitulation.

"We are one and the same, Nyiramacyibili. Thank you for helping me to see who I really am."

"How can I have helped you? I am lost and alone as well."

The silverback lowered his huge form and knuckle-walked over to me. He played with my hair, tenderly grooming me before settling into a sitting position and leaning against my body. "You are stronger than you think, Nyiramacyibili. We are the same in many ways, but I think you may have suffered more. Better that you had been one of us, but that was not to be. Your light was strong enough to bring me back from a despair that was worse than death. To die a spiritual death is the Hell that your human society speaks of. You will survive your murder. You will live on in the hearts and minds of those humans who understand their connections with the damaged earth."

"Where are you going? Will we meet again?"

"I must cross the volcanoes and unite with the groups of gorillas that wander alone and frightened. Your place now is with Digit and his group. Thank you, Nyiramacyibili."

With that he vanished into the mists, and I knew that we would never meet again—in dreams or in death.

10

Truth and Lies

○ ○

When does truth start to hide from the soul
Of a form that must live within itself?
When does the bank become part of a river
Unless subdued by a lapping stealth?
When did our love grow horns to stab
The once-shared purity of heart?
When, my love, did submersion force
Our body and soul to part?[105]

My time with Mgahinga Gorilla was heartbreaking, and his absence made me feel truly lonely. After wandering for a time through the bamboo forest, I felt better. The gentle breezes emanating from the slopes of the mountain caused the wooden plants to brush gently against each other. This created a magnificent effect, as if the entire forest had become a colossal wind chime, producing a purity and clarity of tone that did much to ease my disturbed mental state. I decided I wanted to seek out Digit, and I took one of the old familiar trails down the mountain and through the meadow. I was searching for our favorite meeting place on the lava outcrop at the base of the Pygeum tree. It was clear to me now that my encounters with Mgahinga Gorilla were not a matter of chance and had, in fact, been engineered by Digit. I had many questions for him.

As I entered the open meadowland, I was rewarded by the appearance of a striking bushbuck. He was very old, dark all over, with a grizzled neck, and very fat. Beautiful grey circles surrounded his eyes, and his horns were the largest I had ever seen on this species. He stood motionless in the meadow, and at his side was a young female, still sporting a coat of a remarkable golden color.[106] The old buck sensed my presence on the other side of the veil and flicked his ears once or twice before lowering his head again to pick at the succulent grasses. The scene brought back memories of solitary walks with my old dog, Cindy, and how we often spotted herds of duiker as well as the occasional bushbuck.

When Cindy was born in March of 1968, I had been living in the Virungas for more than a year. I admit I invented the idea that Count Adam Beilski brought her mother from Poland. Cindy's mother was a Rhodesian ridgeback—a dog pathetically named "Happy," whose life was spent tied-up in a driveway. Unlike her mother, Cindy did have a very happy life![107] Besides my African staff and Cindy, my only companions were my chickens, Lucy and Dezi (sic), followed by Wilma and Walter. Walter must have thought he was a person because he liked to sleep in my tent with me, but he was good company. When two-month old Cindy moved to camp, she was an unwelcome visitor as far as the chickens were concerned.

In view of her run-ins with chickens, poachers, and elephants, Cindy was a lesson in courage, although she truly failed as a watchdog. When Sebagari[108] came into my cabin and swiped my valise, which was full of all the money I had in the world, as well as my jewelry, Cindy never barked. Sebagari just patted her on the head and left with it all. Everyone who visited or lived at Karisoke loved Cindy, and she returned the love with morning rounds of wet kisses for everyone—black, white, stranger, whatever. In many ways she was the real heart of Karisoke—the love.[109]

My pet Circopthitis (sic)[110] blue monkey, Kima, was also a great comfort and consolation to me in the often lonely days at Karisoke. I fear that the African staff held no affection for her, but she brought great joy to my spirit. Perhaps Kima's absence has made my heart grow fonder, for she was really a despot at heart and ruled the camp with much drama. There are many, many entries in my diaries that refer to her antics. One of the most legendary was the time when Kima took one of Cindy's puppies and climbed with it into the Hagenia tree outside of the cabin. The African staff and I were screaming our heads off because we had no idea what to do, and that rascal monkey threw the puppy some thirty feet to the ground! Somehow, it miraculously survived. Cindy kept wagging her stump of a tail throughout the whole ordeal and scooped the puppy into her jaws, taking it back to the cabin without any fuss whatsoever.[111] Cindy and Kima had been friends most of their lives, and evidently she had grown entirely tolerant of Kima's extreme antics.

One Christmas season in particular was not a happy time for Kima and Cindy. I was involved in an unhappy love affair with a surgeon from the Ruhengeri hospital, Dr. Peter Weiss, who was also responsible for repairing the damage from my abortion. He was initially very critical of me, and what began as a tempestuous relationship turned to passion after Bob Campbell abandoned me and went back to his wife. Peter and I were on the verge of a break-up due to his inability to commit and his continuing affair with the African woman, Fina, who was the mother of his children.[112] While I was sorting out my futile connection with Peter, Cindy and Kima were undergoing periods of malaise and sickness of an unknown origin. Perhaps Kima and Cindy were mirroring my internal turmoil, for during this unhappy period I began drinking often and neglecting my health more than usual. My smoking increased, exacerbating the symptoms of my emphysema. Many mornings I awoke coughing blood and feeling generally *mixed-up*.[113]

I had always waited until well into January to take down my Christmas tree, since Christmas was my favorite holiday. One evening I had just finished a good dinner and had too much to drink (I referred to drinking in my diaries as "*get X*"),[114] when I decided it was time to take down the tree. I was burning a lot of pine in my fireplace and remembering a similar Christmas when I was in the States listening to African music, dismantling the tree, and wishing fervently that I was in Africa. Well, there I was, in Africa, alone, at Christmas, and the act of taking down the tree was killing me.[115] On top of it all, Kima, as usual, refused to go into her cage for the night, and I spent over an hour in my bedroom grooming her and trying to coax her into her bed.

On another morning during this period, I awoke to Kima breaking the stovepipe in the kitchen, which had caused the chickens and crows to start screaming their heads off. Walter the rooster, who spent his evenings riding the carriage of my typewriter as I completed my field reports, was in frenzy, and the cabin was rapidly filling with smoke.[116] The memory of it all causes me to smile, but it is a bittersweet recollection because I realize that my pets often reflected my agitation and sadness. My behavior upset the delicate schemes of their lives, which in turn had definite consequences in the human realm. Looking back on it all, I think that Kima, especially, mirrored my state of mind in her periodic rampages throughout the camp.

The lonely Christmas season of 1975 was an important turning point in my earthly existence. I became increasingly solitary in my day-to-day activities, preferring the company of my pets and the gorillas to any kind of intimate human involvement. I wrote once that there are times when truth is forced to hide from the human soul. The truth is that I was tortured by intense loneliness, and in order to escape mounting feelings of isolation, my drinking had reached unhealthy proportions. I went to great lengths to escape the torture that loneliness can inflict upon the soul. My predicament was not due to lack of human companionship at Karisoke, but rather it was the lack of quality in my relationships that was most painful. I suppose you could say that I had an alcoholic personality, since I drank to subvert my feelings of sadness and depression. Alcohol only increased my inability to deal with these debilitating emotions. I gradually developed a dependence upon alcohol during my eighteen years alone on the mountain, but because my most serious bouts of drinking occurred at Karisoke, my friends in Kigali and Ruhengeri never observed me drinking more than was the social norm. After my death, reporters often inquired about the exaggerated stories of my drinking that were propagated by my enemies. My friends and social acquaintances from the embassy would reply in an entirely truthful manner that they had rarely seen me drinking to excess. It is unfair that Amy Vedder claimed in her book[117] that I had pilfered camp funds to buy cases of Johnny Walker Red scotch.[118] I would never, never take money from my gorillas. The best denial I can offer to her outrageous claim is that, during the investigation of my murder, Karl Hoffman, the vice-consul of the US Embassy in Kigali, wrote that investigators found only several empty beer bottles and one whiskey bottle—not case after case of scotch as was reported by Vedder.[119]

In an interview given after my murder, Ian Redmond responded to questions about my drinking. I was gratified to realize than Ian was indeed a very good friend in that he did not let me off the hook, but also understood that this particular failing did not negate my worth as a person. The biographer asked Ian if I had a drinking problem, and his reply was to the point. I always liked that quality in him. "It was a problem if you fell out with her when she was drunk. It depends on whether you would call 'getting drunk' a drinking problem. When Dian was depressed and under a lot of pressure she would get blotted. She had very few other methods of relieving the stresses and strains on her, but as far as I know, it was something that she chose to do because of what was happening at the time and not something which she did all the time. I heard an American Ambassador say that when she was his houseguest, she drank no more than any other houseguest. I don't know how many bottles of Johnny Walker came up to camp every week. It's not something which I ever took much interest in."[120]

I became aware of the negative effects of my drinking after a doctor's exam in July of 1985—just months before my murder. Blood tests and laboratory results indicated that my liver was not functioning properly, most likely due to excessive alcohol consumption. The test results were even worse than a report that was completed the previous year.[121] There had also been some concern that the anti-malarial medications that were prescribed at that time could negatively affect liver function tests, but I probably was drinking too much when I was alone, and had become a functioning, though episodic, alcoholic. Unfortunately this sad truth gave ammunition to those wishing to discredit me, and I regret that this information could tarnish my legacy.

At first I was mildly upset when I heard Ian repeat some of my indiscretions, but I must face up to the issue if I am to restore my sense of self-worth. I must learn to accept my flaws and my weaknesses as well as learn to celebrate my strengths. I wish this illness had been under my conscious control, but it was not. I admit to my failing because I am seeking the truth and the spiritual health it may afford me. I find some comfort in the remarks of a biographer who said that, given the circumstances of the stresses I was experiencing, it was no wonder that I did not drink myself into "oblivion."[122]

Time for reflection can be both a blessing and a curse. My search for Digit was proving fruitless, since he was not in the Pygeum tree as I had expected. This was very odd, since Digit always seemed to sense my psychic disturbances and was usually available when I needed to talk things out. I climbed the tree and waited, hoping that the new vantage point would afford a better opportunity to spot him. The mists had lifted, and it was a beautifully clear day. I decided to enjoy the vista, confident that it would just be a matter of time before Digit appeared, and used the moment to consider some of the many criticisms that have been directed at me.

An example of my behavior, which has been twisted to suit the agendas of my detractors, is the fact that I did not allow the gorillas to become habituated to the sight of the black faces of African trackers. Shirley McGreal,[123] founder of the International Primate Protection League, of which I was a member, once asked me if it was wise to "get the animals to trust people." She was firmly asking for a direct quote on this issue. I told her I *never* habituated my gorillas to Africans for the simple reason that the split second it might take a gorilla to recognize an African as a friend or a foe could be the instant that cost the gorilla its life. My Africans totally understood why their faces could not be accepted by the gorillas, so, in fact, did the President of Rwanda. Gorillas only knew black faces as poachers, and my African staff and other high government officials comprehended the facts as they existed. Black faces meant danger; white faces, after eleven years of habituation, meant safety. Unfortunately, Jane Goodall and Birute Galdikas[124] criticized me on this point in their speeches. Without having encountered any of the poacher problems that I faced at Karisoke, they insisted that I should introduce the gorillas to the public. I answered both of them, stating that *I would not be responsible for habituating gorillas to Africans until every last poacher was driven from the park—probably outside of my lifetime.*[125]

I did continue to train Africans in botanical and parasitology studies within the Parc des Volcans. Many of these men saw the gorillas at long range, without the gorillas realizing that they were on the scene. In this way, the Africans remained happy about maintaining their distance from the animals and were able to support their own work interests without jeopardizing themselves or the gorillas.[126] Actions and words can damn us when twisted by the tongues of our enemies, but Digit reminds me that what matters are our intentions. Just as the bluff charge of the silverback can be misconstrued by a terrified tourist, or even a novice researcher, so were many of my negative utterances and actions misinterpreted without any attempt to look at the motivations that gave birth to them. I was an imperfect being, but I was always careful to protect the gorillas and all of the wildlife that inhabited the Parc des Volcans.

Although I often felt isolated and abandoned during my darkest days at Karisoke, in the years immediately preceding my murder I came to understand that my friendships extended beyond the animal kingdom to include many human friends, supporters, and admirers. Most of my friends lived a great distance away, but I was a prolific correspondent. I kept carbons of all my letters and would admonish regular correspondents that it was important to date everything because of the way my filing system was arranged.[127]

Sadly, I mistakenly believed that my student, Kelly Stewart, was my friend. She was quoted in magazine interviews saying that my murder was "a perfect ending," and that I "got what I wanted," further speculating that it "must have been painful," but "didn't last long," since it was "a clean whack."[128] I wondered how she could have had such a precise insight into what it feels like to be murdered by a machete. I can assure her that it was an excruciatingly painful death, if that information makes her happy. These interviews appeared in *Vanity Fair Magazine* and were subsequently picked up by other news media. In a later interview, Kelly backpedaled a bit on her statements, since she felt the quotes made her look "bloodthirsty."[129]

During my tenure at Cornell University in the early 1980's, I was really missing the mountains and the gorillas and was thrilled to receive a letter from Kelly Stewart detailing her family's trip to Rwanda. I wrote to her that life was just barely tolerable being so far from home, camp, and the "beasts."[130] Kelly's father was the actor, James Stewart, and I was pleased to hear that he was well enough to crawl through the bamboo in an effort to reach the gorillas and Group Four. We had a nice correspondence. I asked her about the trip and the gorillas, wondering if she thought the infant Simba would remember the murdered gorillas Digit, Uncle Bert, and the infant Mwelu. I was especially grateful for that particular letter because Kelly was kind enough to tell me where the young gorilla Bonne Année (Happy New Year) was buried.

Bonne Année had been captured by poachers for the Cologne zoo, and she was given to me by the park conservator, Francois Benda-Lema, when she became ill. She was the last infant gorilla I treated before leaving Karisoke for Cornell. Her reintroduction to the wild was a complicated and difficult affair, which I detailed in *Gorillas in the Mist*. In typical fashion, my adversaries in the Mountain Gorilla Project seized upon the difficulties inherent in her care and accused me of self-promotion during the first attempted release of poor Bonne Année.[131] She lived for less than a year before dying, but at that time it was still the longest period that a reintroduced gorilla had been able to survive in the wild.

The story of Bonne Année, or "Charlie," as she was first named, is a primer in the intricacies of gorilla trading. On January 1, 1980, two Africans, one of whom was supposedly an evangelist, went to the home of Dr. Vimont-Vicary in Ruhengeri and asked him if he wanted to purchase a young gorilla for the equivalent of $1,000. This was the second time in seven months that Dr. Vimont had been approached by sellers, and when he realized the infant had already been captured, he pretended to accept the deal. After making arrangements with his wife to contact Prefect Nkubili's successor, Theophike Sebigega, and Jean Pierre van der Becke of the Mountain Gorilla Project, Dr. Vimont drove the two sellers to an area known as Kora, adjacent to the southern facing slopes of Mount Karisimbi. Here, they walked down a small back road leading toward the Zairoise[132] border until they reached a very small potato storage hut in which the baby was contained. They caught the baby with some difficulty (one man was seriously bitten), put it into a basket, and drove to Dr. Vimont's home in Ruhengeri. The doctor then deliberately proceeded to get both of the sellers drunk while awaiting the arrival of the Prefect, using the pretense that he was expecting the delivery of money from friends. When the military arrived, Dr. Vimont arranged to be "imprisoned" so as not to arouse the suspicions of the sellers and also to elicit more information from them. The two men divulged that they'd had the infant, a female thought to be between thirty to thirty-six months of age, for about two weeks, and that they'd fed it corn, bread, pineapples, papaya, raw potatoes, and bananas. It also must have been given some water because it was not dehydrated when I received it. The men also said the mother and father were killed during the capture, but I would estimate that more gorillas had probably been killed because the entire group would have made a stand to defend the infant.

Bonne Année arrived at my camp on the evening of January 1st in a potato basket carried by my porter, Guamhoegasi,[133] and accompanied by van der Becke and an American student, Mark.[134] She was taken immediately to the guest room and, when I opened the basket, she hid under the bed in a dark, cold corner. The Africans brought in gallium, thistle, celery and bamboo. The baby showed no interest in drinking water, but within a half an hour she ate three stalks of bamboo. She had no desire to cuddle, but she did allow me to pet her back before she spent the night under my bed, ignoring two stuffed gorillas I placed nearby for comfort's sake.

Bonne Année spent the following day mostly under my bed, but eventually she went through the usual introductory routine of parallel strutting, scratching, and avoidance of direct visual encounters. In mid-afternoon she indicated her fear of the first African she saw by screaming, even though the African was ten feet away in another room. She also showed apprehension upon hearing the sounds of woodcutting—some one hundred feet from the cabin. This was a recollection, I believe, from her life spent in the forest. Exhausted, she finally slept with me that night.

By the third day, she showed a great improvement in her relationships with Africans who knew proper gorilla vocalizations and responded confidently to her. I hired a new African, a fifteen-year-old boy named Kulekazi, and his rapport with the baby was instantaneous. Several days later, we made a large wire sleeping box, filled it with Veronia branches and moss, and attached it to the upper wall of my bedroom beside the stove. The baby accepted it readily, and we both got our first full night of sleep since she'd arrived.

Bonne Année showed much improvement in health and disposition throughout the month. By January 22 I was able to leave her alone outside for the first time. Instead of throwing the wild temper tantrums that I expected, she briefly tried to get back inside the front door before following Cindy for about fifty feet to feed on gallium. She remained content for about ten minutes before again trying to break down the front door. The paramount question became what to do with her? I preferred releasing her to one of the groups in the wild, but there were many aspects to be considered, and I wrestled with the decision for weeks. Group Four was the best and first choice with regard to group composition, but they were unhabituated and at that time resided in the heaviest poacher area of any of the study groups.[135] My second and final choice of the less remote Group Five was a failure, but not because I was lazy or feeling ill as my detractors have often said. Infanticide was a definite possibility in Group Five because there was no female who would be likely to assume maternal responsibilities. There was no perfect solution.

In *Gorillas in the Mist*[136] I told how Bonne Année's introduction to Group Four had been "jinxed from the start." It was March, pouring rain, and the group had traveled far from the bivouac camp that had been established with the help of my student, John Fowler, and an African assistant. An unidentified fringe group had invaded the territory, and this, combined with the excitable nature of Group Four, made it highly unlikely that they would have accepted Bonne Année. Reluctantly I decided to attempt an introduction to Group Five on the following day, even though I realized that the strong group bond would make infanticide a real possibility. My misgivings were confirmed, and the baby was brutally attacked by two females and one of the younger males. Only the intervention of the old silverback, Beethoven, saved her. She was brought back to camp, where she settled into her sleeping cage and picked at her treat box of fruit. Luckily her injuries were not severe, and she seemed happy to be back in familiar surroundings. In the end, release was accomplished to Group Four after I left for the States. Group Four's lack of strong kinship bonds worked to Bonne Année's advantage, and she was adopted into a new gorilla family. Group Five proved to be the wrong choice, but it was not a casual decision, and was a resolution that I wrestled with for many weeks. It is unfortunate that the time for her release coincided with my return to the States, but I did not approach the situation flippantly. I lost a great deal of sleep over her fate and was intensely involved with her rehabilitation.

Bonne Année's story is a bit like any fable one hears about the relationship between a wild animal and the human(s) that befriend it. The question always arises as to what is the better fate for the animal: freedom, or captivity with its well-meaning benefactors. I have always chosen the risks of freedom versus the certainty and boredom of life in a cage, no matter how grand the enclosure. But sometimes, in some situations, humane captivity is the only solution, however imperfect, that remains. I put my heart and soul into decisions that affected Bonne Année, and it hurts to know that my critics continue to distort and twist my motivations and actions. Those that continue to vilify me often do so without having a clear understanding of the facts that governed my decisions. The disparagement of my memory serves no purpose except to advance the profiles of my detractors at the expense of my legacy.

As I opened my mail at Cornell University many years ago, the news of Bonne Année's death was just about the straw that broke my back. I wondered whether she would have been better off going to the zoo after all and living a bit longer, as Coco and Pucker had. I am inclined to believe that the year she spent free was worth more to her than several years behind bars, but if asked to swear to that, *I must reply that I just don't know,*[137] just as I had years ago. I shared these deep feelings with Kelly Stewart because I thought she was a sympathetic friend, but I was wrong. She would ultimately agree with her husband, Sandy Harcourt, who threw his support and prestige behind the theoretical conservation practices of the Mountain Gorilla Project. Harcourt's betrayal was another blow to my already fragile ego. When Harcourt first arrived at Karisoke as a young graduate student, he showed the most promise of any of the researchers who had arrived up until then. He ultimately became infatuated with me, and I retained many of his notes and tender correspondences over the years.[138] Sandy's first letters to me were often signed "I do love you, Dian,"[139] but by 1981 he was signing "A. H. Harcourt."[140] That same year, Professor Robert Hinde of Cambridge University chastised Sandy for not being "gracious" in his communications with me.[141] Sandy wrote back that he found it impossible to be polite with me, considering his perceptions of my "past and present behavior with respect to (us) and the conservation of the Virungas."[142] He added that he hoped "another buffalo"[143] would soon put an end to our animosities—a reference to an incident in which he was gored by a water buffalo and would have died had it not been for my ministrations. If there was any irony to be gained from this sad situation, it came when Sandy wrote a letter to the publisher of *Gorillas in the Mist*, indicating that he was concerned that he would be defamed by me.[144] I responded to Sandy's letter with one of my own to my editor, Anita McClellan. I pointed out that there were no untruths in *Gorillas in the Mist,* although Harcourt's accusations had tempted me to really add some derogatory information.[145] Happily, I did not succumb to that particular temptation. I took great care in my public writings to never engage in personal attacks or accusations, but I cannot say the same for my colleagues.

As would so often happen in my fragile relationships with those of my own species, Sandy's love and admiration gradually changed to anger and hate. This has happened so many times in my life that I must ask myself whether some basic flaw in my character causes me to be drawn to those who will ultimately reject me with such total resolve. At what point in my varied relationships did my fixations on my ideals and goals drive such an eternal wedge into the hearts and minds of those whom I loved?

In many ways the battle at Karisoke still remains one of Dian Fossey's ideals against those of conservationists who put tourism, fundraising, and administra-

tive costs above and beyond monies going directly to gorilla and habitat preservation. When I lived at Karisoke, the best way to protect the gorillas was to increase
the anti-poaching efforts. Bringing hordes of tourists up the mountain to spread
disease, leaving excrement and used tampons along the trails, was not my idea of
conservation.

Watching history unfold, I realize with much agitation that there are conservation organizations which wrap themselves in the mantle of Dian Fossey's name
in order to raise money for bloated administrative salaries. These organizations
use tainted grants to pay for foreign junkets and add primatologists' names to
their letterheads. Directors are paid exorbitant salaries and report full-time work
with the gorilla organizations on their tax returns, while at the same time holding
down full-time employment in other areas. These "experts" have spent little or no
time in the field and instead rely upon the prestige endowed by advanced degrees
and tenures at renowned universities.

Indeed, there are individuals on the staff rosters of conservation organizations
who have themselves been implicated in smuggling monkeys for laboratory
research.[146] Some of these individuals have been employed at Karisoke. Millions
in uncounted charitable funds are filed away in the archives of the Internal Reve-
nue Service (IRS) on charitable exemption 501(c3) forms. Ian Redmond put it
exactly the way I would have responded, had I been alive, when a biographer
asked a question about conservation ideals shortly after my death. "It was mainly
Dian's publicity that (was used to) launch the Mountain Gorilla Project," Ian
said. "Dian felt very strongly that the little old lady who gives a dollar in some village in the mid-western States (should know) that the money is spent protecting
gorillas, not going to a large fund which was supporting officers and vehicles and
film shows and all the other stuff which is generally considered to be desirable in
the conservation establishment."[147]

I have always been adamant in my belief that Digit's blood money should go
only to the anti-poaching patrols that were supported by the Digit Fund. Of
course, when my anti-poaching activities included burning confiscated snares and
holding captive poachers for interrogation, the local government became
adversely involved. This went against long-established conservation ideals that
local governments must only be sympathetically engaged. Some of my biographers have misrepresented my treatment of the African poachers captured by my
patrols. Shortly before I was murdered, for example, my anti-poaching patrols
were able to apprehend a notorious poacher and bring him to me for questioning.
The patrols had been very successful and had captured four men, in four weeks,
who were all actively working within the confines of the Parc des Volcans. One

poacher's name was Yavani Hategeka, and he was not the least bit cooperative in answering questions. I took away the black magic toys that were sewn into his stinky, frayed jacket. Over the years, I had learned exactly where to look for these things, and I searched him in the presence of my guards, since I was not allowed to touch the prisoners, but could search their clothing.[148] Hategeka's magic consisted of two little pouches of dried vegetation and an inch-square piece of some kind of animal fur. It was like taking a nipple away from a baby and probably not a nice thing to do, but I did it anyway because he refused to give me any information. He shriveled up after losing his charms, and my men told me he would never poach again because I had his "sumu"—or black magic powers.[149] There has been much speculation, never proven, that this encounter was directly tied to my death in some manner. In fact, I would be dead before the New Year.

Innuendo, rumor, and outright lies would affirm that in my zeal to reduce poaching, I was guilty of whipping prisoners, spitting on them, kicking them, putting on masks and cursing them, and stuffing barbiturates down their throats. There was even some macabre speculation about whether or not I had prisoners whipped about the genitals with stinging nettles. Kelly Stewart, who voiced the initial accusation about the whippings, recanted when asked to confirm statements attributed to her. When she was asked whether she actually witnessed any of the atrocities that were ascribed to me, she changed her story, in every instance, either recanting entirely or insisting that she was misquoted.[150] The stories about me became so acrimonious that one friend from *National Geographic Magazine* wrote to me to say, not entirely tongue in cheek, that he hoped I was managing to abide by the "rules of the Geneva Convention."[151]

Fourteen years later, Kelly Stewart wrote an essay for an obscure book, which was planned as a compilation of "field trip fiascoes and expedition disasters."[152] Her hyperbolic recollections reduce me to a caricature of a simple-minded gun maniac who believes it is actually possible to bake a gun within a cake! Perhaps she felt enough time had passed since my death that no one would challenge her account, an account that does not square with even the most vicious tales of my biographers. What remains is another indelible, yet fabricated, part of my memory and legacy in popular literature—one more atrocity added to the growing list of Fossey eccentricities and transgressions. I have no idea why Kelly Stewart dedicated her recently published textbook on the Mountain Gorillas[153] to my memory. Perhaps she felt guilty about her virulent attacks on me. Perhaps she really loved me after all. I have no way of knowing.

In one of my periods of crippling despair in the year after my death, Digit arranged for me to see some correspondences between my biographer, Farley

Mowat, and Jane Goodall, one of the members of the triumvirate of Leakey girls that consisted of Mademoiselles Fossey, Goodall, and Birute Galdikaś. Together, we three were doing the only significant studies on the higher primates—me on the gorillas, Jane on the chimpanzee, and Birute on the orangutan. Mowat was feeling overwhelmed with the responsibility of writing a biography of someone he had never met and wrote to Jane to ask her advice. He explained that he had found himself "appalled at the nest of vipers who inhabit this territory," and said he "had never before encountered such a seething mass of conflicting stories, most of them malicious, if they aren't patently vicious." He added, "I do not know of any magic elixir I can employ to crystallize the truth out of these noxious vapors."[154] Jane wrote back that she was not sure how she could help, but she agreed the whole thing was "a can of worms."[155] In the end, I hold onto the hope that there are some who will understand Mowat's plea to Jane that he was "unsure" who I really was, but he "wanted to know…must know," if he was "to tell the truth."[156]

11

Cinema Verite`

The branches of the stately Pygeum tree cradled me while I dreamed of relation-ships failed. I awoke feeling sweaty and troubled, with Digit gently prodding at the arm I had slung protectively over my ravaged face. He was anxiously attempt-ing to stuff some berries in my mouth, and I gagged and spit because there were too many. The gorillas had witnessed me doing this many times to sick or injured young gorillas in a futile attempt to nourish them. In some instances my minis-trations were successful, as with Coco and Pucker, but at other times they were not. Choking on the berries reminded me that Amy Vedder still blames me for the baby gorilla Mweza's death.[158] Disoriented, and angry at the memory of Mweza, I brushed Digit's hand away from my mouth.

"Nyiramacyibili, your dreams have trapped you within the memories of others."

Digit was right. I reached out and clasped the huge hand with its deformed finger, ecstatic to be in his company and to find him once again whole and healthy. I pressed his hand to my cheek, forever grateful that whatever this place was that we now inhabited, it had healed Digit's body. I felt safe in the tree, safer yet in the loving presence of my old friend. I apologized for my earlier abrupt reaction by eating the berries he had so thoughtfully picked for me. That he had not eaten them himself was testament to his caring soul, for berries are rare, and a favorite food of the gorillas. "I've been looking for you everywhere, Digit. Where have you been?"

"Some parts of your journey must be taken alone, Nyiramacyibili. I will always be near when you truly need me, but I cannot protect you from the consequences of your quest."

"Was Mgahinga Gorilla real, or did I dream him?"

"The gorillas have known about him for many years, both in the previous life and now. You were the only one he would speak with after the death of Jurgen-Sucker. He was told you had come to save the gorillas and he sought you out in the afterworld. He was waiting for you in the lava tunnel."

I had steadfastly maintained that I traveled to Africa to study gorillas and not to save them. Because I came to understand that the gorillas would need saving if they were not to vanish forever from the face of the earth, my legend had spread across the Virungas to Uganda and around the world. Perhaps I would have been less effective if I had not been murdered. My death had imbued me with the double mantle of heroine and martyr, a potent combination, but I felt that Mgahinga Gorilla had somehow misplaced his confidence in me. Perhaps my legend far outweighed the real Fossey.

Digit growled unhappily as he read my thoughts. "Nyiramacyibili, why must you always diminish your sacrifice? You died in an effort to protect us. Is your death any less valuable than my own?"

Once again Digit was urging me to assign meaning to my death. But I could not bring myself to answer his question, and this caused a ripping, searing sensation in the scar that divided my face. A single tear followed the track of the scar, and Digit brushed it away with his misshapen finger.

"I am sorry if these questions cause you pain, Nyiramacyibili, but you must walk this path. I will stay nearby and protect you, but you alone must paint a picture of who you are so that you can recognize yourself. You did it for me after my murder. Remember the movie you planned about me?"

Remember indeed. After Digit's murder, I threw myself into developing a publicity campaign that would tell the world what a needless, senseless death Digit had endured. I wanted his suffering to be palpable and his image to be etched into the world's consciousness. I decided that there were two ways in which this movie, or "personal commemoration," could be structured. In organized Fossey fashion, I called them Plan A and Plan B. Plan A would involve a movie that introduced Digit as a happy youngster before cutting immediately to his fate as a young silverback. This would entail editing that moved abruptly back and forth between scenes of his life and scenes of his battered body after his murder. Plan B would begin the movie with the youthful Digit and follow through to his maturation—only at the end revealing how he was killed for his skull and hands. I was very much in favor of Plan A, since Plan B was too similar to a Lassie show. I wanted the audience to live and die with him. I wanted them to feel his pain. I wanted them to feel his progress toward maturation and ultimate freedom while still guarding his family group. *I wanted the essence of time stressed for the immediate sake of saving what gorillas remain.* Digit lived for his family; he died for a poacher's greed and European trophies. He died in vain, except that he saved his home group from slaughter, ultimate slaughter.[159]

Digit was nodding his head and contentedly belching "naoom, naoom," while I went on in great detail about framing each shot, and how the music would fade in and out with an extensive narration on my part. "Nyiramacyibili, don't you see you have arranged the perfect movie, except for one thing that I would change?"

I was annoyed that Digit would want to tamper with what I felt was the perfect vision of his life. It was my nature to resist changes in my plans, but Digit met my resistance with a suggestion. "I would substitute 'Dian' for each instance of my name. Don't you realize you saved many gorillas from ultimate slaughter? You lived bravely for your goal as much as I did, Nyiramacyibili, and you will find what you are looking for by examining the years after my death."

Digit was correct. Our brief existences were parallel on the corporeal plane. But I didn't feel there was any innate heroism in my death, and I certainly did not think it merited a special commemoration. Those that are murdered experience a great sense of guilt and shame until they discover a means to free their souls. I would remain trapped in my ruminations until I came to understand the purpose of my abbreviated existence.

I was happy, however, to learn that the gorillas regarded me with such high esteem. Digit's confidence buoyed my battered spirit, and I decided to take his suggestion that I assemble the bits and pieces of the latter years of my life as one would lay out a storyboard for a movie. Then, perhaps, I might be able to make sense of the people and circumstances that shaped my life, death, and legacy. And if I were to make a movie of my own life, the death of Digit would be its central theme. I knew instinctively where I must begin.

In a correspondence to a young American tourist shortly before my death, I expounded upon my favorite metaphor for life after she had written about her own plans for the future. I told her that I hoped she would be able to adhere to her plans with the full realization that life may only be considered as a piece of pie. Once you have finished with a quarter or a half-wedge, basically only crumbs remain for most people.[160] I was determined, for the sake of my gorillas, not to be one of those left with only crumbs. There was still much to see, experience, understand, and contribute.[161] Neither Digit nor I had died in vain.

Digit was pleased that I finally had some direction and a solid plan for the examination of the last years of my life. I sensed that he was also apprehensive about leaving me alone, but we agreed that it was a necessary step in my spiritual development. His parting actions as he prepared to join the other murdered members of his group were combined with much vocalizing and rumbling on his part. I knew that he was searching for the proper words to give me strength and guidance in this new undertaking. "Remember that wisdom involves understanding. This will be a difficult undertaking for you, Nyiramacyibili. You will only discover your true nature by finding an anchor in your past actions. I will be near if you need me, and I will not allow you to suffer needlessly. But be prepared that the path you are undertaking is treacherous."

Digit looked into my eyes for one last time and, with a quick glance over his shoulder, slowly knuckle-walked into the fog that was forming around the base of the Pygeum tree. In seconds he had disappeared, and all that remained was the swishing sound of leaf brushing against leaf as his long-dead group members joined him. I knew instinctively that Uncle Bert and Mwelu were near, waiting for him in the mists. How I longed to join them and avoid the tasks that lie before me!

The essence of Digit would remain with me. I was certain of this. However, I had to make this quest unaided, just as I had always been solitary in my total passion and commitment to the mountain gorilla. I was experiencing the same emotions I felt when left alone in the Kabara meadow near Carl Akeley's grave in the Congo in 1967. It was the day before my thirty-fifth birthday, and six months later I would be held captive, brutalized and abused by Congolese soldiers. I don't know whether it was a premonition of what awaited me, but as I zipped myself into my tent that first night in the meadow, I felt extremely terrified. Nevertheless, I heard the hoots and cries of the silverbacks in the night, and I knew that there was no turning back. There was no turning back now, either.

My eccentricities have led to many misconceptions about me. I had a single-minded determination to understand the mountain gorillas. I was impatient with my students. My caustic humor was not recognized as a response to pressure. And, I was as ill-equipped as anyone else to endure the rigors of life on the mountain. Although I eventually adjusted physically to the harsh realities of life in the forest, I never fully developed the thick skin necessary to finesse political situations and deflect personal criticisms.

Rosamond Carr tells a story about me in those early days in Rwanda that she greatly enjoys. I had just escaped the clutches of my Congolese captors by tricking them, after they were drunk on pombi,[162] into driving me to the Ugandan side of the border where it joins with Rwanda. I was destitute and battered, but I'd heard there was an American expatriate named Rosamond Carr living on a plantation at the foot of the Virungas. She and I ended up at the same reception at the American embassy. The wife of the ambassador warned Rosamond to be careful because she was about to meet a girl who had been studying gorillas and wanted to bivouac at the plantation. Mrs. Carr was warned to be careful, because as far as the ambassador's wife was concerned, I was really very odd.[163]

Well, I certainly was dressed in a very odd manner. Rosamond said I was wearing the most beautiful pale lilac linen dress she had ever seen; it was marred only by the filthy sneakers on my huge feet. She still tells everyone how pretty she thought I was in those days. I remember with some pleasure that she thought I was absolutely stunning. I had my hair in a long braid over my shoulder and was very tan from all of the fieldwork I had done before my capture. I had a wild look in my eye, though, and managed to pretty much ruin the reception by interrupting dinner pleasantries while I grilled Rosamond about the possibilities of using her plantation for a base camp. I was convinced that if there were gorillas on the Congolese side of the volcanoes, there must certainly be gorillas on the Rwandan side. I completely ignored the ambassador and his wife and moved the shining crystal and spotless silver aside so that I could better position my cheap, ragged notebook. I was intent upon writing down Rosamond's responses to a series of questions I had already composed, numbered from one to twenty.[164] The brutalities I had endured had strengthened my resolve, but also removed me one notch from civilized behavior. After all I had just experienced during my detention in the Congo, I was totally impatient with the pleasantries of high society. There was work to be done, and I wanted to complete it before my metaphorical pie was consumed. A few months later, in 1967, Karisoke was established. From that day forward the study of the mountain gorilla became my only focus, and Mrs. Carr became one of my dearest friends in Rwanda.

Unfortunately, I was perceived as a threat by academic researchers who came to Karisoke in those early years. They often viewed me as an impediment to the observation time they needed to complete their graduate studies. Sometimes, they felt that my survey protocols were outdated or not academically rigorous enough, forgetting that I was the first human to establish close contact with the mountain gorilla. One young researcher quit in a huff because I did not want to seek endorsements from the manufacturers of off-road motorcycles to use in gorilla surveys! The fact that I insisted that anyone who enjoyed the privilege of working at Karisoke must put in time on anti-poaching patrols was also an anathema to most of them. I had little time for summer-camp romances or lazy behavior, let alone direct interference with the gorilla study groups. My harsh demands resulted in many letters of complaint, which arrived by messenger or porter to Ambassador Frank Crigler's doorstep after his tenure began in 1977.

As I review my actions in the last years of my life, I am obliged to ask myself whether I was too hard on these young researchers. While undergoing these periods of self-doubt and reflection, I must keep reminding myself that I was the sole administrator of Karisoke for thirteen years—a young woman doing pioneering research in a foreign country. The Parc des Volcans belonged to Rwanda, but was created by an international agreement with Belgium in 1925 that prohibited poaching. The fact that I was the only one interested in enforcing the anti-poaching regulations was a heavy burden and not a task that I enjoyed.

During the period when I was trying to organize anti-poaching patrols, I was responsible for five students obtaining Ph.D.'s, with another four in progress. After my death, these same students went on to careers in primatology. They now write textbooks and give lectures attacking my integrity as well as my competence. They say that I did not accomplish much scientific work at Karisoke. Out of the other sides of their mouths, they state that I was either highly eccentric or mad as a hatter because I stayed up all night typing. There was absolutely no other occasion for me to complete the mounds of paperwork that were a necessary part of a research station. As an administrator, I had too little time for scientific writing. There were roofs to repair, stoves and lights to keep in working order, men's salaries to pay and write up, clothing and food to attend to, burned down cabins to rebuild (which were burned by the students), new cabins to construct and constant trips to purchase supplies and equipment.[165] While I was attending to these matters, students were busy writing defamatory letters about me to the United States Embassy as well as my sponsor, *National Geographic Magazine*.

I retaliated and expressed my frustration to Rob McIlvaine of the African Wildlife Leadership Foundation regarding the antics of student Bill Weber, one half of the V-W couple, who were such persistent thorns in my side. I reported that "our intrepid gorilla habituator, Monsieur Weber, well known for his numerous contributions to Kigali's soccer, basketball and tennis clubs, has actually managed, at great physical hazard of Toyota transport along an unpaved road, to set up a WWF (World Wildlife Fund) pre-fab rondavel in the wilds of the Visoke car park!! The gorillas of the world have met their savior at long last. God willing, the soccer, basketball, and tennis clubs of Kigali can spare him long enough."[166] My caustic humor was my way of venting pent-up frustration over the antics of students whom I felt had established their own agendas at the expense of my precious time and that of the gorillas. Incongruously, twenty year after my death, the V-W couple established a cottage industry on the lecture circuit where they now bill themselves as "widely known for pioneering studies of mountain gorillas in the late 1970's."[167] They neglect to mention that Dian Fossey enabled their careers and notoriety by welcoming them to Karisoke in the first place, thereby providing the basis for their livelihood and the opportunity for their deceptions.

Rob McIlvaine was one of the conservationists who tried to organize competing organizations and agendas under the same banner during this difficult period. He was the former United States ambassador to Kenya and was passionate about the preservation of wildlife. His stated goal was to engage cooperation for the conservation of the mountain gorilla within a "sensible program."[168] McIlvaine entered my life because of the misguided trust I extended with regularity and predictability to older men throughout my lifetime. He ultimately took advantage of my vulnerabilities and wrote touching, but manipulative, love letters which preyed upon my need to feel that someone was looking out for my well-being and interests. He would begin a hand-written letter with the words "I worry about you so much," feigning sympathy regarding my conflicts with Sandy (A.H.) Harcourt and the disposition of National Geographic Society funding. He went on and on about the "state of my health," urging me to leave Karisoke as soon as possible, which is what my enemies wanted all along. In a final attempt to lure me down from the mountain he wrote: "I long to hold you in my arms. Hurry back."[169]

Even the Leakey Foundation was capricious with my reputation in those days. An elder trustee, Dr. Harold Coolidge, had written a slanderous letter about me to McIlvaine, accusing me of trading in gorilla skeletons. The truth of the matter was that I had been attempting to collect skeletons with the blessing of the National Geographic Society so that I could ship them to museum collections, which included a project at Berkeley. I had one old silverback skull that I found high on the slopes of Karisimbi in 1967 that I used briefly as a teaching tool. The skull had an energy or aura about it that was more than I could bear, so I eventually locked it away in one of my storerooms. It only reminded me of the animal it must once have been.[170] To say that I was insulted, hurt, and angry when Coolidge implied that I was a trophy collector wasn't the half of it. I was deeply wounded by the accusations that I would trade in the bodies of the gorillas, and I expressed my feelings in no uncertain terms when I wrote to Rob about Coolidge's accusations. I vowed never to ship another bone to the States after that incident, and complained bitterly *that no one else had ever cared enough about the gorillas to invest years without a salary, in rotten weather, eating bad food, and enduring monumental loneliness and despair because of the celibate kind of life I had to lead.* I added that there were too many times when, *just waking up in the morning and realizing the physical and mental strains the day would call for, was more than I could bear.* I had never expressed my deepest feelings in that manner previously, and told Rob that as I was getting older, I was afraid that I was becoming less and less able to deal with the isolation and physical demands of my work on the mountain.[171] The stress of my living conditions and the increasing political pressures were becoming more than I could handle. When I poured out my heart to him on that day, I did not know that McIlvaine would eventually betray me as well as my fund-raising efforts on behalf of the Digit Fund. Despite my complaints and struggles, I never expected accolades for giving up so much of my life to work with the gorillas. Indeed, except for one award from the National Geographic, and their constant, integral support up until that time, I never received any. I wrote at the time that *I lived with, and because of, the full knowledge that if it had not been for the support of the National Geographic and my own work, there would be few mountain gorillas left in the world.* I had never separated research from conservation aims; both should go hand in hand when one is fortunate enough to be able to conduct a long-term study in the wild, and especially when one is working with a rare and magnificent species such as the mountain gorilla. It had been that two-fold aim which had gotten me into difficulties in the scholastic world with individuals who didn't understand why chasing poachers, organizing poacher patrols, cutting traps, and running out cattle took so much time in lieu of filling out time sheets. I vowed that as long as I was alive the gorillas would continue to survive and multiply even if it meant putting me in jeopardy—or *close to extradition.*[172]

After my death, Digit and I broke into the storeroom and retrieved the battered, ancient skull that Coolidge had complained about. Digit asked if he could have it, and I willingly gave it to him. He told me the skull belonged to one of the ancestor's of Group Four. Uncle Bert told me that Digit returned the skull to the high slopes of Karisimbi, where he interred it. When Digit returned from the mountaintop, he refused to ever speak of the incident again, and I have honored his wishes.

It is now my turn to dig up the buried secrets of the past and relegate myth to the twin tombs of deception and fraud. I have rehearsed my rebuttals for twenty years. What follows is the last years of my life as told to friends and recorded in my diaries.

12

1978-1979 Digit's Murder

When Digit was murdered on December 31, 1977, just before my forty-sixth birthday, the pattern of my world and the fabric of my immortal soul were forever altered. Almost eight years later to the day I would also be murdered. Christmas had become a time of violence and retribution, rather than a time of peace and celebration. Digit, who was vital to his group as a sentry, was killed in that service by poachers.[173] We found his body on the second of January, and what was once my favorite season became the incarnation of my worst fears.[174] The Catholic faith, which I had diligently studied with Father Raymond, had warned of the consequences of mortal sin, which, if I accepted its precepts, would forever mark my soul. That same faith had left me ill-prepared to be abandoned by all that was holy; faith offered no protection from a cauldron of malevolent intentions.

Years before those terrible days in late December, evil was a silent entity stalking through the swirling mists of the Virungas, and it slowly, surely, and stealthily assumed form and power. It disguised itself in the form of human greed, environmental degradation, political machinations, and terror, finally unleashing its full control in the maelstrom of genocide less than ten years after my death. I had heeded the warning signs, but even I was not sure what I was sensing. I knew something terrible was afoot in the mountain jungles of tiny Rwanda. I heard its dreadful whispers and felt its hot breath on my neck at night when I tried fitfully to sleep. It tried to hijack my body and soul, causing my emphysema to return with a vengeance. My physical maladies increased my sense of anxiety about the fate of the gorillas, and I agonized over the fearful changes in Digit's countenance that had been chronicled in my photographs.[175] Digit was loyally attending to sentry duty, sitting in a shady glade a short distance from his group, when I viewed him alive and whole for the last time. The resulting photo captured something that was not apparent when the shutter clicked. I only noticed it later, and the resigned, haunted, hunched appearance of his body projected an aura of resignation. I returned to preparations for the Christmas season with great difficulty.

The holiday provided some relief from my apprehensions, since it was an especially hopeful one that year. The annual Christmas party for the African staff went off without a hitch on December 23rd, and I got a little "X," but no one noticed.[176] As usual, the Africans were thrilled with their gifts, and the jungle resounded with revelry and drumming well into that holiest of nights. I was elated, in part, because I was making enormous progress on *Gorillas in the Mist,* and I went to bed content and happy on New Year's Eve. The following days would be filled with preparations for the arrival of a film crew from the BBC, which was to be led by David Attenborough. I wanted to make sure that Karisoke made a good impression, and that things were running smoothly. Little did I know, as I drifted off with Kima and Cindy nearby, that Digit had already made his great sacrifice.

The notes inside the cover of my 1978 diary reveal another, more fearful state of mind. I listed my gun inventory as: Gun no. 187921, Walther model PPK/S, calibre 9mm kurz. My old gun was a 7.65 mm,[177] but no amount of firepower would protect the gorillas or me from what was about to transpire. We had been conducting patrols throughout the forest as a constant precaution, since the need for added income emboldened the poachers at this time of year. Digit had been dead for approximately two days before Ian Redmond found the gorilla's bot-fly encrusted body and ran down the trail to deliver the devastating news. Thank god I did not discover Digit's body on my own. I was probably in shock and entirely overwhelmed, because I initially received the news as if it were an abstract concept, and I did not immediately fall apart. Digit's body was carried back to camp by the trackers on a litter strewn with Gallium vines, and Ian and I immediately set about the task of recording the grisly murder for the world to witness. I realized that it was critical to record the details of the crime. There would be time to fall apart later. We shot 1000 feet of film on the body alone, and finished a tissue sample collection. A young French doctor from Ruhengeri was summoned to complete the autopsy. With the utmost feelings of rage, horror, anguish, and revenge I took the photo of Digit's mutilated body for the final record of his life in *National Geographic Magazine.* His magnificent head had been severed from his body, so, too, his gentle hands. These were the same hands that ever so tenderly played with my equipment, stripped celery for me to eat, and patted me about the head and shoulders. His torso, and the lap where I had rested my head, was lying in an affect of repose.

My trackers and I again carefully bound what was left of Digit to the litter and covered the broken body once again with Gallium vines. Our little procession wound its way around my green cabin, and Digit was interred in the gorilla graveyard. My camp notes from that day are stained with dirt, blood, and tears, as are the remaining notes from Uncle Bert's murder.[178] The shaky maps I drew in a futile attempt to ascertain the direction of the murderous poachers' escape routes are testimony to the amount of damage done to my psyche on that day. Word later came from the village that Digit's body parts sold for twenty dollars on the black market, an incalculable waste, and I spent many rainy nights contemplating Digit's marker.

Digit did not die easily. He must have suffered agonizingly from five major spear wounds that entered his heart, spleen, intestines, lungs, and stomach. I can only imagine the terror of his gorilla group as they fled screaming through the jungle while Digit took his final stand against six poachers and their dogs to ensure the group's safety. Somehow, Digit managed to kill a poacher's dog before he died. After his murder I wrote in my diary that there are certain times in one's life when one cannot accept the facts for "fear of shattering one's being."[179] I had identified with Digit because we were both individuals who had learned to live on the fringes of our societies. Digit's lonely duties as sentry for his group were similar to my own. When Digit died, a light within me died also, and I was forced to retreat to an insulated part of myself.[180] Digit represented much more to me than a subject in a study group. I could not allow myself to think of his anguish, his pain, and the total comprehension he suffered while knowing what humans were doing to him.[181] I realize with clarity now that I identified with his struggles to find a position in the social structure of Group Four. In the end, he sacrificed himself so that his adopted family and his unborn child might live.

But I must go back to Digit's murderers. Just as we were about to begin his autopsy, one of my African staff came running and shouting that a poacher had just been seen on the fringes of the camp. I yelled for my four camp staff members to begin the chase while I grabbed my Walther, which was not legally registered,[182] and ran after the men, leaving the doctor and his assistant sitting in my living room with pale faces. I kept running and shooting into the air as a deterrent to keep the poacher from crossing the main open meadows above camp, where he could disappear into the forested saddle area and never be found. Eventually my four men squeezed him up against the immediate slopes of Visoke and we caught him!

A deadly calm enveloped me, preserving what little physical energy remained in my grief-stricken body. The Twa's (Batwa) name was Kanyarugano, and he admitted to being instrumental in Digit's murder. I kept him in my cabin for one night and confess now to the desire to kill him, especially since his yellow, tattered shirt was fountain-sprayed on both sides with streams of Digit's dried blood.[183] I asked two of the Africans to sleep in the cabin, as I did not entirely trust myself. Somewhere inside me decency took over, and I knew that killing the Twa would do nothing to bring Digit back or truly avenge his murder. At the same time, I did not want Digit to have died in vain, and I was genuinely worried that if I didn't kill the Twa he would return to the forest to kill again.[184] During that interminable evening, Kanyarugano divulged that the motive behind Digit's slaying was that a Hutu had offered to pay the head poacher, my old nemesis Munyarukiko, the equivalent of twenty dollars to get the head and hands of a silverback. The Hutu planned to find a tourist who would pay him much more for the grisly souvenirs. Kanyarugano also told us that we would find Digit's mutilated body parts buried in a clump of bamboo near Munyarukiko's house.

I was so angry, that I wanted the world to witness what had happened in a way that would sicken and horrify. Since Digit had been the "big hero" in the Rwandan tourism campaign, I tried propping him up in the same position he had taken in the poster, but this was not an easy or pleasant task since he had been decapitated and was also without hands. Then I propped Kanyarugano up in exactly the same position, holding a piece of wood. I wanted to make these two photos into posters and splash them around Kigali, Ruhengeri, and Gisenyi saying "Come Visit Me in Rwanda." This may sound ghoulish, but I hoped it would make an impression upon Europeans who wished to buy gorilla skulls and hands.[185] I thought Digit's murder represented the beginning of the end,[186] and I worried constantly that that the majority of the other mountain gorillas within the Virungas had already been killed off, since the poachers had dared to attack one of my major study groups. My worry extended to some of my fringe groups that had been regularly coming into the area for protection from the adjacent mountains; they hadn't been seen since my return from America. Within days, I wrote a lengthy dispatch to the one Rwandan official whom I felt I could trust, Paulin Nkubili, the Military Head of Justice in Ruhengeri,[187] and copied the letter to every Rwandan official I could think of. I wrote in English, since my French was very poor, and detailed the poacher's confession, listing the names, mothers, fathers, and communes of the six poachers connected to Digit's murder. I passionately explained that it was of the utmost importance that the killers of Digit be brought to justice—a resolution which I felt should be death or imprisonment. I told the Prefect that, on the afternoon of January 5, when four of the park guards were told to come into the area to search for the poachers responsible for Digit's death, all four were seen by one of my men in the bar at the base of Visoke; the guards were drunk on pombe.[188]

I began a second letter writing campaign to everyone who wielded power and influence—both within Rwanda and in the world conservation community. Finally, I vowed not to release the poacher I was holding to anyone but the President of Rwanda, Juvenal Habyarimana,[189] who was "a friend of Digit's."[190] The President had viewed the *National Geographic* television special about the gorillas on numerous occasions—once with his wife and children, at the invitation of Ambassador Frank Crigler and his wife.[191] Frank commented that I was at my most fetching and persuasive for the event, as well as handsomely dressed and coiffed. I must admit that I was perfectly behaved and especially charming with Mme. H. and the children. The President's response at the time was very favorable, and he remained a supportive friend of the mountain gorillas thereafter.[192]

Nkubili responded to my initial letter and climbed up to camp accompanied by three commandoes, who were the toughest of the Rwandan military. They repeated the interrogation, armed with pliers I had given them, but did not learn any information that my men and I had not already gathered. I finally agreed to release the prisoner to Nkubili. On the same day, Nkubili and his men went to the spot where the trophies were said to be buried, and they found that Digit's head and hands had been removed.

Digit's death prompted my manifesto, but at the time I had no appreciation of the dangerous political gamesmanship that was being played out both in Rwanda and the western world. Eastern Congo was ripe for diamond, gold, and copper smuggling, as well as the black sand called coltan that is the primary component of microchips. The Virungas provided access to these remote, mineral-rich regions. International politics was not my concern, except as it impacted the protection and preservation of the mountain gorilla. All I knew at the time was that I wanted *our* country, Rwanda, to *set an example for the rest of the African nations who also have valuable heritages to preserve. Rwanda had a stable government and the richest heritage of all, the Parc des Volcans. No other country could boast of a park that contained not only the mountain gorilla, but also many other unique indigenous animals.*[193]

My vision of a stable, peaceful society would prove to be an illusion. Several years later, Nkubili was charged in a conspiracy to murder the President and was sentenced to die.[194] A few years later I was murdered, and within ten years President Habyarimana's plane was shot out of the skies near the presidential palace in an incident that would ignite the genocidal wars of the mid 1990's. Extreme members of his Hutu political party were said to be responsible, although it could have been extremists on either side. As a result, over 800,000 people were murdered, and hundreds of thousands more died of cholera and other diseases in the refugee camps. In the days after Digit's death, my dreams soon began to mirror the violence of current and future realities.

It wasn't until the following Monday, after we had buried what remained of Digit, that the psychic devastation I was harboring manifested itself. At first I thought I had pneumonia. I was sick all night with a temperature of 40 degrees Celsius (104°F).[195] My dreams and thoughts were filled with images from the past: Digit so gently taking my notebook from my hands and then taking my pen before returning them to me and rolling over to go to sleep by my side, and Digit coming up to smell my hand and taking my glove before walking in front of the camera lens. I awoke from these nocturnal remembrances vomiting and coughing blood, my body aching and wracked with chills.[196] I felt as if some kind of malevolence was oozing from every pore in my body. Perhaps I was experiencing the vestiges of Digit's innocent suffering and feeling the cruel dismemberment of his body as if it were my own.

The following morning the BBC film crew arrived, and even though I was in bed when they arrived, I was able to maintain an illusion of calm with them while the staff got them settled into their cabins. I kept coughing blood for three days, and I finally collapsed and cried like a baby for an hour. *Night time really hurt.*[197] Letter writing and keeping careful records of my efforts to avenge Digit were all that kept me sane during this hideous time. I also obsessed over my conviction that Digit's murder was an international event and not just a local matter, since Digit was known and loved by all who saw the *National Geographic* television special. In an action I am not particularly proud of, I requested that the conservator of the Parc des Volcans make sure that the dogs belonging to the poachers be shot. I referred to the dogs as "rabid half-starved mongrels" that fed on the wildlife of the Parc.[198] Whether my conflicts were with people or animals, my anger and desperation caused me to temporarily lose the compassion for helpless animals that was normally part of my psychological makeup. Thankfully, a year later, I found myself nursing a poacher's dog back to health. It had been caught in a trap and its leg was terribly infected. It was terribly sweet and I could not bring myself to kill it, so I decided to feed it, dress its wounds, and then find a home for it.[199] I would not capitulate to the malevolence that was slowly spreading throughout the mountains. Respite from sorrow could only be found within the purity of my own intentions.

13

1978-1980 Aftermath

I am certain that without the friendship and support of Frank Crigler, the Ambassador to Rwanda, and his wife, Bettie, I would have never survived those dreadful days in the aftermath of Digit's death. We did not start our association on the best of terms, due to my extreme response to Digit's murder. However, we developed a friendship based upon mutual respect, understanding, and similar goals—even if we did not always agree on the proper means to achieve those goals.

Frank wrote about our prickly but respectful relationship to one of the writers who has tried to be my voice: "You should also be aware that Dian and I, good friends that we were, did not by any means always agree on either her ideas about conservation or her strategies for protecting the gorillas and their habitat—and least of all about how to deal with the humans that, like it or not, cohabited with them in that tiny, overcrowded ecosystem. But I like to think our differences tended to cancel each other out, and that the gorillas gained in the process."[200]

Frank was my buffer between concerned officials in the State Department and the conservators at the Rwandan Office of Tourism and National Parks (ORTPN). I confided to him that I did not understand how I was supposed to cooperate with what I considered to be a long line of corrupt and inept park officials, let alone work with them![201] The Parc des Volcans was under the jurisdiction of the Rwandan Ministry of Agriculture, and their conservators had authority over park guards, most of whom were afraid of the forest and preferred to remain in the villages. In fact, the guards regularly received their salaries whether they went into the parks or not. Honey gatherers, poachers, and cattle grazers were often friends or relatives of the park guards and were free to come and go as they pleased.[202]

When I first came to Rwanda there were no conservators. The first one that was hired was fired soon thereafter. He was the individual who recruited Munyarukiko, the leading poacher of the park, to kill two groups of gorillas on

Karisimbi so that the babies, Coco and Pucker, could be captured for the Cologne Zoo. In the early days of my research, the poachers would blithely run through the campground, their exit confirmed by the receding sounds of the bells on their dogs' necks.

Meanwhile, my article in *National Geographic Magazine* about Coco and Pucker created an international scandal that did not endear me to officials on either side of the Atlantic. The United States was very interested in maintaining good relations with African nations that were considered to be western-leaning, and Rwanda certainly fit the bill. Even though I did not point a finger directly at the Rwandan government, the implication was clear that they were not engaged in active conservation of the mountain gorilla.

The second conservator was fired because he aimed a shot into Group Six when the gorillas charged him and a group of Africans who were leading an ill-trained group of Japanese cinematographers. The third conservator was sacked because vast collections of ivory were found on the roof of his driver's home, and the conservator was subsequently connected with the killings of many elephants. The fourth conservator, who was in charge when Digit was murdered, was working closely with the shady Belgian "consultant" to ORTPN, Alain Monfort. Just days after Digit's murder, Monfort sent a guard up to camp and proceeded to take my gorilla tracker aside, warning him not to go near the high mountain plateaus where the poachers were hiding.[203] He also told the tracker not to tell me whenever he found signs of poaching such as footprints, visual sightings, and traps. The guard told my tracker quite plainly that, if we continued to work against poachers within the Parc, we would be thrown out.[204] To my horror, I also learned that Munyarukiko was involved in the murder of Digit—so much for his promise to me many years earlier. I detailed all of these suspicious events to Frank Crigler, explaining that the main difference between Karisoke and ORTPN was that I put the conservation of the gorillas first and foremost, and ORTPN put tourism first. It was important to realize that, every day a group of tourists came into the park, there was one less day of unspoiled peace and tranquility for the remaining gorillas. I fear that the Crigler's sympathetic association with me, and their protective stance toward the gorillas, resulted in Frank not getting the promotion he deserved, which led to his transfer to a post in Colombia in 1979.[205] Frank has denied that this is true and says that his transfer occurred predictably at the end of a three year assignment in Kigali.[206] Whatever the reason for his transfer, I felt his loss keenly and I will not truly rest until the Criglers know how much I cherished them and their sacrifices, even though it seemed that I was not as responsive a friend as they would have liked.

It did not take long after Digit's death for ORTPN to come down on me, hard, and its director, Dismas Nsabimana, figured prominently in my life from that moment on. My anti-poaching crusades were always a matter of controversy, and speculation was widespread that Digit's murder was in retaliation for my extreme stance against poaching. Meanwhile, the fact that my exposure in *National Geographic* had created a worldwide love affair with the mountain gorilla was appreciated, but not necessarily respected, by ORTPN. ORTPN's attitude was revealed in an official communiqué from Dismas that said, in part, "We deeply regret the acts of poaching that have been directed against the gorilla 'DIGIT' on December 31, 1977. The ORTPN has been quite indignant at the poaching of this gorilla, perhaps more than you, as this act constitutes a challenge and harm to the patrimony of Rwanda."[207] Dismas then lowered the boom and accused me of engineering the arrival of the BBC film crew in the aftermath of Digit's death for publicity purposes. "We know, from prior correspondence that these photographers depended on your help to produce their film(s). We know from them (personally, firsthand) that you asked them to film the dead gorilla and make a display of it that would discredit Rwanda and its parks...we assume that you had invited them immediately after the death of the gorilla, although they claimed that it was pure coincidence...."[208]

Dismas then extended an olive branch and once again invited me to become part of an open collaboration with ORTPN, even though he admitted that I had not recognized its authority since ORTPN created a program for tourism. But, I was convinced that to allow tourism within the confines of such a small ecosystem would be the equivalent of creating a zoo without cage walls, forever changing the essential quality of the gorillas. I felt that conservation funds should be directed to active programs that would reduce or eliminate poaching entirely, and if Rwanda would not raise the funds, I would do so on my own.

Unfortunately, my efforts to raise money got me into a terrible mess. Survival Anglia Limited, a media organization in London, wrote to tell me that while they were continuing to spread the news about Digit, they were worried about a new aspect of the situation. They'd heard a rumor that the BBC crew had experienced "a very unpleasant situation" when they were leaving Rwanda, and that Digit had been killed in retaliation for treatment I had meted out to a poacher caught and held in my camp. They warned me that if stories like this "got around," it could seriously affect attempts to raise money, and they said they needed the full story before they would continue any efforts on my behalf.[209]

The truth of what had happened to the BBC crew was stranger than fiction, and a dark portent of my future. Two days after Digit was buried, and things had settled down a bit at camp, the BBC crew went out to film Group Five, which had been purposely set aside by mutual agreement as a study group not to be viewed by tourists. My tracker blazed a trail for the film crew, but we discovered that a new, burly park guard named Barekaya had utilized our trail to bring a group of loud Belgian tourists to view the gorillas. When one of my students confronted Barekaya, and explained that the group was off-limits to tourists, the guard became aggressive and pushed him. When the BBC team came back to camp, they were understandably upset that they had missed an entire day's work because of the incident. I fired off an angry note to Alain Monfort, Dismas's "consultant," and sent it down the mountain with the porters. Monfort's home was near the conservation office, and the American government had paid for both buildings,[210] so I thought it might give me some authority, or at least a good enough reason to complain about the use of the BBC trail.

Alain Monfort, who was officially in Rwanda as a technical aid to the Belgians, was a shadowy force in the movement to exploit the mountain gorillas as a source of tourism. I had nothing but contempt for him, since he had been sitting on his rump collecting World Wildlife Funds and going to Europe to vacation every six months or so. Monfort and his wife were supposedly salaried by the World Wildlife Fund to assist the Conservator, but no one in Kigali could really say what their duties were. I had asked Monfort myself what he did, and he could not answer me—neither could Mr. Nsabimana. I was able to learn that Monfort was fired from Rwindi National Park in Zaire and A'Kagera National Park in Rwanda because he did not work hard enough.[211]

Monfort scrawled an angry, almost illegible note in reply to my concerns about the treatment of the BBC crew. In this same note, he ordered me to attend a meeting regarding the grazing of cattle in the Parc des Volcans that was, in his words, "mandatory." If I did not attend, it would indicate that I had no interest in the Parc, quote, and unquote. It was such a ridiculous scrawl that I did not answer it. Meanwhile, the conservator, Nsabimana, typed out two pages to respond to my written inquiry regarding the BBC incident and apologized for Barekaya's behavior, saying that the guard was untrained. He made no mention of the mandatory meeting regarding the cow invasion. I wrote back to the conservator immediately to say that I was sick, had virtually no gas, was stranded by two broken-down cars, and therefore I could not attend the "cow meeting."[212]

Monfort responded with a game of cat and mouse that I have never been able to figure out, but for some reason he tried to lure me off the mountain for a day. He never considered that Nyiramacyibili might disobey his orders, and to this day I have no idea what his full intent was on that Sunday in January. Still, the events that transpired with the BBC crew were certainly a part of his plotting. I won the game by not playing, since Monfort must have taken my lack of reply as acquiescence. In fact there was no cow meeting at all, and my staff reported that Monfort was seen sneaking up the mountain during the time when the meeting was supposedly taking place, along with another African who was unknown to park workers. *Monfort grilled everyone he encountered with respect to where I parked my cars, the main commune of my porters, and the exact time the BBC crew was scheduled to leave the mountain.* He had no idea I was sitting up in camp getting regular reports on his whereabouts and not off on a wild goose chase to a non-existent meeting about cows.

Two days after Monfort's mysterious trek up the mountain, the BBC crew was ready to depart. I ordered a taxi to bring them to Ruhengeri for the night, because in the morning they hoped to catch an early plane to Tanzania. The taxi driver was waiting for them, and they drove about thirty minutes to a spot where the road forks off to go to the conservator's office and the park guard station. The guard signaled for the taxi to stop, but since this was unusual, the driver kept on going, thinking the guard was playing around. Suddenly the guard began firing over the top of the taxi, which sped up, since the driver became frightened and had no idea what was going on. About ten minutes into their flight, the taxi encountered Monfort and his land rover, and Monfort swerved his car in front of the taxi. Of course it was Monfort who had ordered the guard to shoot. A huge verbal hassle ensued, and Monfort ordered the taxi to follow him to Ruhengeri to the military camp. Along the route, they stopped to pick up two commandoes who were planted there by Monfort. The commandoes had been told that the BBC teams were mercenaries cloaked in the guise of photographers, but actually involved in sneaking arms and ammunition over the Virungas and into Uganda. They threw all of the valuable photographic and film gear out of the taxi and searched through it, although nothing was stolen. I heard about all of this because one of my African staff was along and understood the local dialect. Then some-how, and I am not sure how this transpired, the Prefect Nkubili was called. He arrived on the scene very angry because once again he was being called into park affairs. He told Monfort that if the BBC team missed their plane, Monfort would be responsible for buying new tickets for everyone.

Even though I knew quite a bit about this unpleasant incident, a day after the episode I had no idea how it had been resolved. So I wrote to my lawyer, Fulton Brylawski, detailing the matter and assuring him that Frank Crigler would do everything in his power to protect the crew if they made it to Kigali. I noted that Frank was already doing a great deal of work outside of his normal duties since

Digit's murder. I also decided to send our footage of Digit to a couple I knew in Ruhengeri, who could deliver it to the embassy where it would be forwarded via diplomatic pouch to the States. With Monfort on the offensive, I felt I had to "hang low" for a while. This would give me more time to complete an article I was preparing on the life and death of Digit that would be distributed to all of the conservation magazines I could reach. Since I suspected the regular mail was not safe for sending film, I worried that it might also be untrustworthy for regular letters.[213]

During this time of passionate lobbying on my part, and various acts of skull-duggery on the part of ORTPN officials, I invented the idea of a fund that would help pay for the commemorations I was hoping to complete on the behalf of Digit. I christened it the "Digit Fund." Since I had no first hand experience with charitable funds and was certain that I did not want the added burden of trying to manage finances, I asked Fulton Brylawski if he would consider helping me in this endeavor. I had pondered this idea long enough to know for certain that I did not want The Digit Fund to be another vague conservation plan spending half its money on overhead, a fourth going to tickling the egos of top-ranking Africans, and the final fourth going into actual conservation schemes. I told Brylawski that I wanted it all very legal, down to the cost of the last postage stamp. I wrote passionately to Shirley McGreal of the International Primate Protection League (IPPL) and explained that the Digit Fund would be established for active work against poachers within the Virungas. I did not want the money going to support only one gorilla and the gorilla's staff, as was the case of the captured Koko who resided with the Gorilla Foundation.[214] The Digit Fund was meant to be a real effort of active conservation.[215]

I became more convinced than ever that I was the only one who could make certain that Digit had not died in vain. Many other gorillas had suffered a fate quite similar to his, but he was the only one whose life had been documented since infanthood. He could not be a lost cause; he *must not* be a lost cause. I worried people would think that he was just another animal, and that he was not as important as the human beings who were also suffering across the African continent. To me, he was not just another animal. His life typified all that might and could happen to the remaining mountain gorillas, and in telling his story, I felt that the world was being given a chance to save the entire sub-species from being killed by poachers for their skulls. Since international treaties for the protection of the gorillas and other wildlife had established the Parc des Volcans, I felt that at the very least I had international law behind me in my fight to save what was left of the Parc. I wanted to enforce the law like it had never been enforced before.[216]

As I recorded these events in my correspondences and diaries, tiny threads were beginning to appear that now seem intrinsically woven into the fabric of the whole. I did not see it while I was alive, but an ominous element was beginning to emerge if one looked deep enough. The pattern was there, but incomprehensible. Considering again the labors of Mgahinga Gorilla in the confines of the lava tunnel, I can see that just as the mosses had masked the patterns of elephant hides on the tunnel walls, so, too, have revisionist historians buried and distorted the events that culminated in my murder. Taken as isolated events, each moment seems inconsequential, just as the leaf of the moss is so small that it seems trivial. But as the moss spreads, it becomes a veil, and then a thick carpet that is all but impenetrable.

14

Smartie's Party

There is an old Kentucky saying that goes "Smartie gave a party and no one came."[217] My dance card at the anti-poaching party would remain empty as I tried to gather sympathy for the gorillas' plight by lobbying the major conservation organizations. Digit was scheduled to be on the agenda at an important meeting in Portugal of the International Union for the Conservation of Nature (IUCN) in early February 1978, but the meeting came and went minus the four representatives who were considered to be most sympathetic to our situation in Karisoke. Excuses ranged from a bout of the flu, not being there for the critical day of discussion, to being "elsewhere."[218] Thus, no one was around to discuss Digit's case, and those who remained wanted to concentrate on tourism instead. Sandy Harcourt had the gall to suggest to the members that I was aware of the importance of habituating a tourist group, and that is why the World Wildlife Fund's (WWF) hut was built in the Parc. The truth of the matter was that the United States embassy, and not the WWF, had purchased the Parc headquarters as well as the twelve rondavels placed strategically for park guard stations.[219] Adding insult to injury, Richard Wrangham, a friend from King's College in Cambridge, suggested that I should begin by putting together a budget for the tourism project, since if I wanted to "see it happen, it could be arranged."[220] But neither flattery nor coercion would buy my support for these misguided efforts.

"Smartie's Party," in the form of the ineffectual IUCN, had asked the impossible by asking me to support tourism, and Wrangham's budget entreaties drained what little hope remained within me that the IUCN would work on Digit's behalf. I was tired of people missing the point entirely, and I refused to listen to any more lies and decrees from the Harcourt corner. I wanted to see Digit's killers imprisoned before anything else. I was disgusted that so-called conservationists were willing to deflect discussion of his death in order to concentrate on tourism when the Parc was overloaded with gorilla killers. I scrawled my opening response about Smartie's party on the back of the summary letter I received from Wrangham. In big, block letters I carefully printed KANYARU-GANO, as if the sight of the murderous poacher's name would somehow give me the strength to continue to fight what was rapidly becoming a losing battle. I commenced by stating that the IUCN plan simply would not work if the money earmarked for Digit went instead to a tourism program. Seven more gorillas had been murdered since Digit's death, and the same poachers were not involved. But even these details were of little importance to the IUCN attendees, at least those that bothered to show up.[221] I chastised Wrangham for "sitting on his distant perch across the ocean," while talking about tourism and ignoring Digit's poachers.[222]

I wrote in *Gorillas in the Mist* that one of the greatest drawbacks of the Virungas is that it is shared by three countries, each of which has problems far more urgent than the protection of the wild animals that share the ecosystem. My greatest fear was that the world would climb *evangistically*[223] (sic) onto a "save the gorilla" bandwagon upon hearing of Digit's death, and an indignant public outcry would pour large sums of money into the Virungas, with most of it going towards shiny new Land Rovers for park officials instead of anti-poaching patrols. If this were to happen, Digit would become the first in a long line of sacrificial victims, particularly if more dead gorillas meant more money for "tourism."[224]

Even though no one came to my anti-poaching bash, I continued my correspondences to Dr. Russell Mittermeier, who was then chairman of the IUCN Primate Specialist Group. At the end of March, when the baby gorilla Mweza came to us, I was at least able to share part of that experience with Dr. Mittermeier. I was also eager to express my concern that money coming in for the fledgling Digit Fund be directed to Karisoke and not to tourism efforts. In the immediate aftermath of Digit's death, friends in England rallied support for funding that was supposed to go directly into the Digit Fund for anti-poaching measures. The U.K. fund had collected 3,000 English pounds, but 2,000 went to Park headquarters in Kigali, and only 500 were promised to Karisoke. This paltry amount was not going to get the Digit Fund off the ground, given the arduous conditions we were working under, and I told Dr. Mittermeier that the U.S. fund, organized by my attorney, F. Fulton Brylawski, had acquired only $100 to date. This $100 was sent by a lady who had seen a *Wild Kingdom* special. I had written to the lady and explained exactly where her money went, which was to buy medicine for Mweza on the first day we had the baby, and to pay the porters from Rumangabo.[225] I wanted Dr. Mittermeier to know a part of Mweza's story so he would see how important the Digit Fund was. I added that Digit had died in vain, because I had so far been unable to put my plans into effect—including getting the movie of Digit's life out to the public.

When I review this time in my life, keeping in mind Digit's admonition that I try to refrain from blaming myself for every atrocity directed at the gorillas, I understand why Digit took my portrait and rendered it in halves. He always had the ability to see into the deep recesses of my eyes as if he understood instinctively the fragile soul that dwelled within. In many ways it isn't important how history remembers Dian Fossey. My enemies can continue to defame me for their self-interests, if that is what they choose for their own legacies. Truth will prevail in tragedy as well as in small victories for the few remaining mountain gorillas. If the gorillas vanish from the earth, they will still live in the immortal fabric of time, which cannot be erased or altered by lies and deception. Those humans who are left on earth and tragically experience the absence of gorillas are the ones who will truly suffer the greatest of losses.

If my enemies were part and parcel of my spiritual battle, my friends provided the protective armor I needed during these trying times. Bettie Crigler offered solace and companionship, as well as a welcome regular correspondence. I saved many of the letters she wrote—communications sent with reliability and compassion over the years. I so looked forward to the visits of the entire Crigler clan to Karisoke, including sons Nacho and Jeremy. In the midst of frustration and disappointment in the aftermath of Digit's death, it was Bettie who buoyed my spirits with a note that stressed her gratitude for our friendship. She wrote to me that if she could have had a sister, she would have felt lucky if that sister were me.[226] Bettie was touched by a gift I had sent to her son, but she had no way of knowing that I would treasure her simple letter as a welcome spiritual light in my darkest days.

It seemed as if the Virungas were mirroring the state of my soul during these days, as the skies wept well into the summer months. I wrote to Bettie that there was still no steady sun, and that, in eleven years, I had never known such a continuity of rain, drizzle, fog, and mist over such a long period, let alone in July.[227] The weather was so dismal that it contributed to the psychological disintegration of an English boy who arrived on Digit's blood money, courtesy of the British Fauna Preservation Society (FPS). He came back to camp one day and was literally tearing his hair out. I wrote to Bettie that I had not often seen anyone actually tear his or her hair out.[228] I tried my best to calm him by preparing some soup, offering beer, and talking about the great work he was doing. The truth of the matter was that his absence would have been no great loss to the camp, but I was worried about how he would feel later—after his abortive attempt to try and work in the field using Digit's money. I confided to Bettie that I had done my utmost to convince the kid to stay. If he refused, I would have to finish the project with my African staff because Bill (Weber) was far too lazy to do it himself.[229] The FPS boy almost had a nervous breakdown, and he returned to England. Bettie replied to this news with an urgent invitation for me to take a break from the mountain and spend a few days with her. She promised to give me the time and space to recuperate, while at the same time underscoring the fact that it would mean a great deal to her to have me with her.[230]

During this period of correspondences, I confided to Bettie that I was trying hard to meet the expectations of the ORTPN director, Dismas Nsabimana, because I had come to respect his intelligence and his integrity as a person, even though we had serious differences regarding the matter of tourism. I wrote that I believed he was able to see through the self-interests of Harcourt and the FPS and preferred not to get involved in my difficulties with the Mountain Gorilla Project. I felt obligated to send him more frequent reports on the work we were doing at Karisoke, realizing that he appreciated written information, not just talk about getting results.

The news from Karisoke that I would be forced to report to Dismas would be tragic beyond belief. The horror and shock of Digit's murder returned in a manner that I could not have expected and resulted in my fearing that I was about to go mad.[231] On July 24, poachers killed Uncle Bert with a bullet to his heart. In a final act of savage butchery, he was beheaded. My only solace was in the knowledge that the bullet did its job quickly, sparing Uncle Bert the agonizing slow death experienced by Digit. The seventeen year old female, Macho, who was the mother of the three year old infant, Kweli, was shot and killed in the same raid. A bullet went through her right arm, and followed a trajectory through her heart, smashing her ribs before exiting her body. Kweli was wounded in the arm, and was still alive, although he would eventually succumb to gangrene.[232]

Shocked and in grief, I was determined to find the source of the guns that had replaced the poacher's spears. Via slow, sneaky, inquiries I learned that a "big shot" from below the mountain knew about the killings a *day before* they occurred. The poachers were trying to capture one of the young juveniles of the group, probably Kweli, in order to deliver the youngster to the big shot in Gisenyi. He had been on his way, along with two other men, to pick it up an *hour before* the killings occurred. How Kweli managed to elude them was a miracle, except that he probably fled when the poachers were dealing with Macho and Uncle Bert.[233] On the morning of his death, Kweli was found breathing shallowly in the night nest he shared with Tiger. The gorillas returned to his side repeatedly throughout the day to comfort him with belch vocalizations or gentle touches. Once Beetsme even tried to pull Kweli into a sitting position, as if trying to get the nearly dead baby to get up and follow him. Indeed, every animal seemed to want to help, but could do nothing with the insidious effects of the gangrene poisoning the life force that flickered within the tiny infant. *Each member of the group went to Kweli individually to stare solemnly in his face for several seconds before silently moving off to feed. It was as if the gorillas knew that Kweli's life was nearly over.*[234] The final disintegration of Group Four was almost complete.

I wrote about the death of Kweli with great fervor and sorrow in *Gorillas in the Mist*, but I would not share my absolute and total devastation regarding these tragic events in any other public correspondences. My diaries and personal letters retain the only record of these deepest of feelings, and they have been hidden from the world by forces and individuals who still fight over my legacy. Thankfully, my biographer Farley Mowat was able to preserve many of my thoughts before my diaries disappeared. He described my utter terror at the events that unfolded in the aftermath of Kweli's death. Kweli's fate put me dangerously near the chasm which separates the rational mind from that of madness. I went to bed at 11:00 PM and woke at approximately 1:00 AM feeling as if there were a plastic bag over my head and I was about to vomit. I could not catch my breath, and for the first time in my life I was terrified out of my senses. I had awakened from a nightmare in which the board of directors of the *National Geographic* was asking me why I had killed the gorillas.

Not knowing what else to do, I sat up in bed and lit a gas lamp, hoping that the light would vanquish the demons swarming about my room. My body went from a state of sweating to chills, and I finally threw up. Eventually, I could not stand to be alone any longer and asked one of my men to wake Ian Redmond. I don't know what I would have done if he were not in camp because my pride would not have allowed me to ask for help from the V-W couple or David Watts. When Ian finally showed up, bewildered, I asked him to talk to me about anything: movies, books, whatever. Well, he had only seen two science fiction movies, but it sure helped just to hear him talk. I was too terrified to go back to sleep, so I asked him to spend the night in the bed next to mine, which he very kindly did. Shortly after I finally fell asleep again, I woke up screaming because I saw the murdered gorillas in my dreams, but the sound of Ian snoring lulled me back to sleep, this time to dream of spaceships. *I had never known that kind of fear before.*[235]

I understand now that my soul was waging war with malevolent forces that were lurking in the mountain mists. Psychologists will disagree and argue that I was having a severe anxiety attack and nothing more. I was fortunate to prevail in that encounter with evil, but I was ashamed to admit what I had experienced to anyone. I believe I would have lost the battle and gone *bonkers* if Ian had not been around. This confrontation with unadulterated malevolence induced the same shame I experienced after my brutalization by the Congolese soldiers. Nevertheless, my psyche was only battered, and certainly not vanquished.

News of the deaths of Uncle Bert and Macho set off an intense wave of protest in the United States that involved Secretary of State Cyrus Vance, who was compelled to exchange correspondences with leaders of the conservation community. Vance was also a good friend of Dr. Melvin Payne of the *National Geographic*. Dr. Payne would soon send two cables warning me to cease my anti-poaching activities, or my funding would be at risk. This flurry of activity at the highest levels of the State Department inspired Ambassador Frank Crigler to take the bull by the horns and try to direct the energy that had been unleashed in a positive fashion, and I believe that I damaged our friendship by not embracing his efforts wholeheartedly.

Frank was aware that the conservationists were understandably upset that Rwanda's gorillas were not being properly protected. As he thought more about the situation, he thought it seemed prudent to channel international concern into constructive assistance that would help not only the gorillas, but the impoverished Rwandans as well. The IUCN had scheduled another conference in late September at Ashkhabat,[236] and Frank hoped Rwanda might be represented there. Frank thought that I would be happy when he launched a cable campaign, "worthy of a Dian Fossey," by sending personal messages to U.S. conservation leaders and asking them to put together a serious assistance package for the Parc des Volcans that could be presented at the IUCN meeting.[237]

The ambassador did not stop there. He arranged to have ORTPN Director Dismas write a proposal that would address the specific, long-term needs of the Parc, including material support and technical supervision. Frank asked for my "blessing" on the matter, and implored me to cooperate with Dismas. "Please work all your considerable charms on the others concerned, even Monfort and the Conservator…I truly believe that we're on the way to something very important and ultimately very helpful to you, Karisoke, and the gorillas. Trust me."[238]

Dismas did not disappoint Frank, but I probably did. Within a week, Dismas had presented a proposal which the Ambassador admitted did put too much emphasis on roads and buildings and not enough on guard training, but at least it was a start. Frank also thought that the addition of a foreign expert to run things would improve the viability of the aid project. Since I had so far not responded to his letter of early September, Frank probably sensed that it was not going to meet with my approval.[239]

I was not able to see the forest for the trees when I read the Dismas plan. All I could imagine was a Parc surrounded by a tarmac of roadways with pompous officials driving shiny new land rovers, and I told Frank so in no uncertain terms. The deaths of so many of my beloved gorillas made a festering wound in my psyche and I doubt if I would have been able to welcome any proposal except that of total isolation for the gorillas at that point. It bothered me that out of a $208,000 budget, $100,000 was earmarked for roadways. Adding insult to injury, the shadowy Monfort was scheduled to attend the Ashkhabat meeting of IUCN. On the other hand, I realized that my negative reactions would do nothing to improve relations with Rwandan officials or board members at *The National Geographic* who controlled my grant money for Karisoke. I was terrified that they were about to cut off funding entirely and asked Frank if he would talk to Dr. Ed Snider about this issue, as I did not have the courage to do it myself.

My negative response hurt Frank deeply, and he wrote that he felt it was pity we could not work together, especially since we shared the same goals with respect to the future welfare of the mountain gorillas.[240] He reminded me with some urgency that Rwanda was, after all, a sovereign nation with the right to make policies about how its resources should be managed. The Dismas proposal may have been less than perfect, but it was still a plan—a plan that required some give and take on my part. Meanwhile, even with my out and out rejection of his efforts, Frank was still willing to approach Dr. Snider on my behalf when he went back to the States for ten days in mid October.[241] What I did not know at the time was that Frank was growing increasingly concerned about my mental state. His first priority, after all, was his job as Ambassador. Since he felt that I was growing increasingly "unstable," and since Karisoke was a very public U.S. interest in Rwanda, he felt compelled to conspire to get me out of the country before things got out of control. He was afraid that I might do something to get the Rwandan government to expel me, "or worse."[242]

I realize now that there was a great irony in my rejection of the Dismas proposal, especially since Dismas credited me with attenuating the effects of poaching.[243] He also understood that it was a mistake in 1925 to sacrifice half of the parklands by turning over the lower slopes of the volcanic cones to the farming populace. He wrote that it was a courageous decision on the part of Rwandan authorities to retain the upper slopes as gorilla habitat even though there was great pressure from farmers, herdsmen, and poachers in a tiny country where cultivable land was at a premium and the human population was growing exponentially.[244]

Abandoning all hope of support from the IUCN, Frank, or Dismas, I once again turned to the IPPL and told Shirley McGreal that, should her organization succeed in raising funds on Digit's behalf, the funds should be sent to Brylawski, who would direct them to a Ruhengeri bank account. All funds would be used directly for the patrols and other objectives concerning gorilla conservation. I felt it was necessary to document all money regarding Digit on an absolutely legal basis.[245] Getting a letter from Shirley during these times was like receiving a visit from a cherished friend at camp.[246] During this time, I had a new research assistant on the way, so I decided it might be a good opportunity to come down from the mountain and plan a visit back to the States. There was a conference at the Charleston Citadel in South Carolina that I was interested in attending, and the trip would afford the opportunity to visit with Rob McIlvaine and F. Fulton Brylawski regarding the Digit Fund. I would also meet Shirley McGreal there, so it would be a good occasion to administer the struggling fund. A break from Africa would also be a welcome respite from the negative forces swirling around me. There were plenty of individuals and organizations who wanted me gone, including Monfort under the guise of the Belgian Aid Society, the U.S. State Department, officers of some conservation organizations, and a few researchers who had worked at Karisoke—all incited by the infamous V-W couple. Sometimes I felt as though the gorillas were the only beings who welcomed me, and many of those I loved most had been killed.

Looking back upon these events, with the hindsight and solitude that Digit has afforded me, makes me feel small and insignificant compared to the overwhelming political and monetary forces converging upon the gorillas' habitat. I was one woman, alone, plagued by health problems and engulfed in a geo-political situation that was both complicated and dangerous. Perhaps, if I had fully understood the crushing odds I was facing in my dedication to the gorillas, I would have given up then and there, taken Cindy and Kima back to the States, and grown old and fat in an adjunct professorship. But my destiny was not yet fulfilled. Hope, and a belief that I could make a difference, kept me engaged in the battle of a lifetime. Who, after all, did the gorillas have to turn to at this critical juncture? I was operating solely on the energy that purity of intention can provide, even though I was both angry and naive in the process of following my dreams and destiny.

At about this time, an omen that should not have been dismissed so quickly turned up in (of all things) Cindy's bag of rice. I had given Big Nemeye some white rice from Cindy's sack, and he mentioned, but did not complain, that the rice was full of dirt and stones. Since I did not regularly examine Cindy's rice, I could not contradict him, even though I threw it out to the chickens every morning and did not notice the dirt and stones. There was also a substance that looked like vacuum cleaner dust mixed in with the stones and rice. When I asked Basil, the houseman, to look at the remains of what was in the portion I had given to Big Nemeye, I was truly frightened by his response. He became terrified, and began laughing hysterically. This was the same response he'd had when his baby died several years earlier—the same response other Africans had when their relatives died via sumu (poisoning) or natural causes.[247] I knew what the warning meant, but I was more concerned for my Africans and Ian than I was for myself.

Even Dismas was swept up in political maneuverings that were beyond anyone's control or understanding. In October, he donated $2,000 to the antipoaching patrols at Karisoke and was fired shortly thereafter. Amy Vedder wrote that he had surprised everyone in the Mountain Gorilla Project by opposing any tourism program centered on the mountain gorillas, but she indicated his views were rendered "moot" when he was abruptly replaced with a man named Francois Benda-Lema.[248] Frank reasoned that, since the United States had finally turned up the heat on ORTPN after the killing of Uncle Bert, the firing and the 2,000 pounds might be easily explained as a belated show of support for the Digit Fund.[249]

Benda-Lema was educated in the Soviet Union, at Patrice Lumumba University, and received a degree in economics. This would hardly qualify him as an expert in conservation, unless ORTPN was interested in his abilities to manage the monies that could be realized from gorilla tourism programs. My current vantage point, which affords the greatest of hindsight, makes my left eyebrow arch even more when I recall that it was Benda-Lema who "accidentally" met with me within weeks of my murder and offered assistance with my visa difficulties so that I would not have to renew my work permit every few months. History has also shown that Patrice Lumumba University was considered a training ground for the future leaders of the Soviet Union's expansion into third world states.[250]

In early October, more sad news arrived in a letter from Bettie, confirming that the Criglers would be leaving Rwanda. I would be left without the one major official who was truly sympathetic to the gorillas. The Crigler's friendship and moral support meant a great deal to me, and I would miss them greatly.[251] In addition, Sandy Harcourt had ordered my most sympathetic supporter at Karisoke, Ian Redmond, to leave. On stationery with the prominent letterhead of the Mountain Gorilla Project, Harcourt said that that the FPS would effectively disassociate itself from Ian's "illegal work,"[252] in other words, his anti-poaching activities. Writing under the guise of concern for the political sovereignty of the Rwandans, Harcourt could not resist mentioning that he knew all about the 2,000 pounds that Dismas had given to the anti-poaching patrols. In a convoluted and veiled attempt to hide his dismay about the contribution, Harcourt praised Ian for his "admirable" work while, at the same time, decrying the fact that "ORTPN handed over 2,000 to Dian."[253] He went on to admonish Ian that the Ministry of Agriculture had more "power" than ORTPN and appeared to "have the final word." Ever the opportunistic politician, Harcourt was savvy enough to jockey for position early in the game. Dismas had lost favor, and Harcourt knew how to ally himself with those who wielded the most power and influence.

As if I didn't face enough problems with the organization of the Digit Fund, my lawyer, Fulton Brylawski, informed me that my stepfather was contesting the will of my late Uncle Bert Chapin. I had named the now-murdered Uncle Bert of Group Four after him. Like the sumu placed in Cindy's rice, the battle over my uncle's estate would foreshadow the battles over my own last will and testament after my murder. My stepfather, Richard Price, loved a good fight, and contesting Uncle Bert's will was probably a delight for him. I wrote to friends that there was no way I could explain to anyone what a total bastard he was, or put into plain words how he had been using my mother as a lever to get what he wanted—either a settlement or a contest.[254] After my death, Price would effectively negate my will and usurp my estate, which was a potentially valuable commodity because of my murder and the resulting publicity for the movie. I had earmarked everything for the gorillas, but it all went to Price. Ironically, a dead woman's "biography," in the form of a fabricated movie, would be worth far more than the notes and opinions of an aging scientist toiling alone and fighting a losing battle on behalf of the gorillas.

Uncle Bert had a clause in his will stipulating that, should anyone challenge any part of it, they would receive $1.00. Price tried to maneuver me into contesting parts of the will, but I was more than happy to settle for the $50,000 Uncle Bert left for me. The money would go a long way toward improving things at Karisoke and outfitting the anti-poaching patrols. I had a deep aversion to being in debt and was already running up bills with the lawyers regarding the Digit Fund. Any amount I owed was coming from my personal savings account in Louisville, which was co-signed by my old friend Betty Schwartzel. Betty was also dragged into the mess Price created after my murder. But in this matter at least, I was able to avoid Price's maneuvering and ordered my attorney to follow Uncle

Bert's wishes. I was so sick of arguing with my stepfather and watching my mother's disintegration because of him, that I really didn't care one way or the other as long as she could be left in peace. Besides, I had other pressing concerns.[255]

My inheritance gave me some breathing room. When I left for the States and my visit with Shirley McGreal, no one but Bettie showed up to wish me farewell, but there was little time to dwell on my loneliness and political plotting over the gorillas. Since my time abroad was limited, I would use it to help in the proper disposition of the Digit Fund—always an abiding concern. Funds had started pouring in from around the world, especially from the United States, where Walter Cronkite had announced Digit's death on the CBS Evening News. The resources would have to be properly administered, and naturally, as with any endeavor in my attempts to protect the mountain gorilla, a battle ensued between the proponents of active and theoretical conservation. The leaders of the fledgling Mountain Gorilla Project, of course, clamored for their share, as did the management of the Rwandan Office of National Parks (ORTPN). An epic struggle ensued, with a cast of characters that involved the highest officials both in Rwanda and the United States. I returned to Karisoke, after my meetings in South Carolina, thinking that the Digit Fund was in good shape, but once again I was mistaken.

In early December, Rob McIlvaine used the banner of the AWLF to publish a "project" letter detailing a conservation effort that was named the "Digit Fund Mountain Gorilla." A mass mailing of the report ensued, and probably did more to blur the lines between my Digit Fund and the Mountain Gorilla Project than any scheme Harcourt or the V-W's could have concocted. The letter invoked the IUCN conference at Ashkhabat and listed several "complications" that had developed in the interim. For example, although the Fauna Preservation Society of England planned to raise $200,000, they had no IRS status, which prohibited them from raising money in the United States. I was mentioned as "a key figure in the situation," as I was said to have strained relations with the leader of the FPS. Indeed! McIlvaine's project letter was in direct contradiction to my wishes that all funds collected were to be deposited in the bank account of the Digit Fund, Inc. They were to be drawn upon only in accordance with my instructions. I had made this very clear.[256]

When I vehemently disagreed with McIlvaine's claims that the fledgling Digit Fund existed on paper only, he conceded that the International Primate Protection League and the Digit Fund were the only institutions with non-profit IRS status and agreed with IPPL President Shirley McGreal's plans to contact a professional fundraiser. Thus, William Kardash was retained to mount a direct-mail gorilla campaign in the United States. McIlvaine's solution was to establish a special Digit Fund within the AWLF—a solution to which I reluctantly agreed.[257] Shirley was about to explode at the assertion that her organization was in no position to handle the contributions that were sure to flow her way. She sent retired foreign services officer Henry Heyman to meet with Kardash in order to create a fund-raising contract. Hearing of this meeting, McIlvaine summoned McGreal to his offices and tried to get her and IPPL to disappear from the scene. She refused and McIlvaine signed a fund-raising contract with Kardash on his own, from which the Digit Fund was totally excluded. The main prize was the mailing list for the Digit Fund.

I had been very gratified at IPPL's involvement and felt that McGreal's efforts were extraordinary and something to be proud of.[258] I wondered if any other single person had done so much for primate protection as had McGreal. I could only do for the gorillas, but she was helping so many species.[259] In another mass mailing to conservationists worldwide, McIlvaine indicated that he could undertake the project only if funds were completely turned over to the AWLF. He also said that I had asked him to manage the funds, which was not exactly the truth. He maintained that his goal was to get me out of the politically sensitive antipoaching business. Hopefully the institutional framework provided by the AWLF would negotiate a technical assistance program to train a ranger force capable of protecting the Parc des Volcans.[260] That was the public stance, but something secretive and self-serving was occurring in the boardrooms, classrooms, and institutions occupied by individuals who used the mantle of conservation to serve their narrow academic interests and moneymaking schemes. Digit's death had ensured that the mountain gorillas were now a viable commodity, ripe for exploitation.

Both the American and Belgium embassies received the AWLF proposal with relief. Belgium agreed to supply uniforms and supplies for the ranger force. At about the same time, Sandy Harcourt worked behind the scenes to launch a separate appeal in Britain through the Fauna Preservation Society. He returned to Rwanda with $200,000 plus a shopping list that did not even mention the training of a ranger force. This seed money would benefit the Mountain Gorilla Project and the emphasis would be on tourism, as Harcourt and his cronies had wanted all along. The money was supposed to be routed through the Rwandan Park System (ORTPN).

I sent out my own mailing under the letterhead of the AWLF, expressing my understanding that the AWLF would manage the Digit Fund and establish a technical assistance program that would help the Rwandans recruit, equip and train park rangers. The IPPL would join the efforts by sponsoring the direct mail campaign.[261] I never dreamed that Digit's blood money would be siphoned off by the Mountain Gorilla Project to provide vehicles for corrupt park officials involved in "tourism." The stage was once again set for a betrayal of my work. Meanwhile, the AWLF established a framework for poaching the Digit Fund so that contributions would go to the Mountain Gorilla project instead. Things were worse than I could possibly know.

It was shortly before Christmas, 1978, and I had endured what was the most terrible year of my life. I had been humbled, maligned, physically damaged, and psychically broken, but I was still a strong, determined, intelligent woman. I returned to Karisoke from my meetings in the States, determined more than ever that the cause of the mountain gorilla would not be lost, but I was not yet at the end of my sorrows.

15

"Don't Confuse Defensive Behavior with Guilt"[262]

I am beginning to understand why Digit encouraged me to undergo this grueling self-examination, which involves scrutinizing my past behaviors and motivations. When I was alive, I was caught in the forward momentum of history—my time-line punctuated with events, personalities, and my reactions to them. Death has given me an entirely new vantage point, as if I am looking backward through a tunnel with insight tempered by wisdom, understanding, compassion for my weaknesses, and appreciation of my strengths. As I gaze through the tunnel of time, I realize that 1979 provided the roadmap for my eventual exile from Kari-soke.

Christmas was barely over when the new ORTPN director, François Benda-Lema, made his first official visit to camp, along with the Conservator, Banzubaze Laurent, to size me up. He told me that Monfort was still around and planned to stay for two more years.[263] Other than that piece of distressing news, I thought that the visit went rather well, although the officials seemed a little unnerved by the wooden crosses in the gorilla graveyard and weren't enthused about being photographed there. The local religion was Catholic, and my makeshift memori-als for my gorilla friends verged upon sacrilege. Not long after the delegation left, I received a letter from Frank Crigler that detailed Benda-Lema's version of the meeting and his goals for future relations between Karisoke and Parc headquar-ters. I was relieved to hear that that Benda-Lema had the highest regard for my work—but the "howevers" were listed in great detail. Benda-Lema told Frank that while he did not condone poaching, he was concerned that the poachers and their families harbored such serious resentment toward me that he feared for my personal safety and even for my life. He added that there were a growing number of people inside and outside of the Parc who regarded themselves as my enemies due to my strenuous efforts to protect the gorillas.[264]

At that time, I did not take the threat to my personal safety very seriously and figured that any poacher in his right mind would of course not like me, but I could hardly imagine that they would have the nerve to injure or kill me. I suggested that Benda-Lema take the time to talk to the Africans in the Kinigi commune at the base of the mountain. He would not have found a single Fossey enemy there; they had proven their trust and friendship throughout the years.[265] As I look back, I wonder if Benda-Lema's list of "enemies" had nothing at all to do with poachers and instead related to his knowledge of other individuals. Was he offering a veiled warning? My gut reaction at the time was to dismiss any worry about poachers and their extended families. I had no other reason to believe otherwise. I felt safe because I had lived unmolested by poachers for almost twelve years, and they had had ample opportunity to do away with me if they desired, especially when I was alone at camp or on one of my solitary walks to the study areas.

I was responsible for the capture and questioning of dozens of poachers during my years on the mountain. One of the most infamous was Munyarukiko, who would ultimately become one of those responsible for Digit's death and mutilation. Early on in our continuing game of "cat and mouse," Munyarukiko organized a ruse in which he pretended to be captured by me in order to obtain the $120 reward posted for his apprehension. He arranged in advance with the park guards to be brought to the Conservator's home, where he knew he would most certainly be released. When I discovered the ruse I was furious and slid down the mountain with Basil and Nemeye in tow.[266] We raided Munyarukiko's hut, which wasn't easy since he had five wives and innumerable children who became hysterical at our intrusion. I stole about fifteen dollars worth of his possessions and screamed that if he did not immediately return the reward money, I would burn his hut. When he did not reply, I set fire to his possessions, and this made quite an impression on the gathered villagers. I took one of his sons and dragged myself back up the mountain, crawling on my hands and knees with the child in tow. The child was not frightened and seemed happy to get a good meal. When I realized the agitation I'd caused in the poacher's village, I promptly returned the child unharmed. He was so excited to get food and toys that he set up a squall the next day when he had to go home.[267]

Munyarukiko exacted his revenge by filing a civil suit against me in which he was awarded $600. I considered this a fair judgment—compared with the alternative of expulsion from the country—and I also realized that similar actions would not be tolerated a second time. My only recourse was to continue to pressure the local authorities to deal with Munyarukiko, but they seemed afraid to do so because he was the main purveyor of meat and ivory for many of the "important" Africans, all of whom appeared to be afraid of one another.[268] The one exception was the ORTPN director, Dismas Nsabimana, who was surprisingly enthusiastic when I burned Munyarukiko's belongings. He said I should have burned down the whole house and was amazed that I had to pay a fine. He considered my antics an accomplishment rather than a misdemeanor.[269]

As far as "taking the law into my own hands"[270] with poachers was concerned, I thought that I should not be condemned for the rest of my life for breaking the law one night when I raided the village. That was unfair.[271] The depiction of this event in the movie, *Gorillas in the Mist*, was also unwarranted as well as inaccurate. Although the scene certainly provided dramatic cinema, with the flames raging behind Sigourney Weaver's profile, it did little to reveal the true nature of what instigated the situation and the root of my motivation. The scene only reinforced the lies regarding my sanity that my enemies rely upon to ensure their viability on the lecture circuit. In the days after I paid my fine to Rwandan society, the poachers viewed the whole thing as a source of amusement, since Munyarukiko was able to outwit me and win a great victory in their eyes.

Despite Crigler's admonitions, concerns, and sincere worries regarding my welfare, I was somewhat pleased with the way the New Year had begun. Perhaps working with Benda-Lema would not be so bad after all. I also had my book to occupy my thoughts. Finishing it would provide the mental discipline necessary to alleviate my sorrow about the events of the previous year and the growing number of corpses in the gorilla graveyard. In addition, Rob McIlvaine was scheduled to visit in late spring on behalf of the AWLF to supervise the disposition of the Digit Fund. I was genuinely happy with the direction events seemed to be taking, and I believed that that the only difference between Karisoke and ORTPN (if one were to exclude the influence of the V-W couple) was that I put the conservation of the gorillas first and foremost while ORTPN put tourism first.[272]

My unenthusiastic reaction to a French film crew that arrived with Benda-Lema's blessing shattered the calm that had settled over Karisoke during the first few weeks of the New Year. There were nine crewmembers in all, complete with a hot air balloon! Tents and equipment galore enveloped the campgrounds, and some of the crew were staying with the V-W couple. To say I blew my top would be putting it lightly. The group was treated to a Fossey bluff charge and creative use of language that would make a sailor blush. The intrusion was bad enough, but when the leader of the group suggested that I work as their research assistant, I exploded. Everyone scattered when I screamed something like, "Holy hell, is that all you want?" I suggested that it might be more entertaining if I were to hang by one arm from a tree and beat my chest. I didn't give a shit who told the crew they could film at Karisoke, and said so. I wanted them out of Karisoke and out of my sight![273]

During this period of chaos, the V-W's had continued to make mischief by spreading lies about me in Kigali and reminding me every other day that I would be removed from the country in thirty-six hours because of my lack of cooperation with ORTPN. They had been saying this for months. In addition, they continued to use the camp like a hotel and totally ignored all of the extra work it was causing the Africans. The only thing I can say with certainty about the V-W's is that they spoke perfect French.[274] Looking for their ten minutes of fame, the V-W's were also lobbying for prominent roles in the French film. I felt that this suited Amy Vedder just fine, since she loved being the center of attention. I often used the phrase, "a terminal case of the cutes," when describing Amy. She was a beautiful young girl at the time, and I must admit, very capable in the field, but she spent most of her time off the mountain, brown-nosing local officials. I also blew up about an entry in her field notes where she indicated that she relieved herself amongst the gorillas and thought it was funny when they played with the results. She became angry and said she hadn't been able to quit her observations long enough to leave the area. Finally, when Ian Redmond explained why she could not continue this habit in the field, she agreed to stop.[275] Maybe the realization that the gorillas were subject to human diseases and parasites caused her to reconsider her actions.

Meanwhile, Amy's husband, Bill Weber, had the bright idea that he was going to teach the poachers how to raise rabbits. I suggested that he instead use *National Geographic* and *Wild Kingdom* footage of the gorillas to begin a conservation program in the schools. To his credit, he managed to accomplish this in all of the secondary schools in Rwanda, but when he finished his cinematic tour with the schools, he lost motivation and spent most of his time off the mountain speaking against me and conspiring with Monfort to take over the camp. The V-W's personal habits were not really my business, but both of them did *injurious things with the gorillas* that made me extremely angry.[276]

In addition to my problems with the V-W's, I worried that the French film crew was becoming highly unethical in its continual disturbance of Group Five. My worries proved to have a solid basis in reality when the female Effie aborted her fetus. I had observed her for twelve years and she regularly gave birth with no problems every 41 to 44 months. I grieved that there would be one less gorilla in the ever-dwindling gene pool. I was saddened that the Group Five gorillas were being turned into a circus group,[277] and I continued to speak out harshly against the invasion of the French film crew. Scientific research had been severely hampered by their presence because the V-W's were often busy on the film and refused to turn in their field reports. This hurt me a lot. Also, the concentration of outside attention on Group Five was not doing the other gorillas of the Virungas any good. Although it was bad enough that twelve years of work and research was being destroyed, my deepest fear was that Benda-Lema would allow even more film groups and tourists to invade Group Five, and the fate of the other gorillas would hang in the balance.[278]

I realize that I was never very easy to get along with, even in the best of times, and was willing to admit it.[279] But events seemed to be spiraling out of control, and I expressed all of these frustrations in a letter to a friend whom I considered to be my white knight. As I reflected upon the unsettling intrusions of the film crew, the extra work it entailed for my Africans, and the general feeling that I was losing control of the camp; it became clear to me that I was never arbitrary in my social interactions with other gorilla researchers and experts. I loved people who were honest, who worked hard, and who were not hypocrites. For this reason, I made many enemies, but those were jealous, lazy, ham-strung people, and the V-W couple was the worst I had ever met.[280]

So the roller coaster ride continued. On one day, I found myself happily entertaining the Prefect Nkubili and his family and thanking him for keeping the captured poachers in prison. Then, before I could bask in the glow of my newfound serenity, the porters arrived with a cable from Melvin Payne of the *National Geographic*, who found out about my verbal encounters with the balloon-encumbered French, and ordered me to stop embarrassing *National Geographic* and to put myself "totally in Ambassador Crigler's hands."[281] The unspoken threat was that my funding would be in jeopardy, which would play nicely into the hands of the V-W's, whom I suspected were at the root of the punishing cable from Payne. I prayed that the addition of an outside consultant would end the constant chaos, since there had been too much to manage for too long a time.[282]

Meanwhile, because of the students' reluctance to accept the role of patrolling for poachers, I decided to use one of my most trustworthy Africans to do some undercover work in the villages below. His salary was being paid by the Digit fund, and he had worked at Karisoke for five years, but Ian Redmond fired him for cutting live trees for firewood—which was a real no-no as far as I was concerned. I concurred that he should be fired as a woodman, but when he returned to beg for any kind of work, I realized that he looked like a member of the Mafia.

That gave me the idea that I could use him to gather information on poaching activities. In order to establish his "cover," I play-acted hitting him and telling him that he could no longer work at Karisoke. We used catsup on his "wounds" in front of several of the Africans working for the French TV crew. They believed it all, and the subsequent rumor mongering contributed to the gossip that Fossey "beat up Africans."[283] Unfortunately, the students also believed it, but at least it provided an excellent cover for my spy.

Our ruse worked, because our spy was able to glean the name of the man who was guarding Sebahutu's gun, the same gun that killed Uncle Bert, Macho, and eventually Kweli. Luckily, the spy was not addicted to pombe,[284] and was given enough francs to buy pombe for others in the local bars of the main poacher village. The information he gathered was sent on to Nkubili, who would issue convictions against anyone found to be poaching or in league with the poachers. No one will believe this, but my spy also found out that the French crew arranged for the killing of an elephant with the assistance of the Belgian aide, Monfort. The purpose of their footage of the elephant slaughter was to show "poachers," played by policeman of the commune of Kinigi, killing one of four elephants that "raided" the shambas![285] The three remaining elephants were "rescued" by the courageous Parc Guards! It was quite the set-up, and undoubtedly made for good cinema at the cost of an elephant's life.[286] Interestingly, the V-W's did not bother to report this atrocity to the State Department.

Through it all, I learned to like and respect Préfect Nkubili very, very much. He was a man of extraordinary integrity and soundness and was respected by all.[287] Even though I spoke imperfect French, and he very little English, we were always able to communicate beautifully. He was essential to the conservation work and truly cared about the gorillas. Because of his steadfast dedication, nearly all of the poachers responsible for the gorilla slayings were locked up in the Ruhengeri prison. However, not even Nkubili was immune to the machinations of local political interests. For example, Sebahutu, the poacher who killed Uncle Bert and Macho, was released because of a tribunal vote that went over the Prefect's head. The vote was influenced by Rugamba, the bourgmestre of the commune of Mukingo. The nasty, jagged scar on Rugamba's[288] forehead was an outward manifestation of his powerful and antagonistic personality. He represented executive power at the commune level, with a position not unlike that of a mayor in the United States. Like the Préfect, he was appointed by the President of the Republic upon recommendation from the Minister of the Interior. Although Rugamba was supposedly under the hierarchical authority of Nkubili, he retained authority over the civil servants posted in his commune. He also acted as a kind of police chief—in charge of law enforcement and the safety of people and property within the Mukingo commune.[289] By subverting Nkubili's authority, Rugamba was laying the groundwork for Rwanda's ultimate shame, although I had no way of knowing the eventual path that iniquity would take.

During the time when Sebahutu was released from prison, I was more concerned about what I saw as a future tarmac of asphalt encircling my beloved gorillas' habitat. I did not notice the seething opportunism, ethnic resentment, and festering greed that was nurturing the next generation of leaders in the communes—and proliferating with little regard for the sanctity of man or gorilla. After the genocide of 1994, the Mukingo commune would become notorious when Rugamba's successor, Juvenal Kajelijeli, was convicted and sentenced for genocide, extermination, and crimes against humanity.[290] Kajelijeli was born in Mukingo commune in 1951 and learned at the knees of the elders of the commune. He was trained as a foreman in a carpentry shop owned by the Busogo Catholic priest. Three years after my death, Kajelijeli would be appointed bourgmestre at the recommendation of the Préfect, Protais Zigiranyirazo, who would also be arrested on genocide charges,[291] and implicated in my own murder in 2001.

From the vantage point of the tomb, the past bleeds into the future like ink on a page that has been subjected to the rain. My tears would join with the mists of the Virungas, just as the bloody remnants of genocide would soon flow cleanly and surely from evil actions taken and holy opportunities missed. The future was not only written in the past, it was ordained. Yet, within the narrow reference point of my life, the future was as veiled as the mist-shrouded bamboo forests. We soldiered on, fulfilling our earthly destinies. Nkubili remained aware of my poaching patrols and was anxious to give me the names of Rwandese who worked in the Parc whom I could trust. I had no greater friend in Rwanda than Nkubili.[292] Nkubili continued in his efforts to send Sebahutu back to prison, but the poacher continued to make his living in the forests, killing elephants and gorillas with a high-powered rifle that he purchased from Congolese (Zairoise) park guards. At least three poachers were known to possess this type of rifle. Many more arms and munitions eventually found their way through the mountain forests shielding the Rwandan/Congolese border. These arms were shuttled by mercenaries funded by superpower nations with colonialist attitudes and an eye toward the natural resources hidden within and beneath the jungles and plateaus. Sadly, Nkubili would soon be transferred from his position in Ruhengeri. The last I heard, he had been declared an enemy of the state and imprisoned for unknown crimes. Whether his close association with me affected his treatment remains an open question.

I sincerely tried my best to heed the edict from ORTPN that I should no longer conduct anti-poaching patrols from camp. This admonition included my students as well as the Africans who worked under my guidance at Karisoke. I suppressed a tremendous amount of apprehension and anger,[293] but I was able to heed the order for almost two months—even though I felt it was unjust. Unfortunately, at the beginning of March, another atrocity occurred that opened old wounds, created new adversaries, and opened the floodgates of my fury.

The four-year old gorilla I had named Lee, from Nunkie's group, was caught in a wire trap and lost his life due to a resulting infection. I wasted no time resuming patrols, using only Africans I could trust. I avoided using camp workers, so in one way I was adhering to the restrictions that were placed upon me. The Africans and I worked three days a week, varying days and locations so that the poachers were not able to discern a pattern in our movements. We cut over 300 traps and released eight ensnared duiker alive. Whatever the eventual price I had to pay for these actions, it was worth it to see the duiker leap safely into the forest. It was absolutely impossible for me to sit by and have the same tragedies happen over and over when I had the will and the means to do something about it.[294] These actions were what the Digit Fund was all about—active conservation as opposed to just talking about conservation. I can't express what it meant to me to be able to put that money to good use on behalf of Digit and all of the others that rested under the little wooden crosses that so unnerved the Parc officials. I paid my men good wages and fed and clothed them. My only hands-on involvement was typing up their reports when they came in from the bush at night. I felt that by not actually entering the forest, I was obeying the letter of the law and adhering to the rules and regulations.[295] I hoped the Digit Fund would fill the funding gap and negate the competition for conservation grants, erroneously assuming the fund would go directly toward anti-poaching patrols. I was wrong. The gauntlet had been thrown as far as I was concerned when the proceeds of some of my articles on Digit went to the Mountain Gorilla Project.[296] The seeds of mysterious funding, competing agendas and murky associations were sown in the aftermath of Digit's murder. I would spend the rest of my now-short life fighting these secret agendas in a futile attempt to make certain that not one dollar of Digit's blood money go to anyone or anything not directly tied to the protection of the remaining gorillas on the mountain.

I needed all the support I could get because there was also a State Department memo in circulation stating that I had threatened tourists with a gun. This information took the somewhat circuitous route of a report from a Chicago tourist agency to the Parc director, Benda-Lema. Luckily, since I never believed in divine intervention, the Rwandese foreign ministry came to my assistance by saying that there was no actual evidence of my alleged shooting spree.[297] Yet, I must admit that there was some truth to the memo. I had become so angry at the tourists' intrusion that I feigned madness and fired a pistol over their heads. I should hate myself for such a no-no, but I couldn't resist. They were so pompous and so sure they could have anything they wanted because they were from the States. I guess I scared the hell out of them. They went clomping down the trail like a herd of buffalo that had gotten into a bee tree![298]

The only good news that arrived in the summer of 1979 was that the poacher Munyarukiko died. The circumstances were rather muddy, and it distresses me now that I had so little respect or value for his life that I rejoiced thoroughly in the news. In my heart, I knew it was time to make a change and glue myself together both mentally and physically, if there was to be any hope of finishing *Gorillas in the Mist*.[299] Cornell University had offered me an adjunct professorship with very good pay. The only dilemma I faced was the choice of someone to take over the job of interim director for Karisoke while I took a leave of absence. At that point in my life, I did not recognize that Kelly Stewart would become a traitor, so I agreed to let her and her lover, Sandy Harcourt, run the camp. Harcourt then presented a list of demands which included the stipulation that I agree not to return for at least a year, and that if I felt compelled to come back, he was to have final say on whether I could come, and how long I could stay. I found this hard to swallow from the cheeky little kid of twenty whom I spent months training when he first arrived at Karisoke.[300] But it was his second demand, that the V-W's be allowed to return to camp, that sent me over the moon. I flat out refused to cooperate. The V-W's were still trying to slaughter me via scandalous gossip, absolute untruths, and vicious rumors. Their nonstop litany included the accusations that I purposely killed the baby gorilla from Zaire, that I locked myself in my cabin for days at a time with all of the curtains drawn, that I daily beat the Africans, and laughably, that I stole the V-W's notes—which I considered to be basically worthless.

I refused to accept Harcourt's demands and hired another director with my own money. As soon as I left, Benda-Lema attempted to oust my choice of Stuart Perlmeter and install Harcourt in his place. Meanwhile, Harcourt ensconced Weber in a guard's hut at the Parc headquarters and gave him a Honda for transportation. Weber's job was to do census work and habituate other gorillas for tourists. I could not imagine a worse person for the job. Weber hated the forest and was truly terrified of the gorillas. Secondly, he was an extremely gregarious person who needed a constant audience around him, which is why he so detested spending time at Karisoke. I could not stand the idea of Digit's blood money, under the guise of the Mountain Gorilla Project, paying for that lazy, guitar-twanging creep to play a role he was no more suited for than my great-grand-mother. My porters had been keeping an eye on him and told me that he was in Ruhengeri at least every other day, *jowling and filling his belly* at the homes of various Europeans. Meanwhile, his tracker and an assistant were roaming the forests and doing his job for him.[301]

In early December, an unhabituated silverback from Group Six attacked Weber while he was leading a group of thirteen tourists from Air France. He was operating under a direct order from Benda-Lema not to turn anyone away.[302] I was truly sick and sorry for him,[303] in spite of the way his wife had been treating me. The gash on his neck narrowly missed his spinal cord. My reaction at the time was one of compassion and concern, and I wrote a letter telling him how saddened I was about what happened, but I wondered then, as I wonder now, whether there were other factors at work in the unusual attack. Mystics will understand what I'm saying, while scientists will scoff. I submit that there are universal forces and connections that remain uncharted and incomprehensible. Perhaps the consciousness of the gorillas had led them to realize that humans were not their saviors after all. Encounter after bloody encounter in the forests had resulted in injury, death, and the poaching of their offspring. One could not blame an unhabituated gorilla for responding to the scent of fear permeating the unhabituated gorillas' private space—Weber's own fear. Benda-Lema's tourists reaped the bounty of the Mountain Gorilla Project and Bill Weber took the brunt. To put it in layman's terms—the unhabituated gorilla was unsettled, disturbed, frightened, and willing to fight back.

Meanwhile, the battle to get Fossey off the mountain continued unabated. Rumors reached a crescendo by December of 1979, and my editor, Anita McClellan, wrote that the cocktail circuit in Boston was abuzz with gossip about a large movement to replace me with a "more scientific" person, one who would work to develop a gorilla sanctuary as an economic resource. *National Geographic* put "a hold on Fossey news," deciding that I was considered to have gotten too close to the gorillas to be able to remain scientific about them.[304] Anita suggested that I must complete my book if I was to have any chance of generating political support from my sponsors, and I took her suggestion to heart.[305] 10,000 miles away from the cocktail circuit, gorillas continued to be slaughtered in remote areas of the park, and the powers interested in tourism seemed to care little about their fate.

Perhaps it was the right time to leave. My November poacher patrol encountered "warning signs" in the forms of crossed sticks set up near trap lines. These curiosities are supposed to imply trouble and represent a taboo. My patrol was frightened and came back up the mountain late, only returning to work when they were out of money. They were understandably anxious about the signs of sorcery from the Batwa, since they certainly had not made any friends among the poachers who lost a lot of trap material, not to mention game.[306] I was also feeling quite ill and needed to get away. It was nothing serious, but my body felt as though it really could not take too much anymore. My left hip had become quite troublesome since I'd slipped on some rocks, and I was no longer able to go into the field without taking several Darvon, which I realized was a narcotic and a potential bad habit.

But I wanted to leave on my own terms. No one had the right to order me out, since I had done nothing wrong.[307] Feeling defensive, however, I decided to burn many letters and notes that I'd accumulated over the years. The words I wished to shield from prying eyes vanished up my little chimney, joining with the mists that crept across the meadows and seeped through the cracks and crevices back into my little cabin, where I inhaled their vapors. My words and thoughts had returned to join me by way of the very air I breathed.

The stories that remain in my files are repeated here, and they have helped immensely as I outline my life story. I miss Digit and wish fervently that he were with me now as I approach the memory of my exile from Karisoke. I miss his conversations and the warmth of his fur when he sits close to me. I can take comfort from the recollection of his promise that he will not abandon me during this task. As I reflect upon these reminiscences, I realize how insignificant they appear when considered within individual contexts. Deemed as a whole, however, they contain many intricate threads which, when woven together, create a story of human loyalties, betrayals and fragilities set against the backdrop of an impoverished nation with great natural resources. The stain of evil intentions and greed would eventually work its way through the design of the fabric, obliterating all that was once beautiful. The ugly truth of man's self-indulgence would be all that remained. I would be sacrificed to this end along with gorillas past and future. The memory of Digit's face and his gentle rumblings are my constant companions as I carefully consider all of these events.

16

(1980-1983) Exile

I was apprehensive about leaving Karisoke for many reasons. Twelve years of my life had been spent tending to the camp, getting supplies, and building the infrastructure, and I had not been in the States for more than six weeks during the previous thirteen years.[308] If it were not for the fact that I had a contract with Cornell University, which had to be fulfilled, I doubt that I would have been able emotionally to endure the move back to the States. It was especially hard to say goodbye to the Africans. Gwehandagaza, my head porter, gave me a beautifully carved effigy of a gorilla for good luck, but once I reached Cornell, I found my separation from Karisoke required more than luck for spiritual health. I decorated the walls of my bedroom in the small apartment in Ithaca with pictures of Kima and Cindy, who had to be left at camp. I also hung portraits of the gorillas, but it was very hard for me to sleep with all of their eyes looking down upon me, accusing me of abandonment. I felt it was *my fault, my fault, my fault.*[309]

It took weeks to get adjusted to civilized life. Small things, like remembering to flush the toilet or to turn lights on and off, were quite distressing. The noise of even a small town like Ithaca was quite unbearable, and I could not accustom myself to the endless cacophony. Then I received terrible news from Stuart Perlmeter saying that Kima died not long after I left. She was found comatose in the box she had slept in for so many years in my cabin. The Africans tried to find a doctor in Ruhengeri to attend to her, but it was too late. They buried her in a small container near the cabin. I just about went bonkers at the news, and kicked myself for not bringing her and Cindy with me. I never quite got over her death. She had truly been a winsome companion to me over the years, and seemed to have more authority over Karisoke than I did in some ways. Whether it was chasing porters, carrying Cindy's puppy up the Hagenia tree, smearing bananas all over the ceilings of my hotel rooms, or throwing tantrums over her lost dolls, Kima was an unforgettable fixture of my life at Karisoke. The world would never feel the same now that she was gone.

To make things worse, there were more meetings regarding the Digit Fund that required my attendance. Shirley McGreal had a second meeting with Digit Fund trustees Ed Snyder and Fulton Brylawski, flooring them when she produced checks made out to the Digit Fund and cashed by the AWLF! They suggested that McGreal write a letter to McIlvaine asking whether the meager sum of $9,000 in the Digit account constituted the entire assets of the fund. McGreal volunteered to be acting secretary, realizing that I was facing possible back surgery in Canada. She went on to defend me and chastise the lawyers who had not noticed that anything was amiss with the bookkeeping.[310] How I wished that the world were filled with Shirley McGreal's![311] AWLF had received over $100,000 from its direct mail campaign on behalf of Digit and refused to share even the resultant mailing list with IPPL. Shirley told me that the whole thing had her scared because of the amount of money and prominent people involved—ex-ambassador McIlvaine being one of them. Embarrassment of one group could harm all wildlife groups, but at the same time should any of them be allowed to get away with dirty tricks? At the same time, I really needed the money in order to continue the patrols.[312] It seemed that once again my misjudgment of men and my dependence upon those who would be father figures had led to another betrayal. Whether McIlvaine had genuine affection for me or had used my vulnerabilities to accomplish his own agendas will never be known. Shirley McGreal thought that people used the fact that I was unhappy, insecure, traumatized, and genuinely upset about the gorillas dying. I was unable to see that people, especially men, would use this as leverage against me. It often happens in human relationships that the person grieving will be taken advantage of by a host of relatives who are looking for opportunities.[313]

At any rate, McIlvaine resigned his position as Secretary Treasurer of the Digit Fund after I flat-out refused to dissolve the Digit Fund and merge it with AWLF. His romancing of me had come to a bitter end, and I was certainly older and wiser for the experience. Once again the gorillas had been robbed, and the crooks were feasting on Digit's blood money. It was too late to undo the damage, but I arranged to have the Digit Fund transferred to the capable staff of the IPPL. It was all rather depressing.[314] Still, I reiterated my battle cry that not one penny of Digit's blood money would ever go to tourism programs. This kind of chicanery has since flourished after my death, with money donated in my name being used to fund administrative salaries and overhead. Conscientious donors do not see all of their money going directly to the gorillas or habitat, but instead to vehicles, expense accounts, and PR campaigns for quasi-legal "charitable" organizations.

To make things worse, even while in "exile," I could not escape the political situation in Rwanda. Harcourt and the V-W's were trying to gain access to Karisoke, putting poor Stuart Perlmeter in a difficult and tenuous position. Even though I was funding camp operations through my inheritance from my real uncle, Bert Chapin, *National Geographic* provided competing and redundant funding for Harcourt to set up his own study program. It did not matter that I stated in no uncertain terms that Harcourt and the V-W's were not to intervene in any way in camp operations while I was gone.[315] Benda-Lema also wasted no time, and urged Harcourt to return to Karisoke and continue his studies in my absence. The Crigler's had long since been sent to Colombia, leaving no one in official capacity that was sympathetic to my goals and ambitions for Karisoke. Finally, Perlmeter went bushy on me and wrote that he could not take the isolation and political wrangling—finally requesting to be let out of his contract. He blamed his terrible case of the blues on having too much paperwork, but having lived in his position for twelve years, I knew that there was much more involved in his situation than he cared to speak about openly. Perhaps he was also shaken by the news that Paulin Nkubili had been officially charged with involvement in an ethnic coup against President Habyarimana and would probably be executed.[316] The pot was just beginning to simmer. It would eventually boil over into horrifying genocidal war.

There is an old saying that goes something like, "there are no evil people, just evil circumstances." Despite my worries about the political machinations in Rwanda, being physically so far away from the turmoil was like a breath of fresh air. The stench of wicked goals and intentions faded somewhat at this distance, and I attributed my rapid physical and mental recovery to new surroundings. I also found surprising comfort in the short lecture series I gave at Cornell that spring. The give and take between students and faculty was an intellectual boost to my weary spirit. My physical maladies also abated somewhat due to visits with a series of doctors who were able to reduce my back pain and alleviate other bodily symptoms that went along with advancing age. I was only in my early fifties, but a poor diet, smoking, and sporadic drinking binges had all taken their toll.

It was not long after the news of Kima's death reached me that I was able to return for my planned summer visit to Karisoke. I went back with a mixture of excitement and apprehension. I was feeling much better in body and spirit, but I would need whatever strengths I had regained when I arrived in Kigali in late July. Benda-Lema had done everything possible to make sure I was not allowed to enter the country. I also learned that in April he had been advised by Harcourt not to renew the authorization of one of my favorite students, Peter Veit, who had been working on female gorilla fertility studies for a year—since 1979. There was no way Stuart Perlmeter was going to be willing to stay by himself at Karisoke, so it was mandatory that I return. Luckily, the Ministry of Foreign Affairs wasn't interested in participating in Benda-Lema's game of cat and mouse, so I had no trouble entering the country or obtaining Veit's work permit once Benda-Lema realized he had put himself in a position of jeopardy within the Ministry. But, learning about the treachery only served to infuriate me even more.[317] When I tracked Benda-Lema down by phone to rectify the work permit issues, and was finally able to corner him, he didn't mention his attempts to keep me out of Rwanda, and he quite willingly straightened out Peter Veit's work authorization problems, saying he had no prior knowledge about any of the mess. Of course this was a lie. Everyone knew that Harcourt had been insisting ever since I left that he should wield total veto power over all students who might be working at Karisoke, and he had encouraged Benda-Lema in this regard.[318]

Shortly after my arrival, I received word from Mutarootkwa, a Zairoise Tutsi who worked on the Parc patrols, that yet another baby gorilla was being held near a village somewhere near Kibumba. The Parc guards were ignoring their responsibilities of protecting the gorillas and concentrating instead on capturing coffee smugglers who were using the gorilla trails as easy routes through the Virungas. Mutarootkwa also revealed that the guards were dismantling Carl Akeley's old cabin at Kabara meadow in order to steal the lumber and tin sheeting. This was being done with the full knowledge of the Conservator, who would get his own share of the wood.[319] Thus, contrary to the views of revisionist historians, the Mountain Gorilla Project was failing to stop the trade in baby gorillas. A mysterious note from Sergio Bottazzi of Gisenyi was delivered to me by way of the porters and confirmed everything I had been told by Mutarootkwa. Botazzi was a successful Italian businessman who owned a villa in Gisenyi,[320] which was near the border with Zaire. He once helped a pilot friend of mine from Sabena Airlines transfer two African Grey parrots across the border to Rwanda.[321] I remember his note well:

Dear Miss Fossey,

This is to inform you that a baby gorilla has been on sale here for about two weeks; about three weeks ago a merchant from Goma asked my help to find a buyer. About two weeks ago the same request was repeated by other people in Gisenyi. If you want to seize it, tell whomever you are sending on its trail to see at Mr. Barizira, the Tailor. But try not to blow (sic) me, because he will immediately know that's me who gave him away. I expect everybody in the place has seen it. Best luck to you.

Last May, several offers of gorilla skulls were made by the Congolese vendors. Lately, also in Gisenyi, I think a hand was offered.

Yours, Sergio Bottazzi[322]

I never reported this incident to anyone, since I did not want to "blow" the cover of Mr. Bottazzi. His note remained tucked away in my files. It is possible that the mysterious "Tailor" of the letter was connected somehow to my death, but I but have no way of proving it. Perhaps the light of history will reveal his role in gorilla smuggling. There is a reason why this correspondence survived and may be viewed by anyone with access to my papers. I did what I could to have the Africans locate the mysterious tailor, but I was running out of time on my short summer trip, and Cindy was my main concern.

When I finally made it up the mountain to Karisoke, I was greeted very warmly by the Africans, who cried and beat themselves about the head, laughing at the same time because I had gained so much weight. I wasn't laughing when Cindy, who was reduced to skin and bones, greeted me. She could barely walk and was unable to wag her silly stump of a tail. All of the hair on her back was gone, and I resolved then and there to take her back to Ithaca with me. At the same time, I was worried that she would not be able to make the three-day trip in the cargo holds. I asked her if she wanted to go for a long walk, meaning the trip back to Ithaca, and I could tell she wanted to go. Worrying about Cindy took my mind off of the deteriorating state of the camp, as I now had a more immediate concern. Incredibly, even most of the chickens had died in my short absence. Poor Cindy was unable to make the walk down the mountain, so one of the porters kindly slung her tired old body over his shoulders and carried her the whole way.

I managed to get the requisite shots and papers, and Cindy made the first leg of our trip in the cargo hold of the plane. At the Brussels airport, custom officials kindly let me take her out of cargo and into the lounge where disabled people and unaccompanied children were resting. I was able to find some grass for her to relieve herself on, since she had never seen cement in her whole life. After another flight we arrived at Kennedy airport in New York. I opened the cage, and Cindy crawled out, wobbly, dirty, skinny, soiled and wearing an old rope collar. We were finally able to clear customs and grabbed a taxi in the pouring rain to catch our final flight from LaGuardia to Ithaca. My new secretary, Stacy Coil, met us and took us to her parents' summer place on the lake.[323] The rest of the evening was uneventful, at least for us, but Stacy's mother had quite a fright when she saw me arrive with a big crate. When she saw something big moving inside, she thought I had brought along a gorilla!

Cindy settled quite happily into apartment life in Ithaca. There were many parks nearby, and we took long walks together while she recovered nicely from her malnutrition and neglect. I placed a soft mattress on the floor, and my old dog settled into her new home, as did I. I went so far as to buy an electric fireplace for Cindy that replicated in some ways the warmth and glow of the old hearth at Karisoke. Thanks to a wonderful veterinarian, Cindy looked great and remained sleek throughout the long upstate New York winter. She had some difficulties, since her back legs locked whenever she sat down in the snow, but with assistance she could get up and move about. She became somewhat perky when the sun was shining, and enjoyed stretching out like a queen-in-waiting on a pillow in front of the fake fireplace. When she abandoned her station in front of the "fire," I covered her with a little fur rug that Rosamond Carr had hand sewn for me in Gisenyi. That little rug meant as much to Cindy as it meant to me.[324]

I, too, became fatter, though probably not sleek. I decided it was fun to be menopausal and recommended my lack of dietary restraint to Rosamond, telling her it was fun to be plump, and that I had become quite pleasant and congenial![325] Unfortunately, while I was settling into the life of a chubby scholar, Karisoke had literally fallen apart, or as I more succinctly put it in a letter to the Criglers, "gone to hell."[326] Someone broke into my cabin by cutting a hole in the sheet metal near my bed. Important and expensive equipment, which included typewriters, binoculars, pressure lamps and other camp necessities, vanished along with several sets of footprints into the forest night. In fact, my murderer(s) would eventually use this same opening to gain access to my sleeping form. I was so upset when I heard about the burglary that I hastily packed up for the airport, which was located only a few blocks away. To make matters worse, I could not get out of Ithaca because a blizzard was in full force. Then, as now, *I accepted fate on any day of the week* and decided to curtail subsequent impulses.[327]

The long winter months gave me plenty of time to think about the status of the Digit Fund. In view of the fact that I was on the wrong side of the ocean to assure that the work of the Digit Fund was being accomplished, I did not feel justified in soliciting further contributions. I decided to have the remaining funds sent to Ithaca and put under the control of an investment counselor. The fund was kept in an interest-bearing account until I returned to resume the patrol work. By this time, Harcourt was running the camp at Karisoke. Maybe I was mellowing in my role as the distinguished visiting professor, because I did not expend much energy fighting him on his dissection of minutia regarding the relationship between Karisoke and myself. Our arrangements eventually became known as the "Ithaca Agreement."[328] Even in exile, I was still the acting director, and reviewing the monthly summaries was my responsibility. Harcourt would regularly go over each paragraph with a fine-tooth comb, reordering sentence structure and grammar to ensure that his interests regarding the future publications of his work were protected. He unexpectedly admitted that his "paranoia about Dian Fossey is too great."[329] I couldn't have expressed it better myself.

The only major objection I had to Harcourt's reordering of minutia was the fact that he wanted to start burying gorillas outside of the gorilla graveyard. When Bonne Année's body was interred in an unmarked grave, it distressed me terribly, and I explained that the graveyard was not my "Christian endeavor to send gorilla souls to heaven," as Kelly Stewart insisted. My true feelings about the gorillas were incredibly intense, and I doubt I will ever have the ability to describe in any coherent manner what I feel should be the final disposition of their bodies. Although there was always a part of me that wanted them near, the scientist in me knew that keeping them nearby was also a very practical way to conserve subspecies remnants long after I was deceased. I insisted that any future gorillas that died be buried in the graveyard intact.[330]

I tried to enjoy my time away from camp as best I could, and realized that my time in Ithaca was a necessary respite from the hardships of Karisoke. Cindy wasn't particularly enjoying the extreme cold, since she was getting to be quite elderly. It took her quite a while to figure out that there would be no grass for her to relieve herself on, and those twenty-two inches of snow were her best bet, but she would have died if I'd left her at camp. Of course, I missed Kima terribly, just as a mother would miss a child. She and Cindy were all I really had. There was genuine comfort in knowing that I still had Cindy, and that she would not be alone when death came to claim her, as Kima was.

In the end, I was glad the blizzard thwarted my impulse to run back to Karisoke because I was thoroughly enjoying a course I was teaching on the Comparative Behavior of the Three Great Apes. The students were truly alive, noncompetitive, and inquisitive. We all learned together, especially about the orangutans and chimpanzees. I got great evaluation marks from the students, and there was a strong interest in having me repeat the lectures in the spring, but I was already committed to do a lecture tour around the States for the Leakey Foundation. Teaching was fun because it made me learn, and lecturing was fun because I was fortunate to meet so many interesting people. However, I wasn't getting much writing done.[331] I still needed to finish my bloody book, which was more like an albatross around my neck, or, as I liked to call it, "a doomed tome."[332]

My editor, Anita McClellan, desperately wanted me to concentrate on my manuscript and was unhappy that I was not including more personal information and more insight on the political struggles I encountered during my life with the gorillas. I abhorred writing about myself and had no respect for people with huge cases of "meitis" as I called it. I preferred that there be no people in my book at all, good or bad.[333] The gorillas were the heroes of my book, and I managed to keep it that way, although I realize now it would perhaps have been better to protect my legacy by including the personal anecdotes and the politics as well as the behavioral science. Of course, I had no way of knowing that I would be murdered and thus retain no chance of defending myself against those who would write revisionist history to further their own careers and egos. I now long for the opportunity to write my own memoirs.

My diaries and field journals remain hidden from scholars and historians who wish to review them. Some rest in the hands of friends and sympathizers, some in the hands of foundations that have hidden them away, some in private collections, and others in university archives. The boards of directors of the so-called charitable organizations that control these documents include some of my former enemies. My field journals and other correspondences are hidden away in a warehouse in Atlanta, Georgia. Serious researchers have been rebuffed, and their queries remain unanswered with respect to access to these documents.[334] Since I am dead, I have nothing to hide, but perhaps those that control the last links to my legacy fear the truths residing in my writings are better left buried with me!

After my death, biographers wrote a great deal about number of guns that were used by my anti-poaching patrols. I want to set the historical record straight once and for all and say that my Africans were armed with two 22 caliber pistols following the gorilla killings in 1978. During the first two years, they used about eight bullets, all of which were shot up into the air to spook poachers.[335] During my tenure at Cornell, I left the guns at camp for the patrols, since I did not believe that it was right to expect an unarmed body of Africans to work without the protection of an accompanying white face or a noisemaker. The Africans that I trained never got into any trouble with their pistols, but the white people did. Two students, including Harcourt and a photographer, misused the pistols as threat objects, which is something neither my Africans nor myself have ever done.

Despite these facts, Harcourt used the pistol issue as a reason for anti-poaching patrols to be declared illegal by the ORTPN. When he visited Ithaca to hammer out the final details of the Ithaca Agreement, he stressed that it was illegal to cross between the two countries of Rwanda and Zaire. Yet once he arrived back at camp, he crossed the border on a regular basis in order to follow study Group Four, and I am fairly certain that he carried one of the pistols in his backpack for protection. It goes without saying that his idea of what should be legal swayed with the breeze.[336] In one rather comical exchange of correspondence, Harcourt used mangled syntax to delineate between "legal" and "illegal" patrols. He cautioned against confusing *official* patrols by Park Guards (which was what AWLF through the Mountain Gorilla project *was so generously funding*) with *unofficial* patrols that were being run by Karisoke. He said that t*he latter, being unofficial, were illegal, but that was all sorted out.*[337] The only thing that was sorted out was the fact that Digit's blood money was being used to fund the Mountain Gorilla Project! I only wish I had included these facts in my book!

Meanwhile, the question remains: How am I ever to express myself, if many of my archives are under the control of my enemies and those who misuse my name for personal profit? Many of the people who were vile to me in life now sit on boards that control my legacy, and my diaries are in a private collection. Relatives I did not know existed have come out of the woodwork to contest ownership and proper disposition. Even the markers that I painstakingly made for the gorilla graveyard have been removed! These documents, artifacts, and photos are the last and final link to the woman I was—someone who gave her life to secure the future of the mountain gorilla. They contain my intimate words and thoughts, and I was not ready to share them with the world when *Gorillas in the Mist* was published. I exist in time as a flawed, but completely dedicated individual, and that is how I would like to be remembered—if it is necessary to remember me at all. But my legacy has been hijacked, and my personality has been distorted. When do the gorillas cease to be wild and become instead fodder for foundation fundraising? I will truly have died in vain, along with Digit, if these fears become reality.

I am devoured by a dread that man will not recognize his greed and self-interests before time runs out for the mountain gorilla and other endangered animals on the planet. The human race looks to the stars for evidence of sentient life, but fails to recognize the wealth of opportunity for contact with intelligent life in the backyard. In man's self-centered fixation with his own attributes, he has failed to identify intelligence in his closest relatives. He has also failed to recognize himself. Will the revisionists corrupt my legacy and reduce the remaining population of the mountain gorilla to performing circus creatures for tourist groups and movie crews?

Allow me to offer an example of my anxiety over these issues. A troubling decision had to be made about the inclusion of Prefect Nkubili's fate in the final rendition of *Gorillas in the Mist*. My editor thought it important that I include details of his imprisonment and possible death sentence. I was adamant that I did not want to mention his fate, even though I had dealt extensively with my feelings about him as well as his support in the war against the poachers in many chapters of my book. Since I did not know his ultimate fate—whether he was dead or alive—I felt it advisable to leave him as a strong force that would give examples in courage to others who would succeed him, and that it represented a defeatist attitude to focus on his death. I did not want to send a message that the bad guys win, and the good guys always lose. We needed a hero, and that is what Nkubili was. A martyr would not inspire others.[338]

Will I ultimately be regarded as a hero—or martyr? I do not find either mantle particularly appealing. Is Dian Fossey an inspiration to others, or have my enemies succeeded in reducing me to a caricature of the woman I once was? How much of my legacy has been used by fraudulent conservation organizations to collect funds from those least able to afford the contributions, only to have those monies flow into corrupt coffers, never to reach the gorillas? I do not want to be abandoned in the graveyard of political martyrdom. If that were to happen, my life would be reduced to the trivial.

Poor Nkubili was abandoned to obscure political martyrdom, and his name has been lost to history. But, perhaps Mother Nature was watching over the Virungas in my absence when he was incarcerated, because she made her opinions known in spectacular fashion in the spring of 1982. Rosamond Carr wrote a letter to me that included a vivid account of a spectacular eruption of Mount Nyiragongo, the same volcano that tormented me as I recovered from my abortion. Nyiragongo is in the Congo, not far from the border with Rwanda. Rosamond's description was marvelous, and it brought a smile to my face to hear that the lava flow went all the way to the military camp where I was held captive and abused by the Congolese army in Rumangabo. I was only sorry that it did not bury the wretched place.[339] Nyiragongo continues to erupt with regularity to this day. The gorillas are not inconvenienced by the eruptions and are somewhat pleased when the lava flows over the roads and makes further incursions by the tourists difficult, if not impossible. I was sorry, however, to hear that the eruption resulted in the loss of cattle and flowers at Mrs. Carr's plantation at Mugongo. She had created a very profitable business selling fresh cut flowers to hotel chains.

I wondered how she could keep going, and I told her that she must possess a great deal of courage to survive.[340]

My term at Ithaca would expire in September, and the pull of Rwanda became stronger with the urgent realization that Harcourt was about to abandon his contractual agreement with me—an arrangement outlined in the Ithaca Agreement after Perlmeter defected. I was surprised, but I also worried about who should replace Harcourt—even though I thought *a snake might do the job just as well.* I suspected that, having gotten his quota of data and photographs, he wanted to publish it as soon as possible in order to throw his weight around.[341] It also crossed my mind that Harcourt had gotten wind of my lecture content, which told the conservation story as it really was, rather than as he and some of his dodgy friends hoped to present it. In addition, he had constantly neglected to send information about the gorillas in his monthly reports. That oversight was in direct and absolute contradiction to the terms established by the Karisoke Research Committee that hired him in the first place. I was deathly afraid that he was going to hand Karisoke over to Benda-Lema for the use of the tourists. I had always thought that, given enough rope, he might just hang himself. That would have been fine with me as long as he did not take the gorillas with him.[342]

Unknown to me at the time, the Bill Weber half of the V-W couple had returned to Rwanda to assist the Mountain Gorilla Project after spending time as a consultant to USAID. He was ostensibly hired to produce an inventory of wildlife in Kenya, Tanzania, Uganda, Rwanda and Burundi.[343] The V-W's were hired on many occasions by various USAID and conservation organizations to produce wildlife and ecological surveys of countries bordering the Virungas. I have no idea of the value or content of their work, but I question how accurate one can be on a three-month survey of the Burundi jungle with a toddler in tow! The V-W's and offspring, it seemed, were everywhere!

The United States and other world powers were very interested in the important mineral deposits of the African rift. The jungles were crawling with mercenaries supported by these same entities. I knew about the mercenaries in my lifetime, but was not fully aware of the mineral exploration that was taking place. Coltan, in particular, was about to become a staple of the telecommunications industry. Its strategic importance has been ranked on a par with that of the oil deposits of the Middle East. Accurate maps of the area would be welcome, although in recent years more sophisticated aerial mapping techniques have become available. I do wonder, however, whether grant money given to environmental organizations for remote sensing of gorilla and other wildlife habitat might also give strategic information to countries with colonialist interests. A fixed-wing aircraft doing conservation work would not be immediately considered a security risk to a sovereign nation, and yet, perhaps, it should be. Gathering conservation data could provide a perfect cover for covert actions. In addition, other eyes can now roam over Africa at will. There are commercial satellites that do not have restrictions on where they collect (with the exception of the country of Israel). The U.S. Government, due to the Kyl-Bingamin Amendment, does not allow U.S. commercial satellites vendors to sell data that is less than two meters in resolution. With that lone exception, these sensors can and do collect in all areas on the earth's surface. The difficulty with Africa is that there isn't much of a "business case" for the satellite vendors to collect throughout much of the continent.[344]

Back in 1982, I had no idea how technology and subterfuge would eventually affect deepest Africa. I was more concerned with returning to Karisoke as soon as my obligations in the States were completed. I was almost finished with *Gorillas in the Mist*, although I was the only one who liked the title. I was very happy with the proofs of the front cover that showed a head-on picture of Uncle Bert with drops of rain scattered over his hair. The back cover was a rear shot of his head taken on the same misty day. The only thing left for me to tackle was the grind of appendices, charts, tables and references. I deplored that picky work and found it very difficult to know how to divide time on a daily basis between the book, updating course work, analysis of field data, and correspondences. There were not enough hours in the day to do everything, particularly in the States, where there was virtually no incentive to wake up in the morning. I did so miss camp.[345]

In mid-October of 1982, my heart was broken once again when Cindy died. In the first few hours after her death, I sat and wondered what life was all about. I so wished that I had touched her body beneath the blue blanket in the hospital. I didn't because I did not want to accept the fact that she was dead, and I guess I was afraid that I would cry. Cindy and I had a pact that we would never cry in front of one another.[346] Jane Goodall sent me a touching note after she heard the news. She was very sorry to hear about Cindy and remarked how horrible it is when a pet that has been around for so long dies. It reminded her of the death of her own dog and the fact that he was just something very special who could never be replaced, however "super" the dogs may be who come along subsequently.[347]

I began preparations for my return from exile. Cindy's ashes would return with me, and I planned to scatter them along the familiar paths we once roamed in better days. The camp had fallen upon bad times and there would be much to do upon my return.

17

The Return

Upon my return to Karisoke in June of 1983, the mountain mists had hardened into hail that pelted everything with a vengeance. In my heightened emotional state after three years away, I had the macabre thought that perhaps the hailstorm was meant for me, since it was supposed to be the beginning of the dry season![348] Perhaps the weather was an omen of sorts, because I soon discovered that ORTPN had installed the first of many bureaucratic obstacles by requiring that I obtain a work permit. After four days of waiting in Kigali, I was able to secure the necessary paperwork, which was only good for six months. I would endure this inconvenience and harassment until a few weeks preceding my murder.

The climb to camp was arduous, but I made it on my own, oxygen tank in tow, and the sun broke through the clouds shortly after my arrival. I had never been away from camp for such a long period of time, and the familiar sights were quite overwhelming. I felt conflicting emotions, elation at my return, and abiding grief for all of the animals we had lost. I was reunited with most of my African staff, many of whom had been with me since 1967. We hugged one another, shook hands, cried, laughed, and exchanged all kinds of gossip and tales. The Africans kindly told me that I looked ten years younger (thanks to good old Miss Clairol), and they liked my new "fat" look. It only took a month to lose about eighteen pounds of my new physique, thanks to the Karisoke diet of potatoes and eggs, not to mention the energy expended to climb up and down the mountains looking for gorillas. My men looked the same and none the worse for the wear of time. I saw immediately the sadness and embarrassment in their eyes—eyes which reflected the state of disrepair into which Karisoke had fallen.

I managed to get cleaned up and take a good look around by early afternoon. It was heartbreaking to see what the English and Americans under Harcourt's watch had done to the place. Camp visitors had basically taken what they wanted, burned out stoves and fireplaces, never bothering to replace or refurbish anything. The Africans were as unhappy as I about the state of disorder, so we set about repainting, rebuilding, rematting, and restoring everything from lamps and stoves, to windows, roofs, walls, and floors.[349] Eight cabins needed repairs of one sort or another. My own, called "The Manor" by some, was built in 1974, using saplings as supports. Tin sheeting was painted green for outside walls and the roof. Lovely, durable matting formed the inside walls and ceiling, as well as serving as a cover for the plank floors. Every one of the eight rooms had huge windows facing south, west, and even north and east. When I was in the cabin looking outside at the age-old Hagenia trees (which were somewhat similar to oak trees, but covered with shelves of moss and lichen strands as well as orchids) I felt like I was floating outside with all of the shades of the green mountain rain forest. At dusk I could watch the animals of the mountain meadows come out to graze.[350]

The Africans truly lived up to their reputations as the backbone of Karisoke when it came to the renovation of my cabin. Everything I had loved the most, Harcourt had removed. The big fireplace in my living room was closed off and the pipes removed, but at least he left the hearth. All of my monkey cages and the gorilla pens were torn up and thrown away, and the gorillas' graveyard became totally obscured by vegetation that Harcourt forbade the men to trim. Even the picnic tables were allowed to rot outside of each cabin.[351]

Working happily together once again, the Africans and I pitched in and soon had everything back to a reasonable semblance of its former function. I had not told the staff that I was scheduled to leave again in August for a few months on my book tour. It would have broken their hearts, since they were thrilled to see everything almost restored to the way things were before I left. Basil, the houseboy, wanted me to bring back all of my old pictures and carvings, which were still stored in Ithaca. I didn't have the heart to tell him it was impossible, due to the high cost of overseas cargo. I was using my personal funds to restore Karisoke, although I worried that my Uncle Bert Chapin's inheritance would not last forever. But much of my old energy had returned, and I reveled in the fact that I was looking out my windows at trees and vegetation rather than cement apartment buildings.

Everyone felt the absences of Cindy and Kima keenly. Well, at least everyone felt the absence of Cindy and reacted strongly to the news of her death. They had loved the old dog as much as I had. I felt fortunate to have Cindy's ashes with me, and I waited for private moments to distribute them around camp in some of her favorite spots.[352] I am afraid that Kima remained forever frozen in the Africans' memory as the camp's little dictator. Her rantings and ravings over her lost doll and toys became an indelible part of camp lore. Ultimately, she was a monkey that only I could love!

In quiet moments, I was able to spend time at Digit's grave, and I trimmed the vegetation so that it looked tidy again. Digit's name had faded from the little wooden plaque, and I was able to restore it with an ink marker so that it stood out in bold letters, lest anyone forget his sacrifice for his family. Popular accounts of Digit's death focused more on the sensational aspects of the trade in body parts, and I lamented that his true altruistic nature might be forgotten or ignored. I so missed him and the times we spent just sitting next to each other in the mists. Speaking in whispers, I told him of the places I had been and secretly vowed never to leave again. I spoke of this promise to no one.

On one of my solitary walks along the trails I used to share with Cindy, I encountered Group Five for the first time since my return. It was unusual to find them grazing so close to camp, and their presence provided a very welcome surprise. The gift they bestowed upon me that day struck me to the core and made me feel that my life had been truly worth living. My thoughts and experiences during those hours seemed very much out of the ordinary. I did not understand fully what was happening, but I have come to understand that the moments they spent with me were but a shadow of the spiritual union I would share with Digit and all of the gorillas in the next world. At the time, the encounter was an extraordinary gift of trust, and an undeniable testament to the bond we had forged over the years.

I had known and written about this group since 1967. By God, they DID remember me! Six of the females and seven of the young came galloping over to me. Two of them had been born after I had left camp. One minute after I announced myself to the group with my own pattern of soft vocalizations of "mwaas" and "naooms," the moms and kids buried me under their own weight as a way of saying, "Hi!" After much patting, hugging and climbing all over me, the directness of their facial expressions and their prolonged vocalizations were all inclined toward me as if to say: "Where the hell have you been?," "Why did you leave us?," or "What's new?" Once the older females began hugging me tightly, the kids were all over my body—pinching, smelling, hitting and pulling gently. I was having problems hanging on to everything. They wanted the camera, my knapsack, my water jug and my glasses. I lost my heavy gloves as the kids took off to play with them, and nearly lost my camera and knapsack too. The silverbacks, Icarus and Beethoven, and the two immature males looked up the slope where I was being submerged by their harem and offspring. After about a forty-five minute period of watching, they went on their way with a series of commanding vocalizations telling the rest of the group to follow them, but no one followed.

Finally, all of the older animals settled down around me on a very steep slope, cushioned themselves with broken vegetation, celery, Lobelia and thistle, and propped themselves up on forearms to listen to my version of gorilla belch vocalizations. I explained my absence and told them about civilization and Cindy's death. *I realize you cannot possibly believe this, but they understood.*[353] I could have died right then and wished for nothing more on earth, simply because they remembered.[354]

I was so moved by this experience that I tried to find the group again the next day, to no avail. It was a horrid, long, steep route because, for unknown reasons, the group simply wanted to travel far that day. I gave up, sent my tracker Rwelekana to follow them, and basked in the sun for an hour until he returned. *He said the strangest thing when he returned, totally exhausted, since we had been climbing for four hours.* He very seriously said, "Yesterday the gorillas had to go a great distance out of their way to say hello and greet you near camp. Today, they have to get on with their own business." I absolutely choked up at his reasoning.[355]

After my thrilling encounter with Group Five, life returned more or less to normal at Karisoke. I had as much difficulty shaking off the trappings of civilization as I did getting accustomed to society's marvels when I arrived in Ithaca. I comically found myself trying to turn off the manual Olivetti typewriter after becoming happily dependent upon the marvels of the electronic word processor. Oddly enough, I never thought to turn it on.[356] It took me almost three weeks to remember that, if I wanted a copy of something, I had to use that archaic invention known as carbon paper, and I was prepared to be first in line if someone were to invent a battery-operated copier![357] Thoroughly enjoying my return, I didn't hesitate to take time from writing the dreaded monthly reports to hike through meadows where Cindy and the duiker once romped. I had a new pair of lavender Nikes and a matching windbreaker that I loved to wear just to impress the park guards. I christened the meadows in my lavender-encased feet and enjoyed a sense of peace and tranquility that I had not experienced in years.

A special place of reflection was the grave of the old patriarch duiker, Mzee. The spot where he finally fell, along the trail next to Camp Creek, was filled with the evidence of many visiting herds, possibly his progeny. They had trampled the grass and there were hoof prints everywhere. It was a spine-tingling sight, as if the few remaining antelope held nightly séances with the spirit of the wise old sage. Perhaps they sought his knowledge of longevity in their doomed habitat. I decided that I must take some of Cindy to that spot, a location she knew very well.[358]

The summer months were dreamy and carefree, but my book tour was looming on the horizon, and I was due back in Ithaca at the end of August. It was a blessing to be finished with the book since it contained the details of so many tragedies. Reflecting upon my many years in Africa, I realized that the best times had been the early years in the Kabara meadow, followed by my initial work at Karisoke. I was beginning to wonder whether I might be a bit too old to continue at Karisoke—how long would I have the stamina to climb the steep, muddy hills?[359] My health was beginning to fail, and I was having difficulty with my oxygen equipment. It must have been the altitude, but on several occasions the tube just about blew my head off—even on the recommended flow settings.

We achieved a minor victory in July when Rwelekana surprised the notorious poacher, Sebahutu, who was responsible for the deaths of Uncle Bert and Macho. Both Rwelekana and his quarry were wounded in the clash by Sebahutu's spear. Although Sebahutu escaped, I reported the incident to the authorities in Ruhengeri and personally offered a reward of a thousand francs, to be paid by the Digit Fund, to anyone who would aid in his capture. The plan paid off, and Sebahutu was put in prison with a five-year sentence.

In another chilling revelation by my informants, I learned that a wealthy German offered a bounty of fifty-thousand Rwandan francs for assistance in the hunting and shooting of a silverback. This "sportsman" was led to a group on Karisimbi where he shot two gorillas, one of which was believed to be a female. All he wanted was the silverback's head, which he paid the guide to carry out for him. He never got his ill-gained trophy because he was caught. Hunting safaris were still the bloody plague of Africa, and I was determined to end this madness once and for all with the help of the Digit Fund.[360]

I was reluctant to go back to Ithaca in August and leave the two new workers, Director Richard Barnes and Karen Jensen, in charge. They were under the influence of a youthful love affair, and all but ignored the gorillas. In all of June they logged only 77.25 hours in gorilla contacts, and the Africans were reduced to doing little more than tracking. I finally put my foot down and told the couple that no more *National Geographic* money would be forthcoming until they caught up with their expenditures and finished recording field data. On some days I became depressed about the self-absorption of the two American kids, and this sadness was compounded by the absence of Kima and Cindy and the ruination of all that I had worked for over the years.[361]

As I think back upon all of the efforts we put into reconstructing Karisoke that summer, it occurs to me that even though we were a tiny little oasis in the vast expanse of the Virungas, we were in some ways a window on human behavior. Human sentience and intelligence were formed and grew out of the African continent over millions of years. Infinitesimal shifts in chemical compositions and molecular arrangements shaped and molded the creatures that emerged from deepest Africa—and humans were but one species. The great forces of evolution tinkered and toyed with the genetic code until modern man emerged with his unique ability to make choices between self-interests and the common good of society. When the humans at Karisoke were sharing the same visions and goals, it was a scene of magical and beautiful symmetry. Starlight would break through the mists and reveal a harmony born of cooperation. The gorillas share this trait in spades, but do not succumb to the temptation of competition born solely on the back of self-interest, coupled with desire. If a gorilla fights another gorilla for food, territory, or a mate, it is for the advancement of the group as a whole. My only personal goal in the establishment and development of Karisoke was the preservation of the mountain gorilla. Many of the Africans shared this goal, and this was evident upon my return when one saw the absolute determination they possessed to repair what the English and American researchers had done to Karisoke.

I think back on the camp notes I kept from various researchers, most of them young, white, dilettantes who would complain and whine ceaselessly that they did not have enough wood, that their typewriters were broken, that I was not nice to them, or that it was too cold, too hot, or too rainy, and I wonder why I did not completely lose my mind as well as my patience. I was not prepared to be either nursemaid or mother. My focus was the gorillas—period. I expected no more and no less from those who were invited to study at Karisoke, which was not designed to be a summer camp, a honeymoon hotel, catalyst for a doctoral thesis, or a launching pad to fame and fortune. Most of these young researchers came from wealthy families that could afford to indulge their extravagances. Nor was Karisoke designed to be a hotel and production studio for film crews who came and went with little regard for the importance of our work or the solitude of the gorillas. I had built Karisoke over a period of nearly fifteen years, with the help of the Africans and the encouragement and donations of the Leakey Foundation, *National Geographic*, various foundations, and benefactors like Alyette de Munck and Rosamond Carr. I mortgaged my salary and my life to get to Africa. I was raped, abused, imprisoned, and endured health problems that would have sent the hardiest individual screaming back to civilization. I eked what I could from the forest, scraping, begging, and borrowing whatever was necessary to make the camp suitable for a research base station. It enraged me that some of these students saw only eight tidy little cabins that would provide a wonderful moneymaker for tourists too inexperienced or lazy to fight their way through the jungles—if it was gorillas they really wanted to see. It seemed as if everyone wanted something from Fossey. They wanted my research, my prestige, my love, and my approval. They wanted control of the gorillas that had come to accept and love me. They even wanted the money that would flow into environmental coffers after Digit's death and mutilation was sensationalized in the world media.

When my protégés fell short, which was often, I let them know in no uncertain terms that I expected the highest degree of professionalism from them. Instead of respect, I was the recipient of betrayals, ridicule, outright theft of my reputation and accomplishments, and eventually murder. Their lies, fabrications, and complete character assassinations, which continue even after my death, somehow gave tacit approval that I did not deserve to live.

At the end of August, 1983, the world was not yet finished with me and wanted more from the tired old woman who lived alone on the mountain. *Gorillas in the Mist* was a modest success, and during the requisite book tour on behalf of my publisher, Houghton Mifflin, I did over sixty television appearances, including the *Tonight Show* with Johnny Carson. Plus, there were innumerable signings and lectures. By the time I returned to Ithaca for a five-day break, I was totally exhausted. October brought an additional flurry of tours through the southern states, and when it was all over I had lost quite a bit of weight as well as my newfound sunny disposition. My heart was certainly not in publicizing the book. I reckoned that if people wanted to buy a book they would buy it, and they certainly did not need the author *shoving it down their throats.*[362] My audiences received me with enthusiasm, but my heart was breaking since almost all of the gorillas featured in the book and lectures were now dead at the hands of poachers. One stop on the book tour remains pleasantly etched in my memory, since I was presented with a remarkable opportunity to use the information I had learned about gorilla behavior. I had just completed a lecture at the Columbus Zoo, which housed lowland gorillas that had been taken from the wild, and I was particularly interested in how the animals had fared in captivity. I asked Jack Hanna, who had accompanied me on that part of the tour, to take me to the ape house for "introductions." I think the keepers were a bit frightened of me because they stayed well out of the way as I was introduced to the silverback, Bongo. I approached his enclosure cautiously, squatting in the narrow passageway that separated the back wall from the bars of the cage, and I introduced myself with a series of greeting vocalizations. To everyone's surprise and delight Bongo approached the bars, leaning forward on his arms and answering with a similar welcome. I knew immediately that the gorillas in the Columbus zoo were still sane, told everyone as much, and managed to rearrange my speaking schedule in order to spend a few days there. As a direct result of my consultations with the staff and keepers, bedding material in the form of hay was introduced into the enclosure. The formerly wild gorillas immediately began to fashion night nests, while the gorillas who had been born in captivity eagerly watched their elders and gradually learned to do the same.[363]

This small diversion did little to ease the aching in my heart over the senseless gorilla deaths in Rwanda—events which I was forced to relive again and again at every stop on the tour. My constant grief led to my idea for the Guardians for Gorilla Groups Plan. The goal of the plan was to assign a guardian to each of the remaining gorilla groups in the Virungas. Each guardian would be responsible for making contact with their gorilla group every few days, ensuring that the location and status of each group was known. Reports would be submitted to a central registry, and the guardians would be paid a salary as well as merit bonuses. I was anxious to return to Karisoke and discuss this idea with the new Director of ORTPN, Laurent Habiyaremye. I had met Habiyaremye some ten years before, when he was director of an import company,[364] and we had gotten along well in our former association.

Not long after I returned to Karisoke, visiting filmmaker Warren Garst from *Wild Kingdom* informed me that Camp Directors Richard Barnes and Karen Jensen had somehow exhausted the entire *National Geographic* grant monies allotted for the day-to-day expenses of Karisoke. In addition, they were defecting to the Mountain Gorilla Project, leaving Karisoke in limbo and without any researchers. I could not be blamed for causing this defection, since I was still on my book tour when they decided to desert. I can only guess what happened, but I suspected that it had something to do with the fact that Monfort and his wife were still consulting with the Mountain Gorilla Project, and were also working at A'Kagera Park.[365] I was left as the sole caretaker, and *National Geographic* was sure to withdraw any remaining funding because the research camp had ceased to exist. If the camp were not to fall into total disrepair yet again, I would have to fund it from my own dwindling resources. I was totally alone, but strangely happy. I had the animals and the forest for company, and I was healthy in spirit and mind.

It was now mid-December, and my editor, Anita McClellan, was due for a visit. I set about planning my annual Christmas bash for the Africans with an enthusiasm I had not experienced in many years. Eighty-one people showed up, and it was especially memorable because I delivered my first baby! The mother was the wife of my tracker, Kana, and both were Batwa (pygmy).[366] Even with the introduction of new life into the world, ethnic differences and prejudices were in play. Most of the other women were Bahutu and not particularly inclined to help. They thought it best that the mother-to-be retire to the forest, as was the local custom. So I rolled up my sleeves in the best imitation of a doctor I could muster and ordered that water be boiled for the impending delivery. I really had no use for the water, but it gave everyone something to do and provided me with an authority born of emphatic direction. I managed to cut the umbilical cord with my newly sharpened bread knife, but balked at sucking the mucus from the infant's nose and mouth and referred this duty to the mother. Since the assembled guests were still excitedly awaiting their gifts, I went to the Christmas tree that stood next to the door of my cabin every year and began to distribute the booty. Kana suddenly interrupted the crowd with a grand toast and announced that his son would be named Karisoke![367] I will forever treasure that moment as a testament to my true relations with the Africans. Mother and baby spent the night and the next morning at Karisoke. At sunrise, Kana returned with his mother, who chanted prayers of thanksgiving over her new grandson. I was humbled and gratified at this special honor, further evidence that ethnic differences can be put aside in deference to an atmosphere of hope and rebirth. Kana and his family were all related to the Batwas in the infamous poaching commune of Mukingo, and I hoped that word would spread that Nyiramacyibili chose to deliver a Twa baby, rather than chase the mother into the woods to give birth. Maybe I had developed yet another tool for active conservation![368]

While relations with the Africans were certainly improving, the same could not be said about my relations with white society in South Africa. While visiting there on yet another leg of my book tour, I made some disparaging comments about apartheid, and the American embassy in Kigali notified me in no uncertain terms that I would not be welcome there again. As usual, it seemed that I could not find a way to tread the fine line of diplomacy. I found it somewhat humorous that I was labeled a racist colonialist at the same time that I was banned from South African white society for espousing equal rights for the black population. In the end, it doesn't matter. I am beginning to see the portrait of me that Digit hoped would emerge, and I am no longer ashamed of what I see. We are all given the tools with which we may choose to fashion our ultimate salvation, and my saving grace was my moral authority with respect to the wildlife of the African continent. While I was damaged by human society, I still possessed an unblemished and optimistic soul that took solace and comfort in the presence of children and animals. Digit has explained to me that certain members of the human race possess this quality of complete understanding and identification with species other than their own. The animals of the earth have noticed that these pure, sensitive souls are most often found at the fringes of their own societies, sometimes mocked and abused because of their spiritual differences.[369] Digit thinks this is because the humans lacking in these qualities are afraid of what they see and long for their own lost abilities. At the same time, their unacknowledged longing becomes hatred for what they do not possess.

The New Year began inauspiciously. I was trying to find new researchers in order to keep *National Geographic* grant money coming in for upkeep and repairs. The Digit Fund and my own dwindling resources were keeping the successful anti-poaching patrols going. When I'd returned to camp from the book tour, I'd discovered that Barnes and Jensen had not only quit, but that they'd completed no reports since September. Barnes had joined the Mountain Gorilla project for a salary, since I'd only been paying him $300 a month. The Africans were doing their best to keep things going, but they were no match for the Europeans who wished to consider Karisoke a tourists' camp. If I had not returned when I did, I don't know what would have happened.[370]

In March I had some serious radio problems, and I was contacted regarding the repairs by Jean Pierre von der Becke. This was the first time since my arrival in December that I had heard from him. He had become somewhat of a disappointment to me since I'd handpicked him to run the anti-poaching patrols and put great trust and faith in his loyalty. It was only a matter of time before the Mountain Gorilla Project seduced him, and our relationship had since become very strained. Nonetheless, the radio needed to be repaired, and I was glad that he was willing to take the time and interest to help. I was even more concerned about the number of poachers' dogs that were running wild around the camp and killing antelope. The African staff was unable to catch them, and I feared the only solution was to kill them. I no longer had my pistol because Richard Barnes claimed that he'd thrown it into the forest. My men were forced to rely upon little starter pistols that I bought in America with Digit Fund money.[371] I needed John Pierre's help in this matter, and I sent along a note to him with the porters.[372]

Although my health took a temporary turn for the worse (bloody pneumonia again),[373] life at Karisoke took on a positive rhythm and I was able to successfully integrate my research with the anti-poaching patrols. The Digit Fund was covering the patrol expenses, while my book proceeds supported the day-to-day running of the camp as well as the salary of the research assistants. The book wasn't selling that well, but I still had my gold teeth fillings to fall back on. I honestly did not know where to go for more money because the Mountain Gorilla Project was sponging all available contributions from the major funding agencies and private donors. The "little old lady in Iowa" was under the impression that donations she made to the AWLF were going to the gorillas, but tourism was the eventual beneficiary. Most people I spoke with on my tours to America, South Africa, and the United Kingdom also seemed to think that they were donating to Karisoke when they gave to the MGP! In essence the MGP owed its existence to Digit, Uncle Bert, Macho and Kweli.[374] So, too, do the organizations that took my name after my death and still use their funds to pay for tourism, questionable "research," overhead, and travel for bloated executives and their junkets.

I was not killing myself by neglect as some friends had worried. I took very good care of myself, fully realizing that I lived in a rainforest at ten thousand feet, in a cabin whose fireplaces smoked more than I. I took vitamin pills, tried to keep my oxygen machine in running order, and ate a couple of bananas a day to avoid potassium deficiency. I survived on potatoes and eggs because of budget problems, but in most other ways I spoiled myself. *My only regrets* were that I could not visit the gorillas on a daily basis anymore, but my Karisoke trackers and research students did it for me. I felt that as long as I could function to train park guards in duties related to the active conservation of the gorillas, I could exist at camp happily.[375]

In the summer of 1984, the depressing fog had once again rolled in, accompanied by three American Ambassadors and their families as my "camp guests." I felt like a short order cook, and one of the wives kept referring to the gorillas as monkeys, but all in all it was a good visit. I only lost my temper once, when one of the teenagers came in and asked, "What's for dinner? If it isn't meat I don't want it!" I told both the teenager and his Ambassador father off in no uncertain terms. Happily, all had good contacts with the gorillas and it did not rain.[376] Things were going very well. I was able to run anti-poaching patrols seven days a week utilizing the Parc guards and my own people—unless the guards were needed for holidays, visiting "big-wigs," or parades outside the Parc. We totaled 5,546.95 man-hours of patrols and we cut down 1,485 traps.[377] Even though we only succeeded in putting two poachers in prison, the work was generally going very well. Sixteen animals had been released unharmed from traps.

Personal success aside, I was still galled that the Mountain Gorilla Project used my name as well as Digit's in their brochures. I kept telling myself that self-integrity was what mattered in the long run,[378] but the unfairness of it all left a bitter taste that I tried to assuage by sticking to my own brand of public relations. I tried my best to answer all donations to the Digit Fund with a personal letter and inclusion on the Karisoke Christmas card list. I very much looked forward to reading my mail, and asked my secretary, Stacey Coil, to keep track of things for me until my next visit to the States because it was too expensive to forward each piece of mail on an individual basis to Rwanda.

The best news of the summer, although I am somewhat ashamed now to admit to my happiness over this bogus information, was that Sebahutu, the poacher who killed Uncle Bert, was himself killed by a buffalo that he was hunting in the forest. After paying a bribe, he had been freed from prison before the completion of his five-year sentence.[379] I later found out that the rumor of Sebahutu's demise was just that. The ruse was designed for my benefit, but eventually I had the last laugh, when I gained access to damning information that made me swear my staff to secrecy once it was revealed. We had not yet seen or heard the last from Sebahutu, as we were oblivious to the web of intrigue, deceit, and murder that was slowly and inevitably taking shape.

Maybe it was another portent of things to come, or maybe it was the misty weather, but my students had also begun bickering among themselves, their personal and professional jealousies adding fuel to their smoldering fires.[380] At about this time I was fortunate to acquire two African Grey parrots, the victims of poaching in Zaire. An adventuresome hiker I'd met earlier in the year had asked me if there was anything he could get for me. I missed Kima and Cindy, I needed a diversion from my students, and in an offhand remark I mentioned that it would be nice to have a pair of parrots. Well, wouldn't you know that the hiker found two hardy looking specimens in the marketplace at Kinshasa? He was not a bird fancier, but he decided that if the parrots could survive the deplorable conditions at Kinshasa, they must be very resilient.[381] Navigating the complicated border restrictions involved getting some help from Sergio Bottazzi, who had previously directed me to the mysterious "Tailor" in Gisenyi. At any rate, the parrots finally made it to Karisoke via Rosamond Carr's plantation, and they remained with me until my murder. Little did I know that the parrots would become the proverbial canaries in the coal mine in the weeks immediately preceding my murder when they became the victims of sumu. The stage was set, and the characters were cast for the final, tragic scenes of my life.

My three-month visa ran out in September, and I was forced to make the four-hour trek to renew it by slipping and sliding down the muddy paths to ORTPN headquarters. My increasingly frail body could barely make the trip without the help of my porters, who half-carried me up and down the path. The man I counted on to be my friend, Laurent Habiyaremye, abandoned me, and forced me to wait days for the new visa. This was an obvious form of harassment, and I blamed it all on the machinations of the Mountain Gorilla Project and the monies that flowed from the tourism coffers. Fossey had to go, and if making me trek up and down the mountain in my weakened physical state hastened my departure, so be it.

So, 1984 ended on a myopic note in more ways than one. A new Batwa baby brought the hope that accompanies all new life, and the anti-poaching patrols had more success than I could have reasonably imagined. However, there were many things unseen, and menacing intents remained hidden in the mists that descended over my mountain home. Fate continued to spin her sinister web, and there would be no escape from her poisonous grasp.

18

Requiem (1985)

I said <u>NO!!</u>

382

I returned to my old perch in the Pygeum tree to consider the remaining days of my life. I had always felt secure in that ancient tree, since it was the scene of many happy encounters with Digit and the others. My thoughts returned to the day, long ago and not fourteen months into my studies, that I first seriously questioned my right to be in Africa, promoting conservation measures in a foreign land and society. I was on an afternoon's stroll with Alyette de Munck, when the sight of a poacher's camp interrupted our idyll. We were walking along a beautiful, isolated river, which flowed deep within the jungle's grasp of wild orchids, liana[383] and senie. Alyette was a Belgian woman who had known Africa since her birth. She lost her husband, and had her son and nephew brutalized and murdered by rebel soldiers, yet she still managed to love the land. In fact, "love" is a trite word to describe her affinity with the continent. As I stood there, breaking bamboo snares one by one, our previously harmonious association was punctuated with a heated argument. My friend stood apart from me and very firmly asked what right I had, as an American living in Africa for only fourteen months, to invade the hunting rights of the Africans, since by birth, they owned the country. I kept on breaking traps, but at the same time I could not agree with her more. Africa did belong to the Africans, but I felt that written orders, whether they pertained to man or animals, should still prevail. If I could enforce the written rules of a supposedly protected park and prevent the slaughter of animals, then I should do so. As I continued breaking the bamboo, the reliable and flexible death trap of the last wild game of Africa, Alyette continued to plead her argument.

"These men have their right to hunt! It's their country! You have no right to destroy their efforts!"

Perhaps she was right that a destitute African living on the fringes of the Parc had no alternative but to turn to poaching for a living. At the same time, why should we condone a man who openly breaks the law; why shouldn't we take whatever actions we can against him? *The man who kills the animals today is the man who kills the people who get in his way tomorrow. He recognizes the fact that there is a law that says he must not do this or that, but without the reinforcement of this law, he is free to do as he chooses.*[384] I probably lost the full potential of my budding friendship with Alyette on that afternoon, although it would take several more years before we finally drifted apart. In the interim, she was steadfast in her support of Karisoke, helping me in my efforts to establish bonds with the creatures that would guide my life from that day forward. In making my decision to learn as much as I possibly could about the mountain gorilla, I would do everything in my power to thwart poaching, feeling that the law, at least, was on my side. My spiritual connection with the gorillas would be the force that guided my actions.

I was often asked to describe the most memorable encounter I experienced in my years with the mountain gorillas. There were, of course, many stunning moments. But the first encounter formed the spiritual basis upon which all future encounters were dependent. My first true communion of the soul with the mountain gorilla occurred after I had been working in the field for only ten months, at a time when I felt that they still only barely tolerated my intrusion into their private world. One day, I was watching a young male feed about twenty feet away. Unexpectedly, he laid down his foliage and turned around to stare intently toward my face. The depth of the expression in his eyes held me spellbound. His calm gaze combined elements of curiosity and, finally, acceptance. As we fixed our eyes upon each other, I received the impression that some intangible barrier between human and ape had been spanned. Heaving a deep sigh several minutes later, the young blackback slowly resumed his feeding as though a puzzle had been solved. I crept away, humbled and honored.[385]

The memory of that seminal encounter brought tears to my eyes, and the panga scar that divided my face stung with the freshness of a newly opened wound at the memory. The echo of my weeping blended with the wind whispering through the foliage of the Pygeum tree, and joined with a purer sound that was barely discernable as a soft voice within the African breeze. The voice was crooning a song that soared above the highest branches of the forest. Suddenly, a fog began to take form, and one by one, gorillas appeared in the mists, forming a protective phalanx around the base of my Pygeum tree. Beethoven, Macho, the little Kweli, my beloved Coco and Pucker, Bonne Année, Uncle Bert, and the unfortunate Mweza, forever reunited with his unnamed mother, each took a place in a circle that represented all that I loved and all I had wished and hoped for. Duikers I had long ago rescued from traps closed the circle. The presence of all these companions provided a feeling of peace and contentment that soothed my aching spirit.

The song reached a crescendo as my beloved Digit knuckle-walked towards the tree and stood in a fully upright position. His display of chest beating complimented the crooning that grew louder as Digit rose to his full height. His accompanying scream was both terrible and beautiful in its intensity, seeming to come from all directions at once. He ripped the surrounding vegetation out by the roots and beat the ground ferociously, flinging leaves and branches into the mists where they appeared suspended, as if time had stopped.

Digit stopped his display and scrutinized me as I clung to my perch. Then, he rapidly climbed the tree, sat by my side, and peered into my face. His eyes were separated from mine by less than two inches. He held this position for what could have been an eternity before draping his arm over my shoulder. Then he snuggled close to my side and began his own song, which he directed to the group gathered below us in the mists. The murmuring sounds he made had a plaintive quality which summoned the group's members up to me, one by one. Each repeated the close eye-to-eye examination before they, too, settled down beside me with long arms entwining all of us into one black, furry mound.[386] I cried once again as I realized that I was forever part of their family. They would always remember me and I would never, never be forsaken.

"Nyiramacyibili, it is time," Digit murmured.

I could only nod in his direction with a complete understanding of the implication. Still, I was frightened by what was about to unfold.

"I feel your trembling spirit, dear Nyiramacyibili, but for the welfare of the group you must finish this task, as difficult as it may seem. You must save yourself from the convenient memories of your enemies and the morass of myth if the gorillas are to survive. I will do my best to protect you on this journey, but it is yours alone to make."

Digit was right. Prophet or doomsayer, sinner or saint, the definition of my legacy was within my grasp. But I had no idea how to stage the final act of the last year of my life.

As I gazed off toward the purple peaks of the Virungas, another figure formed in the mists and stood on a lava outcropping. It was Nunkie, the venerable old silverback who had a harem four females and ten offspring, and who died not long before I was murdered. While I had been relieved that he had not perished at the end of a poacher's spear, I had been suspicious at the time that his death was due to a parasitic infection caused by contact with humans. An autopsy confirmed my fears that human intestinal parasites and a resultant lung disease had hastened his demise.

Nunkie shyly climbed the tree and offered me a stalk of celery. "When I died, you wondered whether we gorillas have a concept of time and memory. Do you remember this, Nyiramacyibili?"

I remembered writing those words, a distant echo in my own memory.

"Nyiramacyibili, when your men carried my corpse away to your camp, the gorilla group followed them before returning to the place where I fell. They smelled my presence where I had died and remained there until it was clear to them that I would no longer be returning, and that the group must seek its own survival. Do you remember this?"

"Yes, I wondered if the gorillas could grasp the concept or ultimatum of your death."

"Before any of us entered this new life, we were all frightened by the departure of the members of our families. Sometimes we would strike the fallen comatose bodies in an attempt to revive our loved ones. You found this frightening and distasteful."

Nunkie was reminding me of a troubling aspect of gorilla behavior, a behavior that I had reconciled as similar to the reaction humans have when striking or shaking someone who has fainted in an attempt to revive them. The frenzy of the gorillas' actions had an underlying similarity, which I finally decided did not indicate cruel behavior.[387] I looked around at the gathering of gorillas, while memories of earthly times flooded through my consciousness, and sweet remembrance returned with the balm of memories treasured, yet mislaid.

"You were all with me that night in my cabin, weren't you?"

"Naoom, naoom," the gorillas crooned in unison. "Nunkie crossed the river of time shortly before you did, and straddled the two worlds in order to lead us to you."

The psychic shock of my murder had erased memories of the gorillas' intervention in my transition to spirit form. Until this moment, my first recollection of being dead had been my wandering presence at the funeral service. Apparently, there was much more to what had transpired in the moments directly before and after the panga blade did its damage.

Digit took his arm from my shoulder, and with his deformed finger brushed the hair and tears from my face as he held my gaze. "We guarded your body for days while the humans talked and worried about what to do about your death and who was to blame. When we heard them talking about taking your body away, the other gorillas wanted to steal it so it would not disappear like so many of our brothers and sisters. The group would not let this happen because you were our silverback. I finally agreed to go with you down the mountain to the cold place[388] until the humans decided what must be done. The women and the porters thought they were carrying you, but I bore your weight down to the city where I stayed with you until you returned to the gorilla graveyard in the box they made for you. We were frightened because even your spirit was asleep until you returned to the mountain."

I could not imagine Digit being afraid of anything, but certainly my unresponsive spirit would have upset the gorillas' sense of order. Digit's explanation of their plan to steal my body explained the mystery of Beethoven's disappearance after his death. The gorillas must have hidden him so that we could not take the body away for a necropsy. The realization that the gorillas viewed me as such an integral part of their social order was comforting, and the notion that they considered me to be their leader gave my existence extraordinary meaning. The gorillas had given me the gift of self-worth. I now understood completely that my life had meaning because I "meant" something to the gorillas. They recognized me as their protector, and I finally recognized that I had fulfilled my earthly obligations. My worries had been groundless all along. My mythical pie was never reduced to crumbs. My legacy would remain rooted in all that I had accomplished. No one, not even the revisionist historians, could ever erase the fact that Dian Fossey lived, fought and died for the mountain gorilla. For every gorilla that rises from its night nest to greet the sun as it burns away the mists in the Virungas' forests, Dian Fossey has meaning.

I motioned to Digit and the others to remain as I relinquished my hold on their comforting presence. While sliding down the rocks and taking the path that led to the camp at Karisoke, I heard the gorilla chorus. The farther I traveled, the louder the gorilla song became, and I knew I would never feel alone, unfulfilled or unhappy again. As I walked the tangled, nettle-infested pathways and gazed at the mountains, the mists began to part. Clouds rolled past the peaks, and I was startled to see the ghost of Laurent Habiyaremye wandering aimlessly on the forest's edge. He did not notice me, just as he had never noticed me in life. Oh, he'd seen me as an impediment to his grand plans for tourism and smuggling, but he'd never seen *me* in life, or in death. He lost his directorship of the Parc after my murder and was banished to Rome, where he died of AIDS.[389] I wondered what brought him back to these pathways, and why our souls were destined in death to share the proximity of the montane forests once again. I knew I was no martyr, even though that term has been applied to me. I did not purposely flirt with death as a definitive memorial to a lost cause. Death was cowardly in its stalking, a craven entity forced to crawl on its filthy belly through the unguarded openings in my fragile cabin and equally vulnerable spirit.

As I entered the portal of 1985, the gorillas' songs remained with me. With each stride down the path to my death, I was feeling stronger and taller, no longer ashamed of my stature, but reveling in the powers of youth and optimism that once more flooded my being. It was time to banish the old ghosts and take strength once again from my accomplishments and those who loved me. My dear friend Rosamond Carr has steadfastly maintained that entirely too much attention has been paid to the unhappy periods of my life. Her memories hold fast to the times that I was blissfully happy at Karisoke. Rosamond is in her nineties now, and as she recalls our private moments together, it is my sense of humor and our shared gales of laughter that fill the vaults of her memory. She shines light into the cavern called history, reminding all who seek the truth that I was extremely proud of all that I had accomplished—my newfound fame, and the success of *Gorillas in the Mist*.[390] Although I would find the limelight difficult, I endured the scrutiny because of the attention it brought to my beloved gorillas. Deep down I was a private person, and not many people were allowed into my life.

In fact, only two great personal sorrows truly cast a shadow upon my eighteen years of work. One was Bob Campbell's return to his wife, and the other was Digit's terrible death.[391] As isolated incidents, they do little to reveal the constant, day-to-day struggles and anxieties that often affected my ability to fully enjoy the happiness that I felt during my tenure at Karisoke. I loved the mountain more than any place on earth; my diaries and my book are filled with descriptions of the wildlife and vistas that compliment my dedication to the gorillas. There was simply no other place where I could imagine living out my final days. It seemed appropriate, whether by fate or design, that during my final months on the mountain, individuals, events, and history collided in an arc that could have only one ending. Seemingly insignificant occurrences would shelter sinister intents. The sixtieth anniversary of the Parc, the successful apprehension of two poachers, a chance encounter over a plate of greasy, cold French fries, the arrival of a new graduate student, and the gift of a long-awaited visa were events that would shape the arena for my final battle.

My emphysema continued to restrict my breathing in the rarified atmosphere of my mountain aerie, but this did not diminish my determination. In my usual fashion, I wrote detailed monthly summaries of the patrols, as well as a yearly review that showed that these patrols were successful beyond my wildest dreams. Always meticulous in my record keeping, my reports recorded every victory, large or small, in the constant battle against poaching. My records from January of 1985 indicated that in 1984 we managed to cut down 2,264 traps in 347 working days. That translated into over 9,300 man-hours of patrols, during which poachers harmed not one of the 76 gorillas monitored from Karisoke, although signs of poachers' activities were still observed.[392] We were probably more successful in the latter part of 1984 than during the entire course of Harcourt's stay, or, as I wrote to a friend in the spirit of Christmas, "ho, ho!"[393] When I was murdered, I had already won the battle against poachers. Indeed, by 1984 the market for direct gorilla poaching had been all but wiped out.[394]

1985 also afforded me some time to smooth out relationships that were important to me. One of the most important was my communion with my mother. My bond with her had continued to flourish through regular correspondences, even though I had severed relations with my stepfather, Richard Price, in thought if not in declaration. Mother worried constantly about the state of my health,[395] but I appreciated her letters more for the chatty news regarding the details of her life. I was happy to learn that she loved the blouse I sent as a holiday present, and that she wore it on Christmas day.

Along with good news in January, bad inevitably seemed to follow. The silverback, Tiger, was injured in a fight while defending his mate, Simba. I had observed Tiger since he was an infant, and it pained me to see him with a gaping wound in his chest, whimpering as I offered him berries, and wandering alone.[396] It made me feel very cranky[397] and helpless to see him suffering, and I became even more annoyed when two Spanish "tourists," whom I believed to be spies for the Barcelona Zoo, arrived at camp. I did not know that the zoo was interested in acquiring a gorilla for their collection, but I was suspicious and made note of my concerns in my diary.[398] The Spaniards came armed with a letter from my nemesis at ORTPN, Laurent Habiyaremye, basically ordering me to collaborate with them while allowing them to do their "research."[399] I was able to retaliate by giving them lodging in the leaky half of one of the more run-down cabins. It had no furniture or lamps, and the pitiful duo had to make do by constantly running back down the mountain for supplies. I really did not like being so cantankerous, but there were times when I could not help myself.[400]

I confided to Shirley McGreal that the two researchers seemed more interested in what the gorillas ate than in any behavioral studies. I wondered whether they were researching what to feed primates in captivity and asked my trackers to keep an eye on them.[401] There was also something intangible in the air that I felt was upsetting the gorillas and causing them to fight more than usual. With so much interaction and switching between groups, I joked that Peanut's group had turned to "peanut butter." The Swahili term is *hiva-hiva*,[402] or all mixed up. It was a subtle change, but a situation that would continue to unfold as the year progressed, making me feel very uneasy.

My mother must have experienced an ancient maternal connection to my own concern that something was not quite right. In February, she wrote that she was worried about me and said she kept getting "bad vibes," urging me to keep in contact and to take special care of myself.[403] She did not elaborate upon her fleeting apprehension, but went on instead to congratulate me for a glowing article about my work that had appeared in *Town and Country Magazine.* Maybe it felt better for both of us to ignore the niggling warnings wired into the ancient pathways of our ancestral consciousness. When presented with an opportunity to face the demons that lurked under the bed, it was easier to dismiss them as figments of our over-active imaginations. The monsters, however, would turn out to be exceedingly real.

People continued to come and go around camp; some were helpful and some were not. The majority were able to work in the field, thankfully, since my health made it next to impossible for me to do so. Instead, I put considerable effort into unraveling the meanings of the names of hills, streams and rivers within the Virungas—a very constructive way for the old lady to spend her days.[404] The history of these place names dated back to the early days of the Tutsis, but many of the names were still in reverential use by the Hutu. Needless to say, my work goals had to be slipped in between beating the Africans, starving them to death, and/or shooting at tourists. I was amazed that those stories were still circulating at the base of the mountain.[405] My enemies would not let the stories die before they were woven by deceit into myth, which was transfigured into "fact" by the subsequent movie, *Gorillas in the Mist*.

Surprisingly, Director Habiyaremye agreed to grant proper authorization for Karisoke to continue as a research facility for another six months. I took him at his word, and wrote a cordial thank-you that included a summary of the Digit Fund work as well as a preview of my place-names study.[406] If I had not been so off balance due to the unusual activities of the gorillas, perhaps I would have been more inclined to question his motives. Rumors were swirling that he intended to usurp the camp and convert the facilities into a tourist hotel. As things stood, I was more than happy to leave the illusion of cooperation intact while I attended to my field studies.

Other business, which would have been impossible to imagine when I first set foot on the mountain, soon took center stage when I finally signed a contract agreeing to have Universal Pictures film *Gorillas in the Mist*. It was an eerie feeling signing those papers. *I felt I was literally signing my life away.* Still, I felt that Universal was the right choice because they had the budget to do the mountains and the gorillas justice, which was the most important reason for the film. *I really did not care what they did with Fossey, whose only function was to bring the gorillas to the public*, although I sometimes wondered what would have happened if I had studied tree shrews instead![407] I attached a note to the signed contracts, hoping that the actress they chose would have highly developed tear ducts, adding that the producers probably thought I meant highly developed in other areas! My only real concern was that the screenwriter not be a feminist who did not know the difference between a gorilla and a chimpanzee. That would have been tragic.[408]

Feminism was an anathema to me. I truly believed that life held many more responsibilities for men than women. In a discussion about "mid-life crises" with Bettie Crigler, I suggested that, although it is never too late for anyone to begin anew, it is far more difficult for men. They are supposed to be settled into a life's rut/routine by the time they take on familial responsibilities, regardless of any inner compulsions that might demand an outlet. On the other hand, women may spend half of their adult lives caring for their families, and when this is no longer a necessity, they're encouraged and rewarded for pursuing other outlets. It did not seem at all fair to me. That was why I would, and could, never be a feminist.[409] I certainly did not want to be portrayed as a feminist in any movie made about my life with the gorillas. Maybe it was the fact that I was becoming increasingly menopausal, but the idea of an actress portraying me elicited a great deal of introspection upon my part about who I was as woman, let alone as a scientist. A well-known movie critic, Roger Ebert, was disappointed in the film version of my life, which was completed after my murder. He said *Gorillas in the Mist* told the world what Dian Fossey accomplished and what happened to me, but didn't explain who I was. In the end, the critic thought that was what the audience would want to know.[410]

The New Year progressed quite uneventfully into spring, and the only complaint I had was the arrival of researcher, David Watts, whom I considered to be an avowed Marxist and a real rabble-rouser. I didn't consider his presence to be much of a threat, since he was due to stay on only until the end of July, and I would be gone for much of that time, having been invited to California by Ruth Keesling of the Morris Animal Foundation. I prayed that David Watts would rise to the occasion and ensure the welfare of Karisoke. Watts was one of three researchers I interviewed in Chicago when I first met the V-W's. I had to trust him because I was scheduled to visit my mother, and then the Humane Society convention in San Diego. There, I was to be awarded the prestigious Joseph Wood Krutch Medal, which included five thousand dollars. I was rendered speechless, but not tearless, at the knowledge of an important and timely gift that I hoped would go far in the support of my plans for active conservation. I vowed to my benefactors that my work would continue with the same degree of dedication and intensity as years past. I was, simply, overwhelmed.[411] In addition, travel to the States was absolutely necessary because my eyesight was rapidly failing. A visit to an ophthalmologist in California on my previous visit found a growth on my cornea, but when I fully realized the length of convalescence and the need to have my eyes bandaged, I cancelled the surgery.[412] It was more important to me at that time to return to Karisoke and complete an obligation I had to promote my book in Holland along the way, but I could no longer ignore the problem.

Life was more difficult for my mother back in California, since my stepfather fell asleep at the wheel on the San Jose freeway and ran into a truck—totaling his Jaguar. Thankfully, no one was seriously injured. My mother was livid that he was driving without a license while under the influence of medications. Her concern, beyond that of her husband's safety, was that the family would eventually be sued for his continuing reckless antics.[413] I detested hearing that she was upset, but it was pleasant to be in a rhythm of regular communication, discussing matters much as two friends would, instead of the expected, conventional mother-daughter relationship.

Time had afforded me occasion for reflection and healing, and now the first of several decisive events began to shape the end of my life. The capture of the poacher, Sebahutu, was the first. Deceit, subterfuge, character assassination, and corruption at the highest levels of government—all information that resulted from Sebahutu's confessions—were captured on tape and subsequently stored in a simple orange folder that was hidden in the bottom of my luggage. But those artifacts have been lost to history; what follows is what remains from my writings.

On May 2, Vateri's patrol found the fresh footprints of four Batwa poachers, but could not track them down before nightfall. The tracks were encountered along the Susa River and split up in several places between that point, an estimated altitude of 9,800 feet, and the boundary between Zaire[414] and Rwanda. We concluded that the poachers had not yet made a kill, and I divided the next day's first patrol into two parties. Both teams left Karisoke at 7:30 AM to climb the eastern side of the five hills. One team found descending footprints of a poacher, east of the fourth hill, that were probably left from the day before, and they left these footprints to search for fresher track. While circling around, they encountered the first team, which had found a fresh trail climbing up the Susa River. They did not know that it belonged to Sebahutu, Uncle Bert's vicious killer.

Nemeye and Sekaryongo followed the lone poacher's fresh trail, while the remaining team followed the previous day's descending trail. The fresh trail led across the Rugasa River and to the border where the patrol saw smoke. Splitting up, they closed in upon the "ikibooga," or camp. Sebahutu spotted them and fled into a creek bed covered over by vegetation. He abandoned his salt sack filled with red potatoes, corn and beans. Three arrows were left drying by the fire. Sebahutu fled with his bow and his panga, which was an old European model with a fancy, worn handle. My trackers caught him and brought him back to his camp for a slow questioning period. During this time, Sebahutu offered each of them 5,000 Rwandan francs and as many elephant tusks as they could carry if they would let him go. He said it was useless to take him back to Ruhengeri prisons because of his connections in Kigali and Ruhengeri. Whether this association included the prefect of Ruhengeri, Protais Zigiranyirazo, who also happened to be the brother-in-law of President Habyarimana, I am not certain, although history has subsequently assigned motive and opportunity to the Prefect.[415]

During the questioning period in the forest, the patrol learned that Sebahutu had entered the Parc along his usual trail near the home of a cultivator and occasional trap-setter named Basesa, a Hutu involved in poaching. Basesa's home was located 250 meters below the Parc boundary and had continually served as a "launching pad" into the park by poachers. I had frequently informed the ORTPN of Basesa's involvement in poaching and cited his unique method of setting distinctive orange salt sack snares, but no one had done anything about it.

Most notably, Sebahutu gave the names of Batwa poachers currently in the Parc, and all were from Mukingo commune. One of them was the second son of my old nemesis, and Digit's killer, Munyarukiko.[416] Sebahutu's initial interrogation was just the beginning. The patrol brought Sebahutu back to camp, and I kept him tied up in my living room for twenty-four hours. I did not touch him, but he was frightened either of me or my reputation as the lone woman of the mountains, and willingly provided the names of sixty poachers and their points of entrance into the forests. He gave me the names of those who had guns, the manufacturers of the guns, and revealed where the guns were bought, and where they were hidden. Finally, he gave the names and locations of the middlemen who make a living in the trade of elephant tusks and feet, gorilla hands and heads, gorilla infants, and bush meat. In a final, stunning revelation, Sebahutu came up with the names and descriptions of the whites and Pakistanis who exported the trophies out of Rwanda, as well as the prison guards who were in cahoots with them.[417] This eagerly disclosed information seemed almost too good to be true, especially since it was a willing confession, elicited without any threats of bodily harm. At a subsequent interrogation by the Park Conservator, Sebahutu told him that I had been nice to him[418] and had not abused him in any way. I was relieved that I would not have to worry once again about the Mountain Gorilla Project or ORTPN spreading rumors and falsehoods regarding my abusive behavior toward prisoners.

Whether someone got to Sebahutu, or he set me up with bogus information, the poacher soon recanted and denied saying anything about a connection between the poachers and the prison guards. Another possibility was that Sebahutu had been lying in order to get his own competitors in trouble. Mark Condiotti of the MGP sat in on one of the interrogations, and noted that the Conservator, Canisius Shyirambere, took notes, and seemed especially interested in the list of poachers who had guns. Due to lack of proof, however, Mark doubted that any of the guards who were implicated would be fired.[419] I decided it was most likely that Sebahutu was afraid of talking against prison guards while under their security, and I hoped that once he had been in prison a while he might repeat what he'd said in my presence. It was also possible that the comments Sebahutu made were on a tape I'd made on the Friday night when he was in my custody—comments he made in the presence of seven other Africans.[420] But I had not listened to the tape. I tried to make an alphabetical list of all the names taken from Sebahutu, but ascertaining the correct spelling of the Kinyarwandan names made it difficult to complete.[421] Neither Mark nor I said anything to anyone about the involvement of park guards in poaching activities.[422]

One of the most damning pieces of information I learned was that the sister of the poacher, Mporanzi, was the mother of the Conservator who was conducting the investigation. I received the information about Mporanzi from my tracker, Nemeye, who swore by the information, claiming that all the Africans knew about it. It was difficult to separate gossip from fact among the Africans, but just to be certain; I swore all of my Africans to secrecy. I put all of them under oath not to repeat anything they'd heard, during or after Sebahutu's confession. I was worried that Sebahutu would be mistreated after he so decently gave all of the information regarding the Parc and prison guards and their collusion in smuggling.[423] Gwehandagaza, who had been my head porter since 1971, dutifully reported all of the gossip he heard regarding Sebahutu's confession and subsequent denials.[424] Gwehandagaza lived down the mountain and did much of the shopping for Karisoke, but his most valuable function was that he was my chief intelligence source. He kept track of activities at Parc headquarters, Ruhengeri, Gisenyi and even Kigali. He played the triple role of porter, shopper and chief of intelligence.[425] The information compiled from this incident went a long way towards implicating those in power that were smuggling, or who were complacent about those who were smuggling. It was imperative that the information be taken seriously, but I had no control over official reactions, since some of the same "officials" may have been involved. I did rest easier knowing that if there were any tactics afoot to steal a baby gorilla for a Spanish zoo, the plans were at least scuttled for the time being. It was obvious that the Parc and their guards had been set on their ears. Raids began everywhere in previously unknown or "secret" spots in the forests where poachers gathered. Nothing like these raids had ever happened previously. Capturing a poacher in his home or hut, even though he possessed skins, weapons and trophies, was not allowed according to Rwandan law. Capturing them in the forest was an entirely different issue, particularly if they were armed.[426] Basesa was finally arrested, and the authorities were looking for witnesses to prove his complicity. Mark and I thought it might be wise to ask Nemeye to act as a witness against Basesa, and perhaps Sebahutu. Without witnesses attesting to the possession of arms in the Parc, Basesa would have to be released,[427] and his release would put my tracker, Nemeye, in a compromising and vulnerable position.

I was elated about all of these events, and I didn't consider the possibility that it may have been entirely too easy to achieve this major victory against poaching. I did realize the dangerous nature of the revelations, and concealed the tape in the orange folder that was hidden in my suitcase.[428] But the tide seemed to have turned, and I took it as a sign that the old lady and the Digit Fund were destined to make a considerable difference. I realized I could not capture a big poacher every day, but I was at least capable of motivating my daily patrols to produce results. Meanwhile, the other white people in the Mountain Gorilla Project were working for their salaries in conservation, and not for conservation itself.[429]

Surprisingly, however, I was beginning to develop a previously unthinkable philosophical attitude toward the Mountain Gorilla Project. For a long time their sham really upset me, as my life-long work was being deprived of the funding it so badly needed. But one evening, while sitting on the living room floor with my African trackers, counting the snares and traps they had brought back that day, I realized that this was what active conservation was all about. My African staff and I woke up each morning knowing that our day would be fully utilized for the benefit of the gorillas. So, integrity was the name of the game. If you have it, don't worry about what your neighbors are doing. Maybe your own actions will rub off on them in time.[430]

Meanwhile, the weather remained dismal after three months of daily rain and fog. Everything at camp seemed to be breaking down, including the refrigerator, which caught fire. The lamps were useless because they could not be fixed without mantles. It might have been romantic dining by candlelight, but it was bloody horrid to have to fix food in such a dim light when gorilla dung was stored in the kitchen![431] The gathering mists were obscuring more than the blue peaks of the Virungas. One of the many theories surrounding my murder is that the poachers sought revenge against me for all their arrests, and the panga was one of two weapons of choice, the other being poison, or "sumu." And yet, revisiting the events surrounding the capture of Sebahutu, I recall that I was left alone on the mountain at the end of May when Watts went to America for a two or three-week stay, and Peter Clay left on May 20. That left the old lady alone at camp, with only the Africans to do the work.[432] If the poachers wanted to kill me because of Sebahutu's confessions, they sure missed a golden opportunity to do me in. Nevertheless, the number one theory concerning my murder placed the blame on the poachers—but a more careful analysis of my vulnerability to an attack by poachers would not bear fruit by any stretch of reason.

During these spectacular changes at the Parc, the Associated Press stepped forward in the person of a reporter named Barry Schlachter. Schlachter trudged up the muddy path to Karisoke at the end of May, after he had spent time with members of the Mountain Gorilla Project and Rwandan officials, including Director Habiyaremye. I'm sure the background information he gathered about me was quite colorful, and he embellished his article with a nasty description of me hobbling about and chain-smoking my Impala cigarettes.[433] I'm surprised he did not add a broom to the account, to compliment my image of "the witch of the Virungas." My portrait was enhanced with a litany of the old rumors of my alleged racism, abuse, and colorful vocabulary, the least of which was a reiteration of the vulgar spray-painting episode on Tutsi cattle. This was one of the last articles written about me for the international press, and in it the famous Garbo-esque quote of "I have no friends," was fabricated. This incorrectly attributed comment has followed me to the grave, and it is a lie I shall perhaps never overcome.

My response was swift. I thought Mr. Schlachter's article was a bunch of shit, and said so. Actually, it was more like an extraordinary bunch of crap. The sound of that more descriptive phrase was more to my liking after I had thought about my response. I tossed the AP article into a pile of new mail that had arrived with other press clippings. I was at first afraid to open them, but finally I could not resist, and I soon learned that the new batch of articles actually discussed my proposed "sainthood!"[434] I was being reduced to simple-minded caricatures, and I didn't like it one bit.

Soon after Schlachter departed, I was preparing to depart for California. The Morris Animal Foundation's conference promised to bring together 63 of the world's top primate experts, and I was excited about the Humane Society award. Just a few days before I was scheduled to leave, I received word by radio that the gorilla Nunkie had been found dead on a remote slope. He had been a force to be reckoned with, especially when he killed Digit's infant child. Of course I never held Mwelu's death against Nunkie, because I understood that he was following ancestral and evolutionary drives that ensured continuity in gorilla society. At first I suspected that Nunkie had been killed by poachers, but the tracker Rwelekana returned to camp and gave me the welcome news that the silverback had died of natural causes.

Nunkie's death was very problematic for his ten offspring and the four females that were left. The group would not survive without a new leader, and we had a devil of a time trying to herd them towards Tiger's territory. I hoped that the lone silverback, now sufficiently recovered from his wounds, would take up Nunkie's leadership position. Unfortunately, the remaining members of the group kept circling back to the death area, and this once again raised the question I often posed about whether gorillas have a meaningful concept of death. Eventually, Tiger had little success assuming a leadership position, and most of the group members ran off to join Peanut's group. Three of Nunkie's offspring were killed via infanticide. The oldest was three years old and was unexpectedly killed by members of Group Five who absorbed one of Nunkie's females. Thus

Nunkie's group had scattered into three different social units, but I found some solace in the realization that poachers had nothing to do with any of it.[435]

My new friend, Dr. Philippe Bertrand, of the Ruhengeri Hospital, helped me conduct an autopsy on Nunkie that indicated lung disease, and perhaps intestinal parasites, were the causes of death. I recalled Ian Redmond's worm studies that suggested exposure to Western parasites might prove to be a real health concern for the gorillas, and I decided to pack some tissue samples for my trip, hoping that the veterinary experts I would meet at the convention in San Diego would have better access to labs for a more precise analysis. Poor Nunkie was interred in the ever-expanding gorilla graveyard, and in October the experts in California concurred that the mountain gorillas faced a new threat by exposure to human disease.

Several times during my last jaunt to the States I heard that it was prestigious and lucrative to be the subject of an American Express commercial. I was curious about the process because a production company in New Zealand had approached me before I left Africa to film a commercial.[436] After I learned that they wanted to portray me holding a credit card, surrounded by a mound of gorillas, with the requisite "Don't leave home without it," I instructed my agent to negotiate a deal for her usual percentage, but only if there was something to be gained by it.

The San Diego symposium was picketed by animal rights groups who charged that zoo officials were cooperating too closely with research laboratories at the expense of gorillas, monkeys, and chimpanzees. I was happy that the activists left me out of the equation by telling the press that I was the only representative at the conference who had any real interest in saving primates. While grateful for the praise and some good press for a change, I also made a point of publicly stating that I wished the people who were picketing had more precise information, instead of *just taking a big downer on the whole meeting.* The convention wasn't as bleak as the picketers imagined, and if they had had all the facts they might have cooled off a bit.[437]

I headed back to camp at the end of July, having accomplished all of my health tune-ups and having enjoyed an extended visit with my mother. My fitness report included the usual problems with my lungs, added complications of bad liver functions,[438] and severe stress fractures in both my feet due to osteoporosis. It turned out there was a good explanation for my new-found hobble.[439] The liver functions were problematic and could have been indicative of alcohol damage. However, anti-malarial[440] medications might have been partly to blame. Not surprisingly, a bookkeeping error showed my stepfather's true colors when my eye surgery bill for $883 was inadvertently sent to "Mommy and Daddy's" home address. The bill was SWIFTLY forwarded to me, and I asked Stacey Coil to make sure it was paid by my insurance policy.[441]

I was awfully happy to be back at camp. Most everything was going well except for the disintegration of Nunkie's group, and the disquieting news, which I heard via my African staff, that the Mountain Gorilla Project wanted to take the camp for tourists and shove me out. I received this information via my African staff. While I was away, David Watts and the Mountain Gorilla people met with local officials to urge the Parc to take my cabins, furniture, the trained Africans, and the study groups. The nefarious plan was for ex-students like the Harcourts, the V-W's, and Watts to occupy the cabins during alternating time periods. The tourists would take the remaining cabins.[442] My staff assured me that they would quit if such a thing happened, and I knew they could not afford to go without work, but I appreciated their loyalty. Watts told the staff goodbye and that he was leaving on vacation, but went straight to the home of the V-W's in Ruhengeri instead.[443]

I also had some puzzling correspondences to sort out. In early June, the Conservator, Shyirambere, had written me a letter that must have arrived after I departed for my six week sabbatical in the States. In the letter, he asked if I had a rubber mask of a gorilla that he could borrow for a celebration feting the Sixtieth Anniversary of the Parc des Volcans.[444] In a separate letter, he asked that I forward a photo of myself with gorillas to Etienne Nyangezi, who was a water resources specialist with the Parc.[445] The photo would be used in a brochure that would illustrate the conservation activities of the Parc over the years.[446] I was happy to provide the black-and-white photo, as well as the gorilla mask, but I was troubled that an anniversary celebration was planned for the Parc and that I had had no advance knowledge of it. I had dedicated eighteen years of my life to the Parc's inhabitants, and yet it appeared as if I would not be invited! Undaunted, I requested that the Conservator tell me the date of the celebration. Invited or not, I would be sure to attend. To show my good faith, I included the July summary of the Digit patrol reports. My request initially fell upon deaf ears, and my pursuit of something as simple as an invitation to a party was the next step in a chain of events that led straight to a blood-soaked floor in my simple green cabin.

My most pressing and overriding concern was to renew my visa, which was due to expire on August 9th.[447] I was convinced, and so was Mrs. Carr, that Director Habiyaremye continually refused to renew my visa expeditiously in order to harass me.[448] Renewing my visa every two months was an agonizing and tortuous ordeal—and it always took a physical and psychological toll. The climb up and down the rutted paths required an oxygen tank and the help of several porters who were forced to carry me a good part of the way. I had no car and was forced to wrangle two seats on a taxi bus that would get me from Ruhengeri to Kigali. I needed two seats because my legs were very long, and I also needed a place for my luggage, since I was often forced to spend three to four days in the capital. The game was the same every time. I showed up at the minister's office, where I waited most of the day, only to be told that the minister would not be in that day. During each trip I wasted almost a week waiting for the minister to agree to see me, and it seemed as if I no sooner made it back up the mountain than it was time again to start worrying about the next trip back to Kigali.[449] This trip was especially unnerving because Director Habiyaremye dressed me down in the anteroom of his office. In front of most of his staff, he informed me that the Mountain Gorilla project would be taking over Karisoke for the sake of the tourists, and that he would staff it with scientists of his choosing. Then he curtly ended the one-sided conversation and tromped into his office.

I was so shaken by the encounter that I went straight to the American embassy and told the two "secretaries" what had just transpired. The American embassy phoned the Rwandan Foreign Affairs Office and complained that if Director Habiyaremye refused my visa, the entire western world would screech loudly.[450] They were very effective advocates, because I got my two-month visa.[451]

The game of chess with Director Habiyaremye did not end with the encounter in his office. New rules and regulations regarding the operation of Karisoke were issued at an ever-increasing pace, and I did my best to ignore them. What really galled me was that Habiyaremye now wanted every guest who went to see the gorillas to pay $50 directly to the ORTPN. I wondered how he would manage to put that into effect without my cooperation.[452]

In yet another example of obstinacy, the Parc department began working at odds with my anti-poaching patrols. In one instance, my patrols caught a poacher red-handed setting traps in the forest, although his accomplice, armed with a spear, got away. Instead of imprisoning him like Sebahutu, the Parc fined him the equivalent of $200 and allowed him to go home. Of course, the poacher was forced to work twice as hard poaching in the forest to repay his friends and relatives who advanced his fine. Thus, my patrols' motivations were reduced to zilch. Why should they work so desperately hard to put money in the pockets of Parc officials? It was all so wrong. My only retaliation, other than personal letters that I wrote to the officials responsible for the poacher's release, was to release a news note to a rather rapacious AP journalist stationed in Nairobi who delighted in such tid-bits. I wanted the Parc to realize that their unorthodox methods of raising money would be as well-publicized as the plight of the gorillas.[453]

At least Watts was gone—which was a tremendous relief. His replacement, however, was something else again. Wayne McGuire[454] was definitely a very nice young man, but I thought he was as dumb as they come. He would not take any notes, didn't know the animals very well, and overslept every morning. The worst thing about him was that he was one of those people without any sense of direction at all, literally getting lost between my cabin and his own, and on two occasions, overnight in the forests during rainstorms! This was very worrisome for me, and especially for my men who had to go out and search for him. Wayne didn't learn any Swahili, and, in fact, I didn't think it would be possible for him to do so. The worst part was that it was unfeasible to leave him alone in camp, meaning that I would not be able to leave until January when the next person[455] was scheduled to arrive.[456]

McGuire was bothersome, but I was happy in my work. My sense of humor remained intact and even seemed to blossom in those last months. A friend from the states wrote that she had acquired a new cat. Since the deaths of Kima and Cindy, I had been reluctant to get attached to any mammalian pets, and was content to lavish care and attention on my two African Grey parrots. I felt I didn't have the courage to love a pet again. The bloody parrots had still not learned to say "shit," which was about all I took the time to teach them. One, however, did learn to say "I love you"—a phrase I used a lot on an off day. I had to admit they were good company, but totally untouchable and traumatized from capture.[457]

August also brought the visit of two young photographers from the states. Evelyn Gallardo and David Root worked very hard obtaining footage of the more elusive gorillas, Pablo and Poppy. I was happy for their company, especially since they respected my wishes not to be photographed.[458] Many of the roads between Rwanda and Uganda were closed because of turmoil in Uganda. This left Rwanda with dwindling supplies of gasoline and kerosene, making it difficult for planes to refuel. I was glad that the couple had come when they did, and told them that they would be welcomed back at any time after the fuel problems were, hopefully, resolved.[459]

Evelyn and David came close to forfeiting their 35mm and video footage, even though *National Geographic* was interested in the footage at my recommendation. Unfortunately, the infamous V-W's were now working in Kigali, and Bill Weber told the Parc department that there was a couple at Karisoke with professional movie equipment. This accusation was based on the fact that Evelyn and David re-charged the video camera's batteries when they were in Ruhengeri, and the V-W's heard about it. The poor couple was stopped by the Conservator and armed guards the day they left camp, and forced to open their luggage. There were a lot of red faces among the Parc staff when nothing was found. Video tape in those days was not considered "professional" film footage. Apologies were profuse.[460] I would never see them again, but they were instrumental, along with Mrs. Carr and the International Primate Protection League, in orchestrating the delivery of a marker for my grave. The plaque would serve the dual purpose of delineating my resting place, as well as protecting my grave from robbers who might steal my bones for use in their "sumu" pouches. The bones of Nyiramacyibili would carry the strength and power of the great apes she protected.[461]

Meanwhile, plans for the Parc's anniversary celebration proceeded. I received an unexpected donation from a benefactor in the States and used the money to outfit my patrols in new uniforms with "Karisoke" stitched on the back and on the shirt pockets. As expected, the men were very happy and anxious to show off their "official" attire. With their security and pride in mind, I also increased their salaries. I still had not received an invitation to the festivities, but Wayne McGuire and a visiting student, Joseph Munyaneza, did.[462] Munyaneza was an entomology student who shared a cabin with Wayne.[463] In the eleventh hour, the Conservator apologetically sent me a belated invitation, indicating that he was appalled at what must have been an oversight on Director Habiyaremye's part. I knew better.[464] Before the ceremonies, my African staff presented the Conservator with a beautiful board, which illustrated the history and accomplishments of Karisoke, and documented each in English, French, and Kinyarwandan. The Conservator was thrilled to death with it and hung it right next to his office, so everyone inspecting the new Parc headquarters could not help but notice it, including President Habyarimana. I was told later that he was most impressed with the display.[465]

The fete started with the late arrival of the President and his guards, who were incongruously armed with machine guns and M-16 rifles. There was much singing and dancing, which I had always loved, culminating in the national anthem. Long, boring speeches followed, delivered in Kinyarwandan and French. Predictably, since Director Habiyaremye designed the program, my name was conspicuously absent on the long list of benefactors and contributors, but The Mountain Gorilla Project received a tribute. The bloody director, Habiyaremye, then got up to deliver and hour and a half long speech in Kinyarwandan, which I considered to be about 94 minutes too long! I thought even the President was going to fall asleep, despite his cool demeanor. The speech was mainly concerned with the great profits of tourism and how much money was being brought into Rwanda because of the gorillas. Toward the end of the speech, two awards were given out to those declared to be doing the most work for the Parc—two travel bureaus!

Well, after it was all over I went back to the Muhabura Hotel in Ruhengeri, which was really kind of a dive, for a very late lunch. Just as lunch was served, my previous nemesis and former ORTPN Director, Benda-Lema, came running up to my wooden table. He was absolutely incensed and claimed that President Habyarimana had given Director Habiyaremye hell about ignoring me and my work. Benda-Lema said he knew this to be true because he sat behind the President and overheard his comments. Benda-Lema went on to complain bitterly about the fact that the written program had contained the names of persons who worked for the Mountain Gorilla Project. He was really aggravated about it all, and for some reason that made me cry. I suppose I was feeling sorry for myself. In addition, I had never gotten along well with him while he was Director, since money had gone to his head, and I was absolutely dumbfounded at his reactions and grateful to him for going out of his way to express them to me.[466] During our exchange, I learned that Benda-Lema was now a bank manager in Kigali. We bid our goodbyes, and he left the dining room to join a group of very "swanky" African officials who were collected outside. I started in on my cold French fries and tough pork chop, only to be interrupted by one of the swanky ones who asked me in English, "Dr. Fossey, what did you think of today's affair?"

Well, I didn't know who he was, but decided I might as well get some things off my chest. My basic complaint to him was that there had been absolutely no mention of the guard patrols, poachers, and confiscated traps. There was no tribute to the guards, and even the Conservator had not been asked to speak. All of the emphasis had been on the loot the tourists brought in. I was so involved in venting my anger that I failed to notice the man taking notes. He asked me to step outside into the light so that he might take my picture, and it was then that I realized that I had been conversing with the senior reporter[467] for Rwanda's weekly newspaper! I'm sure Benda-Lema's influence had something to do with it. I figured either I would get thrown out of the country for sure, or that some good would come of it. I had no way of knowing that my free-wheeling conversation might have been an invitation to murder.

Back I went to my even colder and now totally greasy French fries—I was famished enough to want to eat them—when another big-wig African[468] in military uniform entered the dining room and sat down at my table. He asked me, in French, what problems Americans had in obtaining visas. I about passed out! I told him, in my horrid French, of my two-month visas, doled out by Director Habiyaremye, and he seemed to understand me. He gave me his card and told me to call him the next time I was in Kigali, and that he would give me any kind of visa I wanted. He ended by saying, "What does he think you are, a tourist?" By then I had to cut the French fries out of the grease, but they tasted like elixir. I wasn't sure what it all these conversations meant at the time, but I felt that it might turn out to be the most profitable lunch I had ever had. At the same time, I tried not to get my hopes up too high, because sometimes the Africans would get caught up in the mood of the day and forget everything once they had their beer. As I climbed back to camp that night and heard the songs of the hyrax and the barks of the bushbuck and duiker, I suddenly realized that these familiar sounds were still part of the forest only because I had continued in my dogged way to protect all of its inhabitants. No awards from any director could have meant as much to me.[469]

Hindsight affords me the luxury of speculation regarding these series of encounters, which may or may not have been the result of chance. Perhaps I had once again fallen into the trap I so often encountered throughout my life. With my guard down, I was willing to accept the guidance and promises of men who possessed authority and experience. They told me what I wanted to hear, and I willingly embraced the possibilities.

There was no doubt that the bloody fete for the Parc meant several days of lost work for all of us, but what really hurt was the disappearance of Beethoven on or about August 28th. I could have sworn I saw Beethoven with his group a day or two before the anniversary celebration. McGuire said he wasn't with the group after we returned, but the men insisted he was. Trying to resolve the mystery for myself, I went out to the gorillas for several days in a row, but did not see Beethoven. He just vanished. I assumed he was surely dead, but the mystery of where his body was really blew my mind, and I was heartsick beyond belief.[470] We hired extra trackers to go over and over the trails on a daily basis throughout mid-September. In an extremely odd coincidence, the silverback leader of one of the Mountain Gorilla Project tourist groups, Charles Darwin, died exactly at the time Beethoven disappeared. I was afraid that perhaps they had found Beethoven before we could, and somehow made a mistake in identifying the body. Gorillas were dying left and right, under circumstances that hindsight would assign premonitory status.

I was starting to get paranoid, especially since Dr. Phillipe Bertrand, who did the autopsy on Nunkie, told me that the MGP asked him not to give me any photos or information on Charles Darwin's autopsy.[471] Phillipe was appalled by their orders, and, as a personal friend of mine, said he was quite angered.[472] The motives for the actions of the Mountain Gorilla Project may never be ascertained.

Possibly, they were still reeling from the repercussions of autopsy results on Nunkie, which were a clear indictment of tourism and the introduction of human hookworms into the gorilla population. If Charles Darwin had contracted a similar disease, it would make sense that they would not want Dian Fossey to hear the results of the medical examination. What other reason would they have to hide Beethoven's body, if indeed they'd found it, unless it was a simple case of misidentification? Still, I kept searching and remained heartbroken. Beethoven was my oldest and dearest friend. I met him in September of 1967, during my initial days at Karisoke.[473]

Two more gorillas had died, most probably due to human worm infestations. The fallout to the tourism industry in Rwanda would be staggering if this were proved. I blamed myself for beginning the whole habituation process, and my guilt produced many sleepless nights. On one dark night I went to visit the gorilla graveyard. *It was black as coal and I could only dimly see the markers. I stood beside Digit a long time still not knowing what to do, but Digit knew, and Uncle Bert and all the others.*[474] Soon after my vigil, I decided to put my faith and trust in the abilities of Dr. Bertrand and veterinarians not affiliated with the tourism industry. It was the only way to get at the truth of the matter. I would not live long enough to see the results of my idea, but a veterinary program would blossom in the years after my death through the efforts of Ruth Keesling and the Morris Animal Foundation. My last trip to California and the San Diego conference yielded unimagined consequences in the form of new regulations that were aimed at protecting the habituated gorillas from human disease.

As I reflected upon these events and decisions, which would perpetually affect the future of the mountain gorilla, I continued to hear the songs of the gorilla chorus as they urged me onward in my final quest. A greater understanding of my life and legacy was within my grasp, if only I could muster the courage to examine the last weeks of my life. In a way, I was performing my own post-mortem. Just as it was always paramount that I find a gorilla's body in order to understand completely the causes that contributed to the animal's death, in a similar manner I was trying to understand my own fate.

The autumn months at Karisoke were filled with the promises of the fast-approaching Christmas season, concrete successes by the anti-poaching patrols, and idyllic moments for the gorillas. But while the season of hope was inching its way into the hearts and minds of all of the residents of Karisoke, black magic was slouching through the forests. I saw the signs, but spoke of them to no one. One warning appeared in the form of a crude carved effigy of one of the most poisonous snakes in all of Africa.[475] The serpent had made its presence known in the garden.

My parrots were the first casualty. I awoke one morning in early October to find them flipped over on the floor of their cage. Immediately suspecting they'd been poisoned, because they had been otherwise healthy birds, I threw out their food supply and substituted a vitamin supplement that was recommended for sick birds. Luckily, they recovered. When I sent my Christmas list to a friend in the States, I requested an additional supply of the vitamins, preferring it to any of the items on my list.[476]

October and November, conversely, brought another major anti-poaching success. The patrols captured four men in four weeks, all of whom were actively poaching within the Parc boundaries. The last man they caught was really nasty. It was mid-November, when Yavani Hategeka was apprehended while skinning a lovely bushbuck caught on his trap line, which was located right next to a gorilla group. I had captured him once before, in 1974, but the strange thing was that he did not look any older than he did during our first encounter. I looked a millennium older now. He refused to answer any questions, but the thought of yet another gorilla becoming ensnared and vulnerable to gangrene, not to mention the fate of the unfortunate bushbuck, emboldened me. So during my questioning of him, I once again took away his black magic toys. I also found a letter in his pocket from a dealer in Zaire who was in the smuggling business with the poacher, and I detailed the contents to Rosamond's Aunt Margaret.[477] Some kind of rare metal, probably gold, was involved.[478] I wasn't going to take any chances that Hategeka be given a slap on the wrist by ORTPN, so I sent him directly to the officials in Ruhengeri and was gratified to learn that he was convicted and given a three year prison sentence. It was music to my ears to learn that one of his relatives showed up with a bribe of 50,000 Rwandan francs, but was unable to secure his release. It appeared as if I was still winning the battle.

It is possible, as some have suggested, that the increasing manifestations of black magic at Karisoke were a ploy to deflect blame for my murder upon the poachers. Magic was always a fact of life in the forests. Ploy or not, something sinister was afoot, and I was either unwilling or unable to heed the warnings.

Late in November, as I was preparing my Christmas list for a friend in the States, someone banged, banged, banged on my front door. I opened it to find a very thin, pale, tall, bearded Belgian fellow whose greenish face matched his drenched rain gear. He was burdened with a heavy rifle, a panga, and a rain-soaked jacket. It turned out he was a new employee of the MGP, although I had never met him before. The poor, bespectacled man squished into my cabin, and collapsed near the fireplace, giving me a harrowing tale. His guide, who was a Rwandese Parc guard named Gasabune,[479] had suddenly and without warning turned on him, attacking him with his panga. The guide shattered the man's eyeglasses on the right side and walloped him on the forehead with the panga before collapsing into some kind of seizure. The Belgian man dragged his attacker to the shelter of a tree, went to find help, and ended up at my cabin door.

I sent him back into the forest with a group of my men and a "teepoy," which is a kind of a heavy, woven straw stretcher. They didn't return until mid-evening to report that the African was not where he had been deposited. He had disappeared. By this time the Belgian was in terrible shape—cold, wet, tired, shaking for good reason—and the lump on his forehead was getting bigger. I fed him and plied him with a good, stiff drink before sending him back down the mountain with my best tracker.

It wasn't until the following day that I learned Gasabune did not have rabies, as I had initially suspected. Although rabies is quite common here, it turned out he had an endemic, hereditary disease known to the Rwandans as *Basimu* (sic).[480] It can show itself in men, women or children, runs in family lines, and evidences itself in either self-mutilation or attacks against the nearest person around. There is no known cure for it, but the next attack may be thwarted or delayed by the sacrificial slaying of a goat in the compound of the family. The guide was finally found, huddled in his family compound, docile as a lamb and totally oblivious to all that had occurred. I never learned any other reason for the cause of the violent outburst, and since black magic was so prevalent in the forests, I tended to believe that Basimu (sic) was the root of his outburst.[481]

Hindsight tells me that I should have been more concerned about this incident. When I was teaching at Cornell, one of my students came to visit me before class and found me in one of my familiar dark moods. My cleaning lady had just removed the hair from one of my combs. The poor woman was just being thorough, but the student caught me in the process of firing her. I explained to the bewildered student that any hair was for me and me alone to dispose of, preferably by burning. I should not have left my hair available like that, since it could be used to work a spell against me. The student asked me if I really believed in such "hocus-pocus." I shot back, "*Where I live, if I didn't I'd be dead.*"[482] Perhaps I had become numb to the darker manifestations of the forest, because I viewed the Basimu episode as a colorful story and did not give it any more credence than the episodes of hiva-hiva experienced by the gorillas in previous months.

Besides, I had other concerns that were more worrisome. Wayne McGuire was either truly sick or a slacker, because he disappeared down the mountain to cash a traveler's check in late November, and I did not hear from him for two weeks. I learned that he had been staying at a friend's house, just eating, sleeping, sunning, swimming and feeding like a leech on other Europeans in and around Kigali. I was really angry! His laziness and incompetence was annoying, especially since it meant I could not take my annual Christmas shopping trip to the States. He could not possibly hold the camp together, since he did not have enough sense to come in out of the rain.[483]

I decided to direct my attention to my annual Christmas list for the men and myself. I went begging for socks in all sizes, waterproof warm hats, and jogging suits that consisted of pants and a top with a hood. Not getting to the States had put a dent into my shopping plans for the men and their families. When I gave them something nice to wear at camp, they usually saved it for a visit to the "big city" of Ruhengeri—all four dusty blocks of it! I had hoped that these items could be found inexpensively at army surplus stores in the States, and since I couldn't travel there myself, I asked my friends to shop for me. My own wish list was quite decadent. I asked first for Triscuits, as well as Merit, non-mentholated long cigarettes, which were a poor substitute for the harsher Impala brand I had been smoking for so many years. Potato chips, nuts, popcorn, Jell-O, a little tinned ham, and "tolls" for my toll-house cookies were also luxuries I could never find in Ruhengeri. I also loved the Instant Quaker Oat mix that came in little sample packages in many different flavors. But the Triscuits were my favorite food. I dreamed of them, literally dreamed of them. The plain salted kind.[484] Obviously, salt was lacking in the Karisoke diet.

After hours spent dreaming of Christmas and the goodies it promised, I bundled my letter to Santa and sent it down the mountain with the porters for the mail run. I dusted off my bearded, felt Santa with the "Howdy" sign and hung it on the front doorknob, little knowing that it would be mentioned in the descriptive accounts of my murder scene, along with the Christmas tree surrounded with still-wrapped presents for my staff and their families. I blocked out December 24-29 at the bottom of the page that listed my Christmas gifts for the children: "Kwa Noel."[485]

I continued to live the last weeks of my life as we all do, oblivious to fate unless we are faced with a terminal disease and have time to prepare for the inevitable. The presence of death was indiscernible from the fresh breezes wafting through the trees and the black smoke from the cooking fires. Perhaps my trip down the mountain in early December to renew my two-month visa opened the door to the Grim Reaper. On December 3rd, I prepared for my trip to ORTPN headquarters by hiding my gun, money and jewelry in the back of my bottom clothing drawer, because theft and snooping was always a concern at camp.[486] I often kept the ammunition clip separate from my gun, a mistake that later allowed the intricate patterns of destiny to reveal a final, perfect image. The following day I was accompanied to Kigali by the Dutch boy, Sjaak,[487] who had been of great help and inspiration to me during his stay. He was one of the best workers I ever had at Karisoke, and I was sad and disappointed that he had to return to Holland and to his job as a gorilla keeper. We spent several days in Kigali, getting supplies for a new weather station, as well as insurance for the car and motorcycle.[488]

The last item on my shopping list was the permanent renewal of my visa, but first I needed the crucial work permit from Parc officials. I dreaded yet another confrontation with Habiyaremye, but gritted my teeth and went to the ORTPN office. The scene played out in its usual manner, and no one deviated from the script, except me. Director Habiyaremye would not see me, and the staff shook their heads in mock sympathy, saying there was nothing they could do without the Director's permission. I was feeling beaten down by this repetitive process, but I did not argue. Instead, I went directly to the American embassy, where the staff stated that they could not provide any assistance. Tired, discouraged and defeated, I fell into old patterns and retreated to the Mille des Collines hotel for what I felt was a badly needed and well deserved drink. I ran into the editor of one of the local papers, who had always written sympathetically of my work, and when I confided my difficulties to him, he smiled broadly and patted my hand. He said, "Mademoiselle Fossey, I think you do not understand. In Kigali you have many friends. But, not at ORTPN. And not, perhaps, among your fellow Americans and some other foreigners. Why do you not ask your friends for help?"[489]

Maybe I did have friends in high places after all. I took the editor's advice to heart and found the business card given to me at the Muhabura Hotel in Ruhengeri when I was laboring over my cold lunch of French fries and pork chops a few months earlier. It wouldn't hurt to try, as I was running out of options, and the Presidential Secretariat's offices were a few blocks away. I entered the building and presented the card given to me by Augustin Nduwayezu. Luckily, he happened to be in and wasted no time graciously inviting me into his office and listening once more to the tale of the unobtainable work permits and visa. He told me that the President himself was supporting my work in the Virungas, and that he saw no problem with extending my visa for two years.[490] He informed me that I was one of the country's cherished guests and could stay in the country as long as I wished. Augustin's secretary took my passport and stamped it with a special visa authorizing me to stay in Rwanda for two years. If I had been handed a ticket to cloud nine, I could not have been happier![491]

Was this encounter a lucky break, or was it too good to be true? The events of that day could not have been staged, as I had no itinerary and my visit to the Mille des Collines for a quick drink was born of serendipity and old habits rather than design. What was certain was that Augustin had access to the highest powers in Rwanda. He was more than an immigration official, and headed what amounted to a national security agency. Our original meeting in Ruhengeri was due in part to the responsibilities of his job, which required him to know the motivations and proximity of anyone who came within shouting distance of the president during the Parc anniversary celebration.

The effects of Augustin's actions would soon become obvious. By the simple act of stamping my visa, he had directly undermined Director Habiyaremye's authority and influence, and this would not go unnoticed. Meanwhile, I loudly broadcast the news of my visa renewal all over Kigali. Friends would later recall that it was the happiest anyone had seen me in public in a long time. Hindsight suggests that it might have served me better if I had been more circumspect about my good news. However, Director Habiyaremye would have heard the news anyway, since his efforts to have me evicted would have run smack up against the president's wishes to keep me in the country. The information I had gathered from Sebahutu, and to a lesser extent, Hategeka, might also have posed a danger to me. Relatives of the Conservator were implicated in smuggling, as well as almost every family in the Mukingo commune. The bourgermeister of the commune had direct civil ties to the governor of the province, Protais Zigiranyirazo, who was the brother-in-law of the President of Rwanda. Every official had competing desires and motives as to whether I should stay in the country or not.

Meanwhile, the interests of my own country were involved. In the 1980's, the United States supported African nations that were considered Western-leaning. USAID pumped money into scores of of them. The Mountain Gorilla Project was one of many community-based projects which benefited from foreign aide; the payoff being good will from local governments. After the genocidal wars in the 1990's, testimony in the United States Congress examined western colonial interests in Rwanda. Ethnic conflicts, wars, and constant civil strife angered the displaced local populace, and they eventually slaughtered gorilla study groups in Congo.[492] In addition, strategic minerals such as coltan could be extracted with a cheap and desperate labor pool. Policy was driven by greed,[493] and the resulting genocide, relocation camps, and cannibalization of the gorilla population was totally unnecessary. I was not imagining things or paranoid when I sensed that nearly everyone had a good reason to depose me from Karisoke.

Even from this vantage point, however, it is impossible to see the entire road-map to my death. I do know that I would probably have not done anything differently. Would I have fled the mountain to spare my life? Certainly not. The gorillas were my responsibility, and no threat would have loomed large enough to force me to abandon them. To this day, Rosamond Carr maintains that if I were still alive, I would be living at Karisoke. Leaving was never a possibility.[494] I had lived on the mountain for eighteen years. Many, many nights were spent alone. Some nights, especially in the early years, were filled with anxiety, terror, and the nightmares that accompany those primitive emotions. None of it, the loneliness, despair, fear or frustration was enough to force me to leave. I think of the snowy night back in Ithaca, when I packed my suitcase and Cindy's kennel, ready to rush back to my gorillas when I felt they were threatened. Nothing in those last years could have persuaded me to abandon my work and my dreams, which were, finally, filled with hope.

So, with my visa happily clutched in my hands, I returned to Karisoke on December 7. The climb took over three hours, and I needed a lot of help, but at least there was no rain. The next three weeks at camp were filled with rather ordinary events. As usual, I was annoyed with uninvited company and officials, but did my best to entertain and made tuna casserole for all. Several days before Christmas, I received gifts from Rosamond, which were quite lovely. The tea tray went on my wall, since I would never have occasion to use it. A bamboo frame would be just perfect for my favorite picture of Digit, and lotion, as always, was just what I needed for my dry skin. Although I had fallen behind in my daily diary entries, I made a note on the back cover that Ruth Keesling would be arriving on January 27, along with five others from the Morris Animal Foundation. We would be discussing plans to open a real, honest-to-goodness veterinary clinic that would benefit research into illnesses intrinsic to the gorilla population.

When I met with Ruth in San Diego in July, I told her that there were only 248 mountain gorillas in the world. I was terribly worried about them contracting human diseases and warned her that they were all going to die, and that I was going to die with them.[495] I came right out and asked Ruth if she would send veterinarians to Africa to help care for the gorillas. Just weeks before her visit, Ruth received word that I had been murdered, but she came anyway. She eventually continued my work as President of the Digit Fund, and a year later founded the Mountain Gorilla Veterinary Center. My diary entry was simple, yet in a way

contained my hopes and dreams for the future of the mountain gorillas: *Jan. 27&
28-Ruth and 5 people.*[496]

I was alone at camp, with the exception of McGuire and my African staff, and
I prepared a Christmas lamb dinner for McGuire and the zoology student, Joseph
Munyaneza. Joseph left camp the day after Christmas.[497]Although specific
descriptions of my daily activities during my last days are missing from my diary,
there are reminders of my thoughts during my final Christmas season. I scrawled
opinions about mice in traps, and how that would equate to a very brutal death.
Mice were always a problem at Karisoke, and I had always resisted most control
options, including poison and traps. Additional random notes and phrases say
that I felt "relief was a cottage industry," "tragedy a growth industry," and the
end result would be that "helping hands help themselves."[498] Surely, I had relied
mostly upon my ability to help myself throughout my extraordinary life on the
mountain. I wondered about threats to the butterfly, and what entailed God's
way for God's creatures. In the very end, I was, ironically, thinking about God
and the value of all life. I wrote my last diary entry with conviction, in big block
letters, stating firmly, "When you realize the value of all life, one dwells less on
the past and concentrates more on the preservation of the future."[499]

So, on the night of December 26, with my diary unusually incomplete and my
life drawing to its final and tragic conclusion, I donned my sweat suit-like paja-
mas and tucked myself into bed. Wayne McGuire stopped by to report on his
visit to the gorillas, and I said good night.[500] The parrots were in the room with
me, and I was surrounded by the soft glow of my kerosene lantern, which illumi-
nated the objects I held most dear. The carriage of my manual Smith Corona
field typewriter held an unfinished note to my beloved friend, Rosamond, thanking her for her gifts and explaining that the yearly Christmas party would be postponed until after the New Year so that the film people involved with *Gorillas in
the Mist* might attend. The tree remained beautifully decorated in anticipation,
with the carefully wrapped gifts around it.[501] The lotions from Rosamond, which
I had just applied to my face and hands, were arranged on the stand next to my
bed. Papers and books tumbled from the simple wooden shelving, and the flick-
ering light of the lantern played against the bright printed fabric of the curtains.
Portraits of gorillas, dead and alive, looked down from the walls of the cabin, and
the songs of the jungle lulled me to sleep. It was the night after Christmas, and I
was surrounded by life, by love, and by the artifacts of a life lived fully, forcefully,
and gracefully to its conclusion.

Deep within the African night during the season of light, death wrapped itself
in the cloak of the jungle darkness and stole into my cabin. Digit and the others

were there in spirit to receive me, and they were silent witnesses to what would remain forever unspeakable. Even the restless parrots cowered, and not a sound was heard from them in the camp that night. The parrots had evolved to forage in the light of day, and the veil of night would provide safety only if they remained silent. A cry for help would have made them vulnerable to the predatory presence moving through the shadows.

When I awoke, feeling the hot breath of evil upon my neck, I tried in vain to retrieve the gun I had hidden in the clothing drawer. Darkness, fear, and confusion overcame me, and I grabbed the wrong ammunition clip, which jammed and fell useless to the floor as the panga was raised above my head. Terror momentarily flooded me with the strength of my younger days, as I struggled with my assailant and fell to the raffia mat which covered the wooden floor—my eyes wide open to the perpetrator. I died clutching fistfuls of my own blood-soaked hair. The bloody panga was abandoned, and footprints led down the Hagenia-lined path before disappearing into to the marshland.[502] The parrots could only click quietly to each other as they huddled in their cage, scratching obsessively at the bottom corner. Soon the smell of death confirmed what they had just sensed, as blood flowed endlessly onto the raffia mat. They would never again say, "I love you."

The spirit embraces death as a passage to a new existence. The agent of death is not as important as the progression, and my violent death made it impossible for me to make a smooth transition to the afterlife. It has taken many years and much searching on my part to come to terms with the violence I experienced. Material form is but a stage of existence, and the separation is difficult even in a peaceful death. Thankfully, the gorillas remained with my damaged spirit for these twenty years until I was given the means and courage to review my life without the specter of character assassination causing additional damage. I am with the gorillas now, and my mother has since joined us.

Ironically, it was Amy Vedder and Kathleen Austin[503] who wrapped my body in sleeping bags for its final journey down the mountain in the company of the unhappy porters.[504] What they did not see during that final descent was the long gorilla procession that accompanied them. Digit bore most of my weight, while the others supported the grief-stricken porters. The last thing I remembered after the light left my wide open eyes was that my casket was covered with Gallium vines.

19

Coda

o o o o o o o o o o o o o o o o o o o o o o o o o o o o o o o o

I truly loved her, miss her, and think of her nearly everyday. I imagine her looking down from heaven with approval at the increase in the gorilla population and the protection of the gorillas in Rwanda

—*Rosamond Carr*[505]

What matters most is the extraordinary quality of Dian Fossey's life and accomplishments, although the details of her murder will consume conspiracy theorists and academic researchers until the murder is solved, if ever. One is reminded of the gorillas' favorite food, the many-layered thistle plant. Without a careful and meticulous peeling away of the dangerous layers of deceit and intrigue potentially involved in Dian Fossey's life and death, injury to reputations, lives and legacies can be the only result. Many Rwandan contemporaries of Fossey are under current indictment by the ICTR (International Rwandan War Crimes Tribunal), but Fossey's death is considered a lesser crime than that of genocide, and remains largely ignored by the courts. Protais Zigiranyirazo, ex-governor of Ruhengeri Province, languishes in custody in Arusha but remains silent on the topic of Dian Fossey.

In the end, the tracker, Emmanuel Rwelekana, and researcher, Wayne McGuire, were formally charged and convicted of Dian Fossey's murder by the Court of the First Instance of Ruhengeri. Rwelekana's mistake was that he was associated with Amy Vedder, who was observed hugging his associate, the tracker Nemeye, at the murder scene. The secret police took that unusual greeting between a white woman and an African as a sign of complicity.[506] Vedder also tried to visit with Rwelekana while he was incarcerated for questioning, but was denied access.[507] The animosity that existed between Fossey and the members of the Mountain Gorilla Project was well known in Kigali and Ruhengeri, and thus

Vedder was questioned, but never charged with anything. She was caring for an infant child at the time and by any stretch of the imagination seemed an unlikely suspect. Rwelekana never had his day in Rwandan court, refusing to sign a confession, and steadfastly professed his innocence until he was found hanged in his prison cell in August of 1986,[508] although there are many who doubt the "official" version of his death. Rwelekana had been employed by Fossey for many years, and it was common knowledge that the two had many disputes.

Emmanuel Rwelekana was hired and fired more than once by Fossey, although she speaks highly of him in her writings. Fossey admitted that she lost her temper with him in late 1979 because he was seven days late and did a poor tracking job. She attributed her burst of temper to exhaustion and overworking. Other camp staff informed Fossey that Amy Vedder's husband, Bill Weber, hired Rwelekana for more money after at least one of their disputes. Fossey stated that although her men were "fiercely loyal," she could not keep matching the salaries Weber was offering.[509] When Fossey was murdered, Rwelekana was working for members of the Mountain Gorilla Project, and he left a wife and five children behind. He had used his tracker salaries to pay for the education of his children.

Incredibly, Wayne McGuire remained at Karisoke for months after Fossey's murder, calmly continuing his research paper on the role of male parenting in gorilla society. He did not flee to the United States until his indictment was a certainty, almost nine months after the murder took place. Why he managed to get out of the country unchallenged remains a mystery, as he flew out on a regularly scheduled airline. Although he had purchased a round trip ticket, his return was highly unlikely since it was possible he would be facing death by hanging or a firing squad. The Canadian author, Farley Mowat, (*Woman in the Mists*) came to the conclusion that an agreement was reached between the United States and Rwanda to allow McGuire to leave Rwanda without a confrontation. This is conjecturing, but entirely possible given the political climate of the times.

After his indictment and flight, McGuire's attorney, Michael Mayock, called a news conference in an effort to clear his client's name. He asserted his belief that the United States and the government of Rwanda engaged in a conspiracy to make his client a scapegoat in the murder. It was more expedient for international relations to have an American rather than a Rwandan charged with Fossey's murder, Mayock said, adding that the U.S. government may have been duped by the Rwandans into making McGuire a "scapegoat" in the murder.[510] State Department spokesman, James Callahan, called Maylock's accusations "totally off the wall," since the United States had never rendered any opinion as to the possible identity of Fossey's killer.[511] Rwanda's Justice Ministry did issue an international arrest warrant for McGuire. Jean Damscene Nkezabo, Rwanda's Director General for the Administration of Justice, told the Associated Press that officials considered McGuire to be the "principal author of the murder."[512] Interpol was asked to help in the search, but the United States' lack of an extradition treaty with Rwanda made this effort moot.

A week or two before Christmas and Dian Fossey's murder, the acting chargé d' affaires of the U.S. Embassy in Rwanda, Helen Weinland,[513] returned to the States for some routine medical exams that took longer than necessary. Her departure left Emerson Melaven as her temporary replacement after the holiday. He may have been ill-equipped for this sudden elevation to a sensitive diplomatic post, since he had previously been the representative of the U.S. Agency for International Development in Rwanda, with no experience in international relations. USAID also employed the V-W's before they were hired by the Mountain Gorilla Project—a potential conflict of interest. In his initial interviews with the international media, Melaven stated that he and his colleagues were impressed by the Rwandan government's response to the murder.[514] But Weinland's memoirs offer another opinion.[515] She followed the initial events surrounding the murder with frustration because she was not back at her post in Kigali, and by the time she returned, very little progress had been made in the investigation. Weinland states unequivocally that "...it is difficult to believe that the trial to find Dian's killer was a rigorous search for the truth."[516] She cites the "lack of investigative diligence" by officials that followed the death of an embassy driver, a Zairois named Valentin, in August of 1985. The suspect in Valentin's murder was eventually arrested, but never formally charged. Weinland says that the suspect had powerful connections to the gendarmerie, and wrote that she "was disgusted" at the outcome of the trial. Oddly, Fossey and Kathleen Austin had accompanied Weinland to Valentin's funeral in August. When Weinland returned, she reassumed her position as acting chargé d' affaires. She remained in Kigali for only three weeks, but was involved in handling the logistics of Dian's death. Her signature is on many of the death cables that flew between Kigali and the State Department during those days in late January.

McGuire had the misfortune to be the only white person in residence at camp the night of the murder. Kanyaragana, Dian's loyal houseman, was the first to enter the corrugated tin cabin. He was going about his usual routine, preparing to light the morning fire, when he discovered the body. Absolutely terror stricken, he at first told the police that he had not seen the body.[517] The panicked staff summoned McGuire from his hut, which was 100 yards away, with frantic cries of "Dian kufa, kufa!" Dian is dead! McGuire's account of that early morning suggests, but does not prove, that all the inhabitants of the camp reacted with confusion, terror and disbelief at what had happened. The tin wall was found to be missing a panel that covered the hole first carved at the foot of Fossey's bed during a 1980 burglary under A.H. (Sandy) Harcourt's watch. McGuire also noted that the same sheet of corrugated metal on the outer wall of Fossey's bedroom had been removed. The front door was usually locked, but was now open. Had someone come in through the opening in the wall and exited through the front door, or had the door been unlocked all along? A contractor,[518] who worked on the reconstruction of Fossey's cabin years after the murder, maintained that it would have been impossible to remove a side panel quietly,[519] but his account does not address the possibility that the smaller, older patched opening had been utilized during the murder. Reports are conflicting as to whether the door was routinely locked. The two rotating housemen had keys to Dian's house and customarily let themselves in during the early morning hours to start the water for coffee. The house appeared to be ransacked, but Dr. Phillipe Bertrand, Fossey's friend, suggested that the disarray could have been caused by Fossey's frantic, last minute attempt to locate her hidden pistol. Dian's diary entry for December 3, 1985, states clearly that she put her gun (not guns), money and jewelry in a bottom drawer of her bureau. Since a gun, Fossey's passport, $1,200 in U.S. currency and over $1,700 in traveler's checks were left behind,[520] robbery seems an unlikely motive.

Augustin Nduwayezu, who was the official who granted Dian's permanent visa in December of 1985, just weeks before her murder, told author Nicholas Gordon that the pistol found at the scene of the crime was marked CIA.[521] Although it's laughable that a clandestine agency would so brazenly identify its property, the ownership of one gun in particular can without question be attributed to Fossey. The Oldham County police department of La Grange, Kentucky, sent a letter to the FBI shortly after Fossey's murder. The police department noted that Fossey directed a friend to purchase a new handgun for her in October of 1984. The gun, purchased from the Oakwood Limited gun shop,[522] was an Astra Constable blue steel .380 caliber semi-automatic pistol. The serial number on the Astra was 1108609(?) (seventh number obscure). This gun was to replace Dian's Walther.380, which was previously stolen or lost in Africa. The Kentucky police noted that Fossey made it known that she always carried a weapon for personal protection while living in Africa, and they hoped that Rwandan officials could track the firearm to the assailant. But the Astra (or one like it) was found at the scene and was not stolen.

There is also great confusion and controversy regarding accounts of the gun and clip found beside Fossey's body. Eyewitnesses say the gun was a 9mm. The first theory was that she had hidden her gun, and, as was her custom, stored the clip(s) separately. When she was attacked, she ransacked the drawer where the gun was hidden and grabbed the wrong clip, making it impossible to load and fire her weapon. On the other hand, popular gossip maintained that she kept her gun under her pillow. If this were the case, why would it not be loaded?

With both theories there are many problems and inconsistencies, which reveal the lack of a careful forensic examination and the preservation of evidence. Fossey was meticulous about record keeping. She dutifully registered her most recent handgun purchase. According to rumor, she kept an arsenal at Karisoke, but there is no record to support this. There was gossip about one gun, three guns and even a rifle, but nothing supports those claims. Nicholas Gordon reported seeing a picture of two handguns on a chair.[523] These photos were in the files of the Procurer, Mathias Bushishi, but the photos have no concrete link to the crime scene and could have been staged. Fossey spoke of two .22 caliber starter pistols purchased for her patrols in 1978, but there is no mention of these pistols after she returned from her professorship at Cornell. Other than the .32 pistol Fossey said she hid in a Kleenex box after her capture by Congolese soldiers,[524] there is no available record of additional side arms except the 9mm Walther PPK/S, which was stolen or lost by 1983. Fossey stated in a letter to Shirley McGreal that Richard Barnes threw away her only pistol in 1983, leaving her patrols with only the starter pistols. Farley Mowat quotes Fossey in *Woman in the Mists*, *"…I asked about my .32 Walther pistol…he (Richard Barnes) responded, "I threw the gun away in the forest."*[525] A 9mm Walther and the Astra are remarkably similar pistols and could easily have been confused by crime scene witnesses who did not have a professional knowledge of handguns.

527

Astra is an old and widely recognized Spanish firearms manufacturer with a history dating back to the early 1900's. The Constable was a more recent Astra design, exported to the USA from 1965 to 1991. The Walther PP (*Polizei Pistole*) was introduced in Germany in 1929 as a holstered sidearm for the German police forces. Matthew Boyd[528], who has conducted extensive research regarding gun characteristics, was asked: "Is it possible that the only gun at the crime scene was the Astra Constable, and people with little or no knowledge of firearms would call it a 9mm?" Boyd says that scenario is possible, since the average person would not know about the Astra .380 unless they had handled one, or read about it. Rwandans would most likely not have seen one, much less handled one, since it is a Spanish pistol chambered in an American designed cartridge. The 9mm Walther originated in Europe and would have been more familiar to the Rwandan authorities and also easily confused with the Astra. The only way authorities would have been able to tell the difference is if they took a close look at the stampings on the side of the pistol, or examined its ammunition.

Boyd adds that there could have been some confusion about the cartridges unless investigators looked closely at the ammunition casings and/or the magazines. He speculates that if there were two sets of ammunition and Dian picked up an old magazine for the Walther and tried to use it in the Astra, it would not fit because the cartridge (for the Walther) is longer. Magazines for automatic pistols are not normally interchangeable unless both pistols are from the same family/style of firearm. If Dian Fossey tried to load a magazine for any other type of firearm, even if it was chambered in the same cartridge, it would either not stay in place or get stuck in the firearm.

Why is this information important? Clues at the scene give additional information regarding Fossey's character. Contrary to reports circulated by her American enemies, throughout her years in Africa Fossey did not exhibit the characteristics of a gun-wielding maniac. The Astra was a well-made, small pistol, but considered a "ladies" gun that a serious shootist would never purchase. It is not known for its accuracy. Further, when Fossey stored her ammunition separately from her gun, she was practicing good gun etiquette, which does not jibe with a "shoot at anything" mentality. The assessment of the Kentucky authorities that Fossey purchased the gun only for personal protection supports this idea. Terry Fairbanks of the Central Lakes College Criminology Department[529] takes these observations one step further and suggests that if Fossey had committed herself to self-defense, her Astra would have been loaded and ready, and she would be alive today.[530] Considering her kidnapping at the hands of Congolese rebels, carrying a handgun in the jungles of Africa would seem a prudent decision. And why would she go to the trouble to register one gun and not two or three others, especially if she exhibited apprehension at using one gun?

Misidentification of important evidence also supports the contention that forensic science was undeniably sloppy at the crime scene. Did the Rwandan government make a serious attempt to find Fossey's killer(s)? A letter from the vice-consul of the U.S. embassy, Karl Hoffman, states, "…my recollection is that not all of her guns were hidden,"[531] yet there is no mention of any other gun in any of the initial eyewitness reports or literature, other than the supposed 9mm found next to the body. Hoffman's comments were written almost a year after the murder and rely upon memory and speculation, rather than facts. At Wayne McGuire's trial in absentia, prosecutor Mathias Bushishi read an exposition of the government's case, which included a description of two, not three, guns that were found at the scene. One was "from the CIA," he stated.[532]

An examination of an Astra Constable blue steel .380 handgun reveals a stamping on the barrel that reads "ASTRA UNCETA CIA-GUERNICA (SPAIN)." It seems that Rwandan authorities erroneously assumed that a simple Spanish trademark proved a connection between Fossey and the Central Intelligence Agency. The truth is far less interesting. The firm known as Astra was founded as "Esperanza y Unceta" on July 17, 1908, in the town of Eibar by Don Juan Esperanza and Don Pedro Unceta. This original company changed to Unceta y Cia in 1926 when Esperanza dissolved the partnership and moved on to found his own company.[533] The non-existent CIA connection had become another strand of the Fossey myth. Whether this was the result of incompetence or design remains unknown. There are no records that Procurer Mathias Bushishi's inventory included an accurate description of the one handgun known with certainty to be in Fossey's possession, the Astra. However, a careful examination of the same model would strongly suggest that it was indeed the Astra that was found near the body.

Dr. Philippe Bertrand conducted the initial and only forensic examination of the body. He examined the body by lamplight, since there was no electricity. Wayne McGuire remembered that the body was very cold when he first approached it. He held Fossey's wrist and checked for a pulse, but found none. He later asked Dr. Bertrand about the manner of death and the doctor assured him that death had not come instantaneously, but that Fossey must have died within minutes. Dr. Bertrand determined that the cause of death was a fractured skull and bleeding, but here, once again, the accounts of the volume of blood differ. McGuire remembers there being lots of blood on Fossey's face, in her hair, and on the mat beneath her. Others have said that there was blood on the walls as well, but at this juncture all is hearsay. Ruth Keesling, of the Morris Animal Foundation, recalls that there was still blood on the floor and mattress weeks after the murder.

Glass littered the floor, and remnants of broken kerosene lanterns and pressure lamps were everywhere. According to McGuire, the table in Fossey's bedroom had been overturned, and the mattress had been pulled partially off the bed. Yet Kathleen Austin conveyed a different picture of the crime scene to Nicholas Gordon. She said there was "a slight disorder" in the room, and that Dian's body was lying on the floor, but nothing had been overturned, even though the furniture was slightly out of place. Austin concluded that there had not been a great struggle.[534] This would support the supposition that Fossey herself caused the "disorder" in a frantic search for her gun and ammunition. The rest of the disparate descriptions provide nothing but a gruesome picture of a brutal murder. What matters is the manner in which the descriptions vary, especially as to the amount of blood. A complete forensic examination would have provided blood tests as well as an accurate accounting of the amount of blood lost from the body.

This lapse raises the question of the manner of death and casts doubt upon conventional wisdom that death was the result of multiple blows from the panga blade. Poison cannot be ruled out without complete blood profiles. It is possible, but by no means proven, that Fossey could have been drugged to render her incapable of a fight. McGuire has said that she was suffering from insomnia, which has lead to speculation that she took sleeping pills. However, official reports indicate that there were no barbiturates found in her cabin. Varying accounts of the amount of blood would directly impact possible conclusions as to the manner of death. Very little blood would indicate that she was either poisoned or strangled, or both. Rosamond Carr believes firmly that she was strangled. Carr met Kathleen Austin for lunch at the Muhabura Hotel after Austin accompanied Fossey's body down the mountain. Although, neither woman could eat, Carr remembers vividly that there was discussion of possible strangulation.[535]

Death by multiple panga blows would produce much blood spattering, and at this point in time, crime scene photos appear to be lost. Eyewitness accounts are in total disagreement as to the amount of blood and splattering. Meanwhile, Ruth Keesling, who arrived at Karisoke shortly after the funeral, maintains that she spotted a bloody panga still lying under the bed. Concerned about possible fingerprints, she says that she pointed it out to some military types who were guarding the scene and one of them carelessly picked up the blade, wiped it with a cloth, and handed the cloth to her. "Here are your fingerprints," he smirked.[536]

Did Rwandan officials conduct a thorough and serious investigation? Was it simply bungled, or deliberately mismanaged? On the morning of the murder, police were duly summoned on the antiquated radio and eight hours later a procession of Rwandan officials made their way up the slippery, rugged porter's trail to Karisoke. The group included the Prefect Protais Zigiranyirazo, the public prosecutor Mathias Bushishi, the police captain Karangwa, and a contingent of commandoes.[537] The political and personal associations within the ranks of the Rwandan officials at the scene are noteworthy. Rwanda is divided into Prefectures headed by a local Prefect, or governor, appointed by the President. Each Prefecture is divided into Communes that are headed by a Bourgmeistre. In this case, the investigation fell under the Prefecture of Ruhengeri, which was governed by Protais Zigiranyirazo, who also happened to be the brother-in-law of the President of the country, Juvenal Habyarimana. Augustin Nduwayezu, the official who granted Fossey her final visa, did not participate in the investigation, because as head of the secret police this case would not require his services. Nduwayezu told Nicholas Gordon that it was a very public murder and did not require the services of the Sûreté, which had direct organizational links to the President and the Prefect. Nduwayezu maintained that he would have been accused of putting political pressure upon the investigation, if he had participated.[538] Captain Karangwa was in charge of the gendarmerie, which is, essentially, a military branch of the government. He was also a friend of the governor, Zigiranyirazo. Bushishi's role was to act as the public prosecutor—he would eventually bring the case to Rwandan court and try McGuire in absentia. He spent the night after the murder at Karisoke and began the official investigation the next morning. Dian's most recent nemesis, Laurent Habiyaremye, the Parc

Conservator, was not involved in the initial investigation; at least he was not present at Karisoke in the hours immediately after the body was found.

Amy Vedder was summoned to the scene at the request of Kathleen Austin, who was the duty officer in charge of the American Embassy during the Christmas holidays. Farley Mowat's personal archives suggest that there was a unique window of opportunity to murder Dian Fossey between December 26 and December 28. The student, Joseph Munyaneza, left on the 26th and his replacement, Jory Hess, was not due to arrive until December 27. Meanwhile, the American embassy was operating with a skeleton crew over the holidays, and Helen Weinland, the most experienced diplomat at the embassy, was home on medical leave. To her credit, Vedder's accounts of the initial investigation recall her frustration at the manner in which evidence was being collected and/or ignored. When she suggested that an investigator place a pen or some other measuring device for scale next to a set of footprints that were being photographed, the investigator retorted that it was not necessary because he already knew the length of the pen![539] An attempt was made to collect fingerprints from the dresser, but the panga had been handled so often it was ignored, which might explain why Ruth Keesling saw it under the bed.

The bloody panga was determined to be Fossey's own and had previously hung on the wall as a kind of decoration. Everyone was more interested in the hair clutched in Fossey's fists after Kathleen Austin brought attention to it. Austin maintained that separate hair samples were sent to the FBI labs in Washington and to the Paris police laboratory, in the Quai de l'Horloge.[540] The FBI and French reports differ in some critical ways. The French forensic medical examiner, Professor P. F. Ciccaldi, indicated that hair samples found in Fossey's right hand differed from hair taken from her left hand and from her head, which matched. Initial comments made by Rwandan investigators said that the hair samples in Dian's right hand were from a different white person, not an African. The implication was that McGuire was the only white person in camp that night, so the hair in the right hand must have been his. French experts concluded that Fossey tried to defend herself and pulled out the hair of her attacker, but this explanation does not clarify why someone who was being attacked would pull out her own hair as well as that of her attacker.

Nicholas Gordon explains in his book, *Murders in the Mist,* that the three samples, which included one sample from the victim's head, all exhibited the same microscopic characteristics. The only difference was that the unknown hairs were characterized as being reddish-brown, came from the right hand only, and no color was assigned to the hair known to come from Fossey's head. The conclusion of the FBI report was that all of the hairs COULD have come from Fossey's own head, but did not constitute a basis for absolute personal identification of the hairs.

Gordon goes on to rightly point out that if the French analyzed hair from two hands, and the FBI analyzed hair from only one hand, it would be unclear which hand the FBI chose. Adding to the confusion, the French report clearly stated that the hair found in the right hand was from a white person other than Fossey. In the end, the investigation was left with two differing reports and no control with which to evaluate the results. Was this error the result of malfeasance or a simple mistake? The labs were forthcoming with their results, so it would appear that there was no cover-up involved.

McGuire's death sentence, literally, hung by a hair. The Rwandan court determined that since the hair taken from Fossey's right hand was from a white person, and that it was established that McGuire was the only white person in camp that night, the hair must have been his. No DNA tests were conducted, or at least none survive in the public records. Prosecutors assumed that Fossey must have pulled out the hair of her attacker while trying to defend herself.

There are two conflicting reports in files recently released through the Freedom of Information Act. FBI files pertaining to the hair analysis indicate that there were indeed hair samples in each hand and they all matched the hair on Fossey's head. This is contrary to the initial report, viewed by Gordon in the Harold Hayes' archives, that mentioned only one hand. The more recent report indicates that additional tests washed blood from the hairs, but there was not enough blood to conclude that it belonged to Fossey.[541] The newly released FBI documents also include the incomplete initial report, viewed by Gordon, which states that there were only two hair samples: "One hair sample was found grasped in her right hand. The other hair sample was taken from the hair on her head." Gordon was reporting on the only file available to him at the time.

However, the newly released written lab report clearly makes a new reference to three samples: (Q1) "Hairs received in sealed white envelope marked 'right hand;' (Q2) hairs received in sealed while envelope marked 'left hand;' and (K1) Hairs received in sealed white envelope marked 'head.'" All of the samples were examined with a stereomicroscope. Fibers were examined and removed from Q1 and Q2, and the hairs were returned to the envelope for serological (blood) examination. There were no fibers found on K1, and the sample was returned to the envelope for more study. The textile fibers were preserved on glass microscopic slides for possible future comparisons. (Lab No. 60129020 S UJ WM) (FBI File 95-271119-3) Q1 consisted of three hairs, and the examiner noted that the color was reddish brown with characteristics similar to the head sample (K1). Q2 consisted of numerous reddish brown hairs with no roots. The question "broken?" is jotted in the notes. K1 consisted of numerous hairs that appeared to be cut. All of the hair samples were "slightly stained" with blood, and the lab soaked the blood off for comparison purposes. Grouping tests were conducted on the human blood identified on Q2 and K1 were inconclusive. Human blood, too limited for conclusive grouping purposes, was identified on Q1.

The report remains maddeningly inconclusive, since the blood grouping was useless and the lab concluded that hair comparisons do not constitute a basis for absolute personal identification. McGuire, however, was sentenced to death by a hair that the French lab considered to be his, although the FBI lab enigmatically stated that all of the hairs "could have" originated from Dr. Fossey. Of course there was no control when the hairs were sampled, and the chain of evidence remains murky at best and broken at worst. One is tempted to wonder what modern forensic science could do with any remaining lab slides.

McGuire's motive, assumedly, was that he wanted to procure Fossey's research documents. Fossey maintains in her writings that she was not actively involved in research at the time and would not consider doing any additional articles unless she were paid upfront. McGuire admitted to taking two boxes of Fossey's papers after the murder for safekeeping. As far as a possible conspiracy between McGuire and Rwelekana is concerned, McGuire did not speak the local language and Rwelekana did not speak English, so it is hard to imagine that the two were able to concoct an elaborate murder scheme. McGuire maintains that he was not even acquainted with Rwelekana, who had been fired by Fossey months previously.

The case against Rwelekana was based in part upon human blood found smeared on a flashlight, a piece of rubber, and a piece of green fabric found in Rwelekana's room. The blood was determined to belong to Group A, which matched Fossey's blood group. There are conflicting reports in the records as to whether the bloody objects were found in Fossey's room or the tracker's. The motive assigned to Rwelekana was that he had cut a deal with McGuire to regain the job he lost due to a previous falling out with Fossey. Rwelekana steadfastly proclaimed his innocence and maintained that the blood found on his clothing was animal blood, not Fossey's. He was found hanged in jail—the apparent victim of a suicide—yet suicide is very uncommon in Rwandan society.

Other African camp personnel, who were detained by gendarmerie and released, returned to camp with tales of torture and coercion, with bruises as proof. The tracker Nemeye, who was instrumental in the capture of the notorious poacher Sebahutu, recounted the incidents of torture to journalist Nick Gordon.[542] Nemeye's accounts of the murder are quite graphic, but his descriptions of the body do not square with other accounts. One remembers Dian's skepticism at the accounts of the African trackers; she often referred to their propensity to exaggerate or bend the truth. The Orinfor journalist, Jean-Baptiste, maintained in later interviews that he was threatened by Captain Karangwa after he tried to interview McGuire. The authorities, in general, were obstructionist; they refused interviews and withheld other information regarding the investigation. Jean-Baptiste maintained that he also got into trouble with Zigiranyirazo when he refused to read a prepared news bulletin regarding the murder on the radio.

In the hours and days immediately following Fossey's murder, Director Laurent Habiyaremye was conspicuously absent from the investigation, but very much in presence at the American embassy. A delegation from ORTPN, headed by Habiyaremye, called on the acting chargé d' affaires, Emerson Melaven, on the morning of January 2, 1986, and the world watched as one of Dian's worst enemies presented condolences to the people of the United States. It was important that Rwanda not be blamed for the murder:

"Ladies, Gentleman. It was with great sorrow that the trustees, the board of directors and the personnel of the Rwandan Board of Tourism and National Parks learned of the death of Dr. Dian Fossey while working in the National Volcano Park. Dr. Dian Fossey was murdered during the night of December 26 to December 27, 1985 at the Karisoke Research station which she herself created in 1967.

"An eminent scientist of international renown, Dr. Dian Fossey remains the person to have made the greatest contribution towards the protection of the mountain gorilla (gorilla gorilla beringei)[543], a rare species in danger of extinction now found only in our range of volcanoes. For the past eighteen years she had defied the jealous and discouraged wrongdoers in order to bring the entire world to finally understand the importance of protecting the national volcano park, privileged habitat of this anthropoid (sic), our distant ancestor.

"Poaching was considerably and noticeably overcome thanks to her on-the-spot interventions, as well as through international opinion. It is to this that Rwanda owes its reputation as a champion of conservation. Dr. Dian Fossey was also the creator of a selective form of tourism based on the visiting of groups of gorillas accustomed to the presence of humans (sic), according to scientific data which she gave in keeping with this species.

"Scientists and research workers from all corners of the world found in her a devoted and unselfish person whose principal concern was the survival of humanity in an ecologically balanced world. The fact that she specified before her death that she wished to be buried beside these primates to which she had devoted her life is sufficient proof of her attachment to our country.

"The Rwandan Board of Tourism and National Parks recognizes that she did not deserve what happened to her that night; but she should know where she is resting in eternity, that she is still alive in the hearts of the board and of the Karisoke research station. The work she did in Rwanda will live forever among present and future generations. The investigation of this vile murder continues. And once the culprit has been found, he will be punished according to the law."[544]

How curious that Director Habiyaremye would have such an instantaneous change of heart after banning Fossey from the Parc's anniversary celebration four months earlier. She probably rolled in her grave to hear that she was responsible for tourism, but the protection of Habiyaremye's money-making schemes, and the future of international relations, mandated the tribute. Ironically, Dian's nemesis provided her most glowing tribute: "A devoted and unselfish person whose principal concern was the survival of humanity in an ecologically balanced world." Sincere or not, these comments are telling, especially since Director Habiyaremye omitted the gorillas in his description of a grand vision for an ecologically balanced world.

Even more troublesome were the contents of a cable sent from the U.S. embassy in Kigali to the Secretary of State's office in Washington.[545] Melaven took the opportunity of Habiyaremye's visit to ask the ORTPN director about future plans for Karisoke, and the director indicated that the camp and its work would continue. Yet Melaven's classified "FYI" to the State Department, after he said goodbye to Habiyaremye, indicted that at least in the short term, operations at Karisoke were in confusion. The gendarmes had rounded up all of the camp workers for questioning, and Melaven thought it unlikely that they would be released anytime soon.

Jean Pierre von der Becke and his colleagues from the Mountain Gorilla Project were taking turns going up the mountain and bringing food to Wayne McGuire, who except for the police guard, was the only person remaining at camp. An appeal was made directly to Protais Zigiranyirazo to try and get some of the workers back, but the governor said there was little he could do. This was an interesting expression of impotence, coming from the brother-in-law of the Rwandan president. Everything was coming to a halt, and it was clear that despite Habiyaremye's flowering tributes, he was unwilling to commit resources to Karisoke.

After the service at Dian's gravesite, Protais Zigiranyirazo intoned a blessing in Latin and added that Fossey "placed her life at the service of Rwanda."[546] Zigiranyirazo was possibly the "big man," Dian often referred to in her letters about poaching and smuggling. Certainly he remains a man of imposing stature and flamboyant presence. At his first appearance in the Arusha international court for war crimes, he wore a dark suit, a blue shirt, and a bright yellow tie. The fancy clothes said much about the man. Whether he ensured Dian Fossey's fate remains to be discovered, but he had the capability. Mr. "Z," as he was known in Rwandan circles, was the Prefect from 1974 to 1989, and was also known as a wealthy businessman. The International War Crimes Tribunal's indictment says that he was perceived as a member of the "Akazu," a powerful circle around the former president, Habyarimana. It also links him to death squads and the so-called "Zero Network," which carried out systematic attacks against civilians, mainly Tutsi and Hutu opponents of the Habyarimana regime.[547] Zigiranyirazo has been charged in international court for ordering his own son, Jean Marie Makiza, to shoot and kill three Tutsi gendarmes during 1994. In addition, he was specifically accused of conspiring with influential and powerful persons, including Habyarimana's widow, Agathe Kanziga, to commit genocide.[548] His trial has been postponed numerous times as of late 2004, but Zigiranyirazo may have a long reach and influence that extends far beyond his prison walls in Tanzania. The prosecutor in the case has had to ask for protection for witnesses who reside in Rwanda, other countries in Africa, and those who reside outside of Africa who have requested protective measures.[549] The judge granted the request. Zigiranyirazo's ability to wield deadly power coincides with a propensity to avoid getting his own hands dirty. He was a university student in Montréal when he was deported for threatening to order the killing of two exiled Rwandan human rights activists. Did he also have the motive, means and stature to order Fossey's murder? Probably, but the International War Crimes Tribunal will not engage the issue, and the FBI remains silent about the scope and intent of its investigation of Zigiranyirazo. The murder of one is diminished in comparison with the extermination of 800,000.

Melaven noted in the 1986 cable that Zigiranyirazo's lack of enthusiasm for the fate of Karisoke did not bode well for the gorillas that had been tracked and observed by Fossey's patrols. The Christmas season was time of year when poaching was heaviest, and this fact could not have been missed by the Parc officials. By accident or design Fossey's murder played handily into ORTPN's desires to confiscate the cabins at Karisoke for their tourism programs.

Meanwhile, tributes to Dian Fossey continued to pour in from all over the world, and a memorial service was held at which Joan Goodall, one of the original "Leakey Girls," and Dian's frequent correspondent, gave a moving eulogy.[550] Goodall, perhaps more than anyone, understood the challenges and passions that Fossey wrestled with every day during her studies with the mountain gorilla:

"I, along with thousands of others, will always remember Dian best sitting, half-hidden in lush vegetation, dwarfed by the proximity of a huge silverback male gorilla. He accepts her totally: and her face is radiant with love for him and joy in his nearness. No wonder that Dian, having finally won the trust of these magnificent animals, was shocked, grief stricken-and enraged-when "her" gorillas were killed by poachers. Sometimes these killings were unintentional, as when a gorilla was accidentally caught in a snare set for other game. Sometimes it was deliberate, as when a gorilla was slaughtered so that various parts of his anatomy could be used for magical rites or (worst of all) for sale to tourists as souvenirs. But the end result, the suffering inflicted on the victim, was the same.

"And so Dian, for better or worse, tackled the poaching problem in a variety of often unorthodox ways. But the methods she used initially, as when she leapt out at poachers with Halloween horror masks, gave place over the years to the careful training of dedicated game guards. If the poachers had been after "my chimps," I too would have been desperate to stop them. But I doubt I would have had the courage to stop them in that way.

"Dian's persistence, her determination to stay in the field whatever the cost, led to her greatest scientific contribution: the carefully documented case histories of individual gorillas that in some cases cover nearly twenty years. Was this contribution to our scientific knowledge of gorillas her most important legacy? The fact that through her work our understanding of these apes has increased a hundredfold? Or was her contribution towards the survival of the gorillas themselves even more important? History will be the ultimate judge of this, I suppose. But it is probably true to say that, had Dian never gone to Rwanda, there would be far fewer mountain gorillas in the Virungas than there are today. It is possible, even, that the last would have gone."

So, as Goodall says, history must be the final judge. Those of us who embrace silence when faced with attacks on Dian Fossey's legacy share the experience of Dian's beloved parrots, who remained the only eyewitnesses to the murder. Experts on avian intelligence say there is anecdotal evidence that parrots retain some memory of violence they've witnessed or experienced, and there is general agreement that birds have the ability to recognize people they have lived with for a long time. Indeed, they can exhibit extremes of behavior, from outright attacks to cowering, when reunited with the object of their fear. The atrocity perpetrated upon their beloved owner was such an insult to their avian acumen that Dian Fossey's parrots refused to speak the phrase they had learned from her on what she termed her "bad days": "I love you." Hopefully there will be others who will continue the search for veracity in an effort to preserve Dr. Fossey's good name and incredible legacy. Evil will not triumph if the truth is spoken.

Significant African Staff at Karisoke

Bambari: Tracker, circa 1974.

Basil: Houseman from 1968. Stuart Perlmeter accused him of stealing in 1980 and he was probably fired. He was back with Fossey in 1984.

Basili: Tracker, circa 1974.

Big Nemeye: Seemed to come and go, but was head tracker in 1983. Hired by Bill Weber in 1979.

Burumbe: Woodsman.

Byandagara, Frederick: Built weather station in December 1985.

Celestin: Tracker circa 1985.

Guamhogazi: Camp worker, circa 1970.

Gwehandagoza: Head porter from 1971 to 1985.

Kana: Tracker.

Kanyaragana: Head houseman from 1971 to 1985.

Mukera: Head woodman circa, 1970; drummer and dancer.

Mutari: Porter.

Mutarutkwa: Anti-poaching patrol 1979

Nemeye: Hired as a teenager in the early days and stayed with Fossey until the end. Currently in prison for crimes related to genocide.

Rwelekana: Tracker. Hired and fired many times.

Sanwekwe: Congolese park guard and tracker. Introduced to Dian in Kabara meadow.

Sebarari: Stole Fossey's valise in 1968.

Sekaryongo: Patrol.

Semitoa: Houseman circa 1978.

Seregere: At camp in 1970-72. He was fired for the theft.

Vatiri: Leader of anti-poaching patrols since 1978.

Bibliography

Ackerman, Diane. *A Natural History of Love.* New York: Random House Vintage Books, 1995.

African Wildlife Foundation. "Saving One of the World's Most Endangered Primates." Available. Online: <u>http://www.awf.org/news/4138</u>

Aristotle. *Generatione Animalium,* 384-322 BC.

Aristotle. *Historia Animalium*, 385-322 BC.

Arusha Times. "Former Mayor begins Own Defense." The Arusha Times. Available. Online: <u>http://arushatimes.co.tz/2003/15/un_tribunal_1.htm</u> ISSN 0856-9135

Associated Press. "Judge Rules Dian Fossey's Will Invalid." Wire Services. January 15, 1988.

Associated Press. "Scientists Working with Gorillas to Evacuate Rwanda." Associated Press, April, 9, 1994.

Audry, Robert. *African Genesis.* New York: Dell, 1961.

Bishop, Barry C. *Research: Dian Fossey (1932-1985), 1986.*

Carr, Rosamond. *Land of a Thousand Hills: My Life in Rwanda.* New York: Viking, 1999.

Cockburn, Alexander. *Washington Babylon.* New York: New Left Books, 1996.

Crary, David. "Rwanda Officials Praised for Response to Dian Fossey's Murder." Associated Press, December 29, 1985.

Crary, David. "Woman Who Spent Life With Gorillas Killed By Assailants." Associated Press, December 28, 1985.

Crichton, Michael. *Congo.* New York: Knopf, 1980.

Dalai Lama. *Ethics for the New Millennium.* New York: Penguin Putnam Inc., 1999.

Deutsch, Linda. "Researcher Proclaims Innocence in Fossey Murder." Wire Services. August 29, 1986.

Drabble, Margaret. *The Oxford Companion to English Literature.* Oxford: Oxford University Press, 1985.

Faul, Michelle. "Rwandan Official Confirms N.J. Man Sought in Fossey Murder." Wire Services. August 22, 1986.

Fine, Doug. "The Misty Future of Rwanda's Mountain Gorillas." Washington Post, April 30, 1995.

Fossey, Dian. "More Years with the Mountain Gorillas." National Geographic Magazine, October 1971.

Fossey, Dian. "Making Friends with the Mountain Gorillas." National Geographic Magazine, January 1970.

Fossey, Dian. "The Imperiled Mountain Gorilla." National Geographic Magazine, April, 1981.

Fossey, Dian. *Gorillas in the Mist.* Boston: Houghton Mifflin, 1983.

Fossey, Dian. Archival Papers. The William Ready Division of Archives and Research Collections. McMaster University Library. Hamilton, Canada

Froelich, Warren. "Life Is Much better Among the Gorillas." *The San Diego-Union Tribune,* June 27, 1985.

Goodall, Jane. *In the Shadow of Man.* Boston: Houghton Mifflin, 1971.

Gourevitch, Philip. *We Wish to Inform You That Tomorrow We Will Be Killed with Our Families.* New York: Picador, 1998.

Gun's World. "Astra M900 Pistol." Available. Online: http://www.gunsworld.com/spain/astra900_us.html

Hayes, Harold T.P. *The Dark Romance of Dian Fossey.* New York: Simon and Schuster, 1990.

Heritage Warner Books Press Release. "Fossey Diaries." Heritage Warner Books, September 3, 1986.

Karisoke Research Station Press Release. "Rwanda's War Hits 'Gorilla's in the Mist' Research Station." August 31, 1994.

Kelly, Sean. "American Naturalist Buried Among Her Beloved Gorillas." Associated Press, January 1, 1986.

King, James. *Farley: The Life of Farley Mowat.* Toronto: Harper Collins, 2002.

Leakey, L.S.B. *By the Evidence.* New York: Harcourt Brace Jovanovich, 1974.

Madsen, Wayne. Congressional Testimony for Congresswoman Cynthia McKinney. Available. Online: http://www.muhammadfarms.com/Covert_Action_in_Africa.htm

Milton, Pat. "New York Researcher Chosen to Continue Dian Fossey's Work." Wire Services. September 20, 1989.

Mitchell, Henry. "At Home in the Wild: Dian Fossey: Fond Hearts and Furry Friends." The Washington Post, September 30, 1983.

Morris, Desmond. *The Naked Ape.* New York: McGraw-Hill, 1967.

Moses, Jonathan. "Sobering Account From Lawyer Prosecuting Rwandan Genocide." Auckland District Law Society. Available. Online: http://www.adls.org.nz/news/archive2/issueno29/augnews18.asp

Mowat, Farley. Fonds. The William Ready Division of Archives and Research Collections. McMaster University Library. Hamilton, Canada

Mowat, Farley, *Woman in the Mists.* New York: Warner Books, Inc, 1987.

Netherlands Institute of Human Rights. "The Prosecutor vs. Juvenal Kajelijeli." Available. Online: http://sim.law.uu.nl/SIM/Dochome.nsf?Open ICTR-98-44A-I

Ngowi, Rodrique. "Gunmen Kill Rare Mountain Gorillas and Steal Baby in Rwanda." IP, May 14, 2002.

Ohlsson, Leif, 1999, _Environment, Scarcity, and Conflict—A study of Malthusian concerns_, PhD dissertation (12 February), Dept. of Peace and Development Research, University of Göteborg

Rosenblum, Mort. "Naturalist May Have Been Slain Over Witchcraft Amulet." January 17, 1986

Shlacthter, Barry. AP News Feature. Associated Press, July 8, 1985.

Schaller, George B. _The Year of the Gorilla:_ Chicago, University of Chicago Press

Shoumatoff, Alex. "Dispatches From The Vanishing World: Fatal Obsession: The Jungle Death of Dian Fossey." Vanity Fair Magazine, 1986.

Smith, William E. "Rwanda Case of the Gorilla Lady Murder." Time Magazine, 1986.

Smyth, Frank. "People in the Mist." Escape, January, 1995.

Smyth, Frank. "Rwanda's French Connection." The Village Voice, May, 1994.

Snow, Keith Harmon. "Proxy Wars in Central Africa?" Available. Online: http://www.worldwar3report.com/proxy.html

Snow, Keith Harmon. "Central Africa: Hidden Agendas and the Western Press." Available. Online: http://www.allthingspass.com/docs/HiddenAgendaCongo.htm

Stewart, Kelly J. and Pascale, Sicotte. _Mountain Gorillas: Three Decades of Research at Karisoke._ Cambridge: University Press, 2001.

Swain, Jon. "Arrest Made in Killing of Dian Fossey:" CanWest Global Communications Corp., July 30, 2001.

The William Ready Division of Archives and Research Collections. McMaster University Library. Hamilton, Canada

Vedder, Amy. _In the Kingdom of Gorillas: Fragile Species in a Dangerous Land._ New York: Simon and Schuster, 2001.

Warner Brothers. Production notes from *Gorillas in the Mists.*

Warren, Adrian. "Mountain Gorillas." Available. Online: http://www.lastrefuge.co.uk/data/articles/gorilla_p5.html

Warshaw, Andrew. "Digit's Death (Unnamed Article)." Associated Press, February 3, 1978.

Weinland, Helen. *Living Abroad with Uncle Sam.* Bloomington: 1st Books, 2003.

Wolper Productions. "Search for the Great Apes." [video recording] Stanford, CT, National Geographic Society, Veston Video, 1989.

Yamagiwa, J., 2003. Bushmeat Poaching and the Conservation Crisis in Kahuzi-Biega National Park, Democratic Republic of Congo. J. Sustainable Forestry, 16: 115-135.

Endnotes

Sources for this book were biographical texts, Fossey's own writings, interviews, wire service reports, Freedom of Information Act (FOIA) communications, and archival documents located in the McMaster University Library in Hamilton, ON. Permission to access the McMaster archives was graciously granted by Farley Mowat. Following each chapter heading the reader will find a listing of the principle sources, although there may be minor references that are only listed as text in the endnotes. Any comments in this book that can be directly attributed to Dian Fossey are referenced as such in the endnotes.

Prologue

[1] Fossey, Dian. Fossey Archives. Obituary for her "Old Dog, Cindy." f. 5: McMaster.

[2] Mowat, Farley. *Woman in the Mists.* New York: Warner Books, 1987, p.367.

[3] Poison or sorcery

[4] Carr, Rosamond. *Land of a Thousand Hills.* New York: Viking, 1999, p.177.

[5] Leakey Foundation Audio Recordings.

Chapter One: "The Family Group"

[6] Friend of Dian Fossey during her time in Louisville.

[7] Fossey, Dian. Fossey Archives. Obituary for her "Old Dog, Cindy." f.5: McMaster.

[8] Each of Fossey's study groups was assigned a number as a matter of record keeping.

[9] Mowat, Farley, *Woman in the Mists.* New York: Warner Books, 1987, pp. 84-85.

[10] Dian, as well as others, used many variations in the spelling of her Kinyarwandan name. I have chosen to use the proper Kinyarwandan spelling, although "l" is sometimes interchangeable with "r." The meaning is "woman who lives alone on the mountain."

[11] Gordon, Nicholas. *Murders In the Mist.* London: Hodder and Stoughton, 1993, p.1.

[12] Rosamond Carr, Shirley McGreal and the International Primate Protection League, Evelyn Gallardo, Ruth Keesling and David Root procured the marker.

[13] Fossey, Dian. *Gorillas in the Mist.* Boston: Houghton Mifflin, 1983, p. 116.

[14] *National Geographic Magazine*, January, 1970.

[15] Fossey, Dian. Leakey Audio Archives

[16] Fossey. Dian. *Gorillas in the Mist.* Appendix.

[17] Fossey, Dian. *Gorillas in the Mist*, p. 14.

[18] Fossey, Dian. Fossey Archives. Obituary for her "Old Dog, Cindy." f. 5: McMaster.

Chapter Two: "Forming Bonds"

[19] Phone Interview with Ruth Keesling. July 30, 2004.

[20] Fossey, Dian. "More Years with the Mountain Gorillas." *National Geographic Magazine*, Vol.140, No. 4, p.581.

[21] Hayes, Harold T.P. *The Dark Romance of Dian Fossey.* New York: Simon and Schuster, p. 120. Comments made by Betty Henry Schwartzel.

[22] See comments made about Dian Fossey in: Vedder, Amy. *In the Kingdom of Gorillas: Fragile Species in a Dangerous Land.* New York: Simon and Schuster, 2001.

[23] Mowat Fonds. Fossey Diary. August 27, 1975. Box 242. f.8: McMaster.

[24] At this writing, Mary Henry is living in Florida.

[25] Fossey Archive. Letter from Dian Fossey to "Mrs. Morell." October 15, 1984. f. 18: McMaster.

Chapter Three: "Breaking Bonds"

[26] Deep prolonged rumbles that Fossey called "belch vocalizations." It was most frequently heard from stationary gorillas at the end of a long, sunny resting period or when in a lush feeding site.

[27] Fossey, Dian. *Gorillas in the Mist*. p.206.

[28] Fossey, Dian. *Gorillas in the Mist*. pp.182-83.

[29] Search for the Great Apes. *National Geographic Video Classics*. 1975.

[30] Aristotle wrote about Africa in *Historia Animalium* and *Generatione Animalium*, to explain the wild mélange of animals in Africa.

[31] Schaller, George B. *The Year of the Gorilla*. Chicago: University of Chicago Press, 1988, p. 3.

[32] Ackerman, Diane. *A Natural History of Love*. New York: Random House, 1994, p. 189.

[33] Hayes, Harold T.P. *The Dark Romance of Dian Fossey*. New York: Simon and Schuster, 1990, p. 217.

[34] Mowat, Farley. *Woman in the Mists*. pp.64-65.

[35] Carr, Rosamond. *Land of a Thousand Hills*. p.167.

[36] Mowat, Farley. *Woman in the Mists*. p. 176.

[37] Vedder, Amy. *In the Kingdom of Gorillas: Fragile Species in a Dangerous Land*. New York: Simon and Schuster, 2001, p. 25.

[38] Fossey, Dian. "Making Friends with Mountain Gorillas." *National Geographic*, January 1970, p.67.

[39] Fossey's medical records include no diagnosis of alcoholism. She herself admits that she would get drunk, but close friends never witnessed this behavior when she was off the mountain.

[40] Fossey Archives. Camp Notes. Note from Amy Vedder to Dian Fossey. f. 8: McMaster.

[41] Vedder, Amy. *In the Kingdom of Gorillas: Fragile Species in a Dangerous Land.* New York: Simon and Schuster, 2001, p. 41.

[42] Mowat Fonds. *Virunga: The Passion of Dian Fossey.* Box 243.: McMaster.

[43] There is some conflicting information regarding the sex of Mweza. Vedder refers to Mweza as "her" and Fossy as "a male gorilla" in their respective writings.

[44] Dr. Lolly Preciado

[45] Fossey Archive. Letter from Dian Fossey to Russell A. Mittermeier, March 23, 1978. f. 18: McMaster.

[46] Mowat, Farley. *Woman in the Mists.* p. 179.

[47] Fossey identified intergroup vocalizations called hootseries which were used in long range communication. They were low pitched and often undetectable to the human ear at the beginning of the series, but usually built up into plaintive sounding and longer hoots toward the end. See *Gorillas in the Mist,* Appendix B, p. 256.

Chapter Four: "The Bonds of Happiness"

[48] Fossey, Dian. *National Geographic Magazine*, January 1970. p. 52.

[49] There are varying accounts of exactly what happened during this period, but Fossey described each of these incidents at different times to friends. It appears that she shielded some of her friends from the worst details and they will maintain that it never happened. Fossey is the only one who knows for certain what took place during her captivity.

[50] Fossey Archives. Notes on a Work In Progress. Box 242. f. 35: McMaster.

[51] Letter from Rosamond Carr to Georgianne Nienaber. August 8, 2004.

[52] Mowat, Farley. *Woman in the Mists.* p. 54.

[53] Carr, Rosamond. *Land of a Thousand Hills*, p. 157.

[54] Mowat Fonds. Notes on a Work In Progress. Box 242. f.35: McMaster.

[55] Fossey Archives. Letter to Parents, July 5, 1983. f.18: McMaster.

[56] A greeting, similar to "hello."

[57] Not to be confused with Kanyarugano the poacher. There are conflicting spellings of each, but the tracker Nemeye confirmed in January 2005 that there were two individuals with the same name.

[58] Fossey Archives. Letter to Parents, July 5, 1983. f.18: McMaster.

[59] Mowat Fonds. Notes On A Work In Progress. Box 242. f.35: McMaster.

[60] The local language, *Ikinyarwaanda,* of the Bantu in Rwanda.

[61] Fossey Archives. Letter from Jeffrey Short to Dian Fossey, May 7, 1985: McMaster.

[62] Mowat, Farley. *Woman in the Mists*, p. 65.

[63] Mowat, Farley. *Woman in the Mists* p. 70.

[64] Fossey, Dian. *Gorillas in the Mist.* Appendix B, p. 252.

[65] Sigourney Weaver, *Gorillas in the Mist.* Movie version.

Chapter Five: "The Bonds of Fate"

[66] Williamson, Liz. "Update from the Karisoke Research Center, Rwanda, January 1998," Gorilla Journal, 1998.

[67] Williamson, Liz. Field Report. *Ambarwanda Newsletter* (Embassy of Rwanda, UK), No.6, November, 2002.

[68] Fossey, Dian. *Gorillas in the Mist.* p. 20.

[69] Population growth will eventually outrun food supply

[70] "Those who Attack Together." They slaughtered Tutsi men, women and children.

[71] Williamson, Liz. *Gorilla Journal* 23, December, 2001.

[72] Fossey, Dian. *Gorillas in the Mist*. p.x.

Chapter Six: "The Bonds of Love"

[73] Mowat Fonds. Letters from Louis Leakey to Dian Fossey. Box 241. f.1: McMaster.

[74] Eyden, Sally. "Lovers in the Mist," *The Mail* on Sunday, June 27, 2004.

[75] Letter from David Watts. August 9, 1987.

[76] Production notes from *Gorillas in the Mist*. Warner Brothers and Universal Pictures.

[77] Weaver, Sigourney. Production notes from *Gorillas in the Mist*.

Chapter Seven: "The Children of Antiquity"

[78] Mowat, Farley. *Woman in the Mists*. p. 94.

[79] One who has not borne offspring.

[80] Fossey, Dian. *Gorillas in the Mist*. pp.70-71.

[81] Kelly Stewart, in an interview with Alex Shoumatoff, "Dispatches From The Vanishing World: Fatal Obsession: The Jungle Death of Dian Fossey." *Vanity Fair Magazine*, 1986.

[82] What is a friend? A single soul dwelling in two bodies. Quoted in Des MacHale, *Wisdom* (London, 2002).

Chapter Eight: "The Faces of Death"

[83] Aeschylus, Agamemnon

[84] Fossey, Dian. *Gorillas in the Mist*. p.41

[85] Fossey, Dian. *Gorillas in the Mist*, p.14.

[86] Fossey Archive. Letter from Dismas Nsabimana to Fossey January 27,1978 translated by Ryan Barrett. f.12: McMaster.

[87] Fossey Archive. Fossey's "Rough Draft of Rwandan Trip," f.18: McMaster.

[88] Fossey Archive. Fossey's Notes on "Return to Rwanda," f.18: McMaster.

[89] Fossey, Dian. Gorillas in the Mist, Illustration at end of Chapter 10.

[90] Mowat Fonds. Letter from Ian Redmond to Wade Rowland, October 7, 1986: McMaster.

[91] Mowat, Farley. *Woman in the Mists.* p. 14.

[92] Fossey Archive. Camp Notes. f. 8: McMaster.

[93] Camp note from David Watts to Dian Fossey July 28, 1985 Mowat archive Box 240, f.24: McMaster.

[94] Cassandra (also called Alexandra) was the Trojan seer who uttered true prophecies, but lacking the power of persuasion, was never believed. Cassandra was twice cursed, cursed with the gift of prophecy and cursed because no one believed her. She was the daughter of Hecuba and King Priam who ruled during the Trojan War.

[95] Fossey, Dian. Draft of *Gorillas in the Mist.* Fossey archives Files 1-2: McMaster.

[96] Carr, Rosamond. *Land of a Thousand Hills*, p. 34.

[97] Percival, Valerie. "Environmental Scarcity and Violent Conflict: The Case of Rwanda. 1995. American Association for the Advancement of Science and the University of Toronto.

[98] Mowat Fonds Box 242: McMaster.

[99] Fossey, Dian. *Gorillas in the Mist*, p. 58

[100] Fossey, Dian. *Gorillas in the Mist*. Appendix. In both free ranging and captive young gorillas, the cries build up into temper tantrums if the stressful situation is prolonged.

Chapter Nine: "Death and Dreams"

[101] When under the pressure of extreme anxiety, Fossey would have vivid and extraordinary dreams that extended to rides in spaceships. This chapter does not

represent an actual dream, but is a compilation of worries, fears and imagery expressed in her diary excerpts. The lone silverback and Hans Sucker were real.

[102] Mowat Fonds Box 242 f. 25: McMaster.

[103] George Schaller was the first serious primatologist to visit the Virungas, and Dian Fossey was selected by Louis Leakey to fill his shoes.

[104] Salopek, Paul. "Africa's Wildlife Runs Out of Room." Chicago Tribune. March 12, 2000.

Chapter Ten: "Truth and Lies"

[105] Mowat Fonds. Unpublished Poem by Dian Fossey. Box 242. f.5: McMaster.

[106] Mowat Fonds. Fossey Diary Entry, Box 242 f. 5: McMaster.

[107] Letter from Rosamond Carr to Georgianne Nienaber, January 23, 2005.

[108] Dian's spelling. Sebagari or "Sebarari" was at Karisoke from 1970-1972. He was fired for the theft of Fossey's valise and papers. He was sentenced to three years in prison after being caught with a pistol in 1978. Not to be confused with SEMBAGARE, Rosamond Carr's trusted friend.

[109] Fossey, Dian. Fossey Archives. Obituary for her "Old Dog, Cindy." f. 5: McMaster.

[110] Cercopithecus

[111] Fossey, Dian. Fossey Archives. Obituary for her "Old Dog, Cindy." f. 5: McMaster.

[112] Mowat Fonds. Dian Fossey Diaries. Box 242: McMaster.

[113] Ibid.

[114] Mowat, Farley. *Woman in the Mists*, p. 124.

[115] Mowat Fonds. Dian Fossey Diaries. Box 242: McMaster.

[116] Ibid.

[117] *In the Kingdom of Gorillas*

[118] Vedder, Amy. *In the Kingdom of Gorillas*, New York: Simon and Schuster, 2001, p.240.

[119] Mowat Fonds. Box 241. f. 43: McMaster.

[120] Mowat Fonds, Box 242. f. 20: McMaster.

[121] Fossey Archive. Oslerwelch Laboratories Test Results, f. 47: McMaster.

[122] Mowat, Farley. *Woman in the Mists*. p.191.

[123] Founder of the International Primate Protection League (IPPL) and eventual supervisor of the Digit Fund after Robert McIlvaine resigned.

[124] One of the original "Leakey Girls", including Fossey and Jane Goodall. Galdikas studied orangutans.

[125] McGreal Files. Letter From Dian Fossey to Shirley McGreal. May 19, 1978.

[126] McGreal Files. Letter From Dian Fossey to Shirley McGreal. May 19, 1978.

[127] Fossey Archives. Letter to Kelly Stewart, March 7, 1973. f.38: McMaster.

[128] Shoumatoff, Alex. "Fatal Obsession, the Jungle Death of Dian Fossey," *Vanity Fair Magazine*, September, 1986.

[129] Mowat Fonds. Interview with Kelly Stewart. Box 242: McMaster.

[130] Fossey Archive. Letter from Fossey to Kelly Stewart, October 19,1981. f. 18: McMaster.

[131] Vedder, Amy. *In the Kingdom of Gorillas*. pp. 213-14.

[132] Congo

[133] Fossey's spelling. Sometimes spelled "Guamhogasi" in the literature.

[134] Probably Mark Condiotti of the Mountain Gorilla Project

[135] McGreal Files. "Story on 'Charlie.' January 1-January 23, 1980," by Dian Fossey.

[136] Fossey, Dian. *Gorillas in the Mist*. pp. 224-25.

[137] Fossey Archive. Letter from Fossey to Kelly Stewart, October 19, 1981. f. 18 McMaster.

[138] Fossey Archives. Letters from Sandy Harcourt to Dian Fossey. f.19: McMaster.

[139] Mowat Fonds. Letter from Sandy Harcourt to Dian Fossey. Box 241. f.3: McMaster.

[140] Mowat Fonds. Box 241. f.4: McMaster.

[141] Fossey Archives. Letter from Robert Hinde to A. H. Harcourt, September 21, 1981. f.18: McMaster.

[142] Fossey Archives. Letter from A. H. Harcourt to R.A. Hinde, October 10, 1981. f.18: McMaster.

[143] In 1974 Harcourt was gored by a water buffalo and nearly died but for the ministrations of Fossey.

[144] Fossey Archives. Letter from A. H. Harcourt to Hodder and Stoughton, copy to Dian Fossey. May 6, 1982. f.18: McMaster.

[145] Fossey Archives. Letter from Dian Fossey to Anita McClellan. May19, 1982. f.18: McMaster.

[146] International Primate Protection League. The Baby Monkey Case. April, 2001.

[147] Mowat Fonds. Interview with Ian Redmond. Box 242: McMaster.

[148] Fossey Archive. Letter to "Pat." November 21, 1985. f.18: McMaster.

[149] "Sumu" can also mean poison.

[150] Mowat Fonds. Kelly Stewart Transcript. Box 242: McMaster.

[151] Fossey Archive. Letter from W. Allan Royce to Dian Fossey. August 8, 1985. f.32: McMaster.

[152] Stewart, Kelly. "The Gun." *I've Been Gone Far Too Long*. RDR Books: Oakland, 1996.

[153] Stewart, Kelly J. and Pascale Sicotte. *Mountain Gorillas: Three Decades of Research at Karisoke.* Cambridge: University Press, 2001.

[154] Mowat Fonds. Farley Mowat Letter to Jane Goodall.1986 Box242:36. McMaster.

[155] Mowat Fonds. Letter from Jane Goodall to Farley Mowat. August 28, 1986. f.36: McMaster.

[156] Mowat Fonds. Farley Mowat Letter to Jane Goodall.1986 Box242:36. McMaster

Chapter Eleven: "Cinema Verite`"

[157] Fossey Archives. Letter to Mr. and Mrs. Richard Price. f.49: McMaster.

[158] Vedder, Amy. In the Kingdom of Gorillas: Simon and Schuster, 2001. pp.39-45

[159] Fossey Archives. Transcript from "Proposed Digit Cine for his Personal Commemoration." f.47: McMaster.

[160] Fossey Archives. Dian Fossey Letter to Evelyn Gallardo, September 20, 1985. f. 18. McMaster.

[161] Ibid.

[162] Banana beer

[163] Carr, Rosamond Halsey. *Land of A Thousand Hills: My Life In Rwanda.* New York: Viking, 1999, p.154.

[164] Carr, p.156.

[165] Fossey Archives. Letter from Dian Fossey to Anita McClellan, January 24, 1980. f. 18: McMaster.

[166] Fossey Archives. Letter from Dian Fossey to Rob McIlvaine, October 16, 1979. f.18: McMaster.

[167] Empire State College. Press Release for Amy Vedder. February 19-21, 2004.

[168] Fossey Archive. McIlvaine, Robert. "Report On Mountain Gorilla Protection: Digit Fund or Project Survival," African Wildlife Leadership Foundation, May 1979. f.47: McMaster.

[169] Mowat Fonds. Letter from Rob McIlvaine to Dian Fossey. November 29 (1978 or 1979) f.8: McMaster.

[170] Mowat Fonds. Letter from Dian Fossey to Rob McIlvaine, December 8, 1977. Box 241 f.8: McMaster.

[171] Mowat Fonds. Letter from Dian Fossey to Rob McIlvaine, December 8, 1977. Box 241. f.8: McMaster.

[172] Mowat Fonds. Letter from Dian Fossey to Rob McIlvaine, December 8, 1977. Box 241. f.8: McMaster.

Chapter Twelve: "1977-1979 Digit's Murder"

[173] Fossey, Dian. *Gorillas in the Mist.* p. 206.

[174] Fossey Archive. Letter Regarding the Death of Digit to "Brylawski" January 17, 1978. f.18: McMaster.

[175] Fossey, Dian. *Gorillas in the Mist.* Photos of Digit and cuts.

[176] Mowat, Farley. "*Woman In the Mists,*" p. 158.

[177] Mowat Fonds. Fossey Diary 1978. Box 241 f. 25: McMaster.

[178] Fossey Archive. Camp Notes. f.8: McMaster.

[179] Fossey, Dian. *Gorillas in the Mist.* p. 206.

[180] Mowat, Farley. *Woman in the Mists.* p. 161.

[181] Fossey, Dian. *Gorillas in the Mist.* p.206

[182] Fossey Archives. Letter to Brylawski from Dian Fossey. January 17, 1978. f.18: McMaster.

[183] Fossey Archives. Letter to Brylawski from Dian Fossey. January 17, 1978. f.18: McMaster.

[184] Ibid.

[185] Fossey Archive. Letter regarding the death of Digit to "Brylawski" January 17, 1978. f.18: McMaster.

[186] Ibid.

[187] Fossey Archives. Letter to Fulton Brylawski from Dian Fossey. January 17, 1978. f.18: McMaster.

[188] Fossey archives. Dian Fossey Letter to Monsieur le Prefet de Prefecture (sic). January 7, 1978. f.18: McMaster.

[189] The genocide began on April 7, 1994, a day after Rwandan President Juvenal Habyarimana was assassinated.

[190] Fossey archives. Dian Fossey Letter to Monsieru le Prefet de Prefecture (sic). January 7, 1978. f.18: McMaster.

[191] Fossey Archives. Letter to Brylawski from Dian Fossey. January 17, 1978. f.18: McMaster.

[192] Email from Frank Crigler to Georgianne Nienaber. November 13, 2004.

[193] Fossey archives. Dian Fossey Letter to Monsieru le Prefet de Prefecture (sic). January 7, 1978. f.18: McMaster.

[194] Mowat, Farley. *Woman in the Mists.* p.250.

[195] Fossey Archives. Letter to Brylawski from Dian Fossey. January 17, 1978. f.18: McMaster.

[196] Mowat Fonds. Fossey Diary 1978. Box 241. f.25: McMaster.

[197] Mowat Fonds. Fossey Diary 1978. Box 241. f.25: McMaster.

[198] Fossey archives. Dian Fossey Letter to Monsieru le Prefet de Prefecture (sic). January 7, 1978. f.18: McMaster.

[199] Fossey Archives. Letter from Dian Fossey to "Rob" McIlvaine. December 16, 1979. f.18: McMaster.

Chapter Thirteen: "1978-1980 The Aftermath"

[200] Email from Ambassador Frank Crigler to Georgianne Nienaber, May 30, 2004.

[201] Fossey Archives. Dian Fossey Letter to Frank Crigler. February 1, 1979. f.18: McMaster.

[202] Fossey, Dian. *Gorillas in the Mist.* p.26.

[203] Fossey Archives. Dian Fossey Letter to Frank Crigler. February 1, 1979. f. 18. McMaster.

[204] Fossey Archives. Letter to Fulton Brylawski from Dian Fossey. January 17, 1978. f.18: McMaster.

[205] Fossey Archives. Letter from Bettie Crigler to Dian Fossey. October 2, 1978. f.12: McMaster.

[206] Email from Frank Crigler to Georgianne Nienaber. November 13, 2004.

[207] Fossey Archives. Letter from Dismas Nsabimana to Dian Fossey. January 27, 1978. Translated from the French by Ryan Barrett, McMaster University French Honors Student. f.18. McMaster.

[208] Ibid.

[209] Fossey Archives. Letter from Survival Anglia Limited to Dian Fossey. February 24, 1978. f.39: McMaster.

[210] Fossey Archives. Letter to Brylawski from Dian Fossey. January 17, 1978: McMaster. It should be noted that the United States does not make a practice of purchasing real estate in foreign countries. Exactly what Fossey meant by this statement is unclear. Former Ambassador Frank Crigler says that rondavels were purchased by the U.S. prior to his tenure in Kigali. He thinks that the park headquarters may have been refurbished with "self-help" aid funds. (Email to Georgianne Nienaber. November 13, 2004.)

[211] Fossey Archives. Letter from Dian Fossey to F. Brylawski, January 17, 1978. f. 18. McMaster.

[212] Fossey Archives. Letter from Dian Fossey to F. Brylawski, January 17, 1978. f. 18: McMaster.

[213] Fossey Archives. Letter from Dian Fossey to F. Brylawski. January17, 1978. f. 18: McMaster.

[214] Founded in 1976 by Francine "Penny" Patterson to foster interspecies communication. No affiliation with IPPL.

[215] McGreal Files. Letter from Dian Fossey to Shirley McGreal. March 3, 1978.

[216] Ibid.

Chapter Fourteen: "Smartie's Party"

[217] Fossey Archives. Letter from Dian Fossey to Richard Wrangham. March 3, 1978. f.41: McMaster

[218] Fossey Archives. Letter from Richard Wrangham to Dian Fossey. February 21, 1978. f.41: McMaster

[219] Former Ambassador Frank Crigler says that rondavels were purchased by the U.S. prior to his tenure in Kigali. He thinks that the park headquarters may have been refurbished with "self-help" aid funds. (Email to Georgianne Nienaber. November 13, 2004.)

[220] Fossey Archives. Letter from Richard Wrangham to Dian Fossey. February 21, 1978. f.41: McMaster

[221] Fossey. Archives. Letter from Dian Fossey to Richard Wrangham. March 3, 1978. f.41: McMaster.

[222] Fossey Archives. Letter from Dian Fossey to Richard Wrangham. March 3, 1978. f.41: McMaster

[223] Dian's spelling

[224] Fossey, Dian. *Gorillas in the Mist.* p.207.

[225] Fossey Archives. Letter from Dian Fossey to Russell A. Mittermeier. March 23, 1978. f.18: McMaster.

[226] Fossey Archives. Letter from Bettie Crigler to Dian Fossey. March 2, 1978. f.12: McMaster.

[227] Fossey Archives. Letter from Dian Fossey to Bettie Crigler. July 8, 1978. f.12: McMaster.

[228] Ibid.

[229] Ibid.

[230] Fossey Archives. Note from Bettie Crigler to Dian Fossey. Summer, 1978. f.12: McMaster.

[231] Mowat, Farley. *Woman in the Mists*. p.184.

[232] Ibid. p.187.

[233] McGreal Archives. Letter from Dian Fossey to Shirley McGreal. September 19, 1978.

[234] Fossey, Dian. *Gorillas in the Mist*. p.220.

[235] Mowat, Farley. Woman in the Mists. pp.198-99.

[236] City in former Soviet Republic of Turkmenistan.

[237] Fossey Archives. Letter from Ambassador Frank Crigler to Dian Fossey. September 1, 1978. f. 18: McMaster.

[238] Ibid.

[239] Fossey Archives. Letter from Ambassador Frank Crigler to Dian Fossey. September 8, 1978. f. 13: McMaster.

[240] Fossey Archives. Letter from Frank Crigler to Dian Fossey. September 22, 1978. f.18: McMaster.

[241] Ibid.

[242] Email from Frank Crigler to Georgianne Nienaber. November 13, 2004.

[243] Fossey Archives. "The Protection of Rwanda's Gorillas," by General Nsabimana Dismas, September, 1978. f. 18: McMaster.

[244] Ibid.

[245] McGreal Files. Letter from Dian Fossey to Dr. Shirley McGreal. May 19, 1978.

[246] McGreal Files. Letter from Dian Fossey to Shirley McGreal. February 8, 1979.

[247] Fossey Archives. Letter from Dian Fossey to Bettie and Frank Crigler, September 19, 1978. f.18: McMaster.

[248] Vedder, Amy. *In the Kingdom of Gorillas.* p.156.

[249] Email from Frank Crigler to Georgianne Nienaber. November 13, 2004.

[250] The infamous terrorist, Carlos the Jackal, was a student there in 1968.

[251] Fossey Archives. Letter from Dian Fossey to F. Fulton Brylawski and Cleary. December 22, 1978. f. 18: McMaster.

[252] Fossey Archives. Letter from Dr. A. Harcourt to Ian Redmond. November 24, 1978. f.31: McMaster.

[253] Ibid.

[254] Fossey Archives. Letter from Dian Fossey to F. Fulton Brylawski and Cleary. December 22, 1978. f. 18: McMaster

[255] Fossey Archives. Letter from Dian Fossey to F. Fulton Brylawski and Cleary. December 22, 1978. f. 18: McMaster

[256] McGreal Files. Letter to Shirley McGreal from E. Fulton Brylawski. June 3, 1978.

[257] McGreal Files. "Digit Fund Mountain Gorilla Projection Project" December, 1978.

[258] McGreal Files. Letter from Dian Fossey to Shirley McGreal. December, 1978.

[259] McGreal Files. Letter from Dian Fossey to Shirley McGreal. February 8, 1979.

[260] Fossey Archive. McIlvaine, Robert. "Report On Mountain Gorilla Protection: Digit Fund or Project Survival," African Wildlife Leadership Foundation, May 1979. f.47: McMaster.

[261] McGreal Files. Letter from Dian Fossey to AWLF Members. December 14, 1978.

[262] Mowat Fonds. Note in Back Cover of Fossey's 1985 Diary. Box 241. f.41: McMaster.

[263] McGreal Files. Letter from Dian Fossey to Shirley McGreal. February 8, 1979.

[264] Fossey Archives. Letter from Frank Crigler to Dian Fossey. January 19, 1979. f. 18: McMaster.

[265] Fossey Archives. Letter from Dian Fossey to Frank Crigler. February 1, 1979. f. 18: McMaster.

[266] Mowat, Farley. *Woman in the Mists.* p. 144.

[267] Mowat, Farley. *Woman in the Mists.* p.145

[268] McGreal Files. Letter from Dian Fossey to the International Primate Protection League. July 19, 1978.

[269] Mowat, Farley. *Woman in the Mists.* p.170.

[270] Fossey Archives. Letter from Dian Fossey to Frank Crigler. February 1, 1979. f. 18: McMaster.

[271] Fossey Archives. Letter from Dian Fossey to Frank Crigler. February 1, 1979. f. 18: McMaster.

[272] Ibid.

[273] Mowat, Farley. *Woman in the Mists.* p. 209.

[274] Fossey Archive. Letter From Dian Fossey to Allen(?). February 9, 1979. f.18: McMaster.

[275] Fossey Archive. Letter from Dian Fossey to Shirley McGreal. September 18, 1979. f. 18: McMaster.

[276] McGreal Files. Letter from Dian Fossey to Shirley McGreal. February 8, 1979.

[277] Fossey Archive. Letter from Dian Fossey to Mr. and Mrs. Jeffery Short. April 12, 1979. f.18: McMaster.

[278] McGreal Files. Letter from Dian Fossey to Shirley McGreal. March 1, 1979.

[279] Fossey Archive. Letter from Dian Fossey to "Allen." February 9, 1979. f. 18: McMaster.

[280] Fossey Archive. Letter from Dian Fossey to "Allen." February 9, 1979. f. 18: McMaster

[281] Fossey Archives. Telex No. 892398. Melvin Payne to Dian Fossey. f.18. McMaster.

[282] McGreal Files. Letter from Dian Fossey to Shirley McGreal. March 1, 1979.

[283] McGreal Files. Letter From Dian Fossey to Shirley McGreal. March 1, 1979.

[284] A local beer

[285] Gardens or small farms

[286] McGreal Files. Letter from Dian Fossey to Shirley McGreal. March 1, 1979

[287] Fossey Archive. Letter from Dian Fossey to Jean Pierre von der Becke. July 26, 1979. f.43: McMaster.

[288] Fossey Archives. Letter from Dian Fossey to Jean Pierre von der Becke. July, 10, 1979. f. 43: McMaster.

[289] Netherlands Institute of Human Rights. ICTR-98-44A-1. January 25, 2001.

[290] ICTR Press Release. "The Former Bourgmestre of Mukingo Convicted of Genocide." December 1, 2003.

[291] The Arusha Times. "Former Mayor Begins Own Defense." ISSN 0856-9135. April 17, 2003.

[292] Fossey Archive. Letter from Dian Fossey to Jeanne Pierre von der Becke. July 26, 1979. f.43: McMaster

[293] Fossey Archive. Letter from Dian Fossey to Mr. and Mrs. Jeffery Short. April 12, 1979. f.18: McMaster.

[294] Ibid.

[295] Ibid.

[296] Mowat, Farley. *Woman in the Mists.* p.173.

[297] Fossey Archives. Letter from Dian Fossey to Anita McClellan. January 24, 1980. f. 18: McMaster.

[298] Mowat, Farley. *Woman in the Mists.* p.231.

[299] Fossey Archives. Letter from Dian Fossey to Shirley McGreal. September 18, 1979. f.18: McMaster.

[300] Fossey Archives. Letter from Dian Fossey to Shirley McGreal. September 18, 1979. f.18: McMaster.

[301] Fossey Archives. Letter from Dian Fossey to Shirley McGreal. September 18, 1979. f.18: McMaster.

[302] Vedder, Amy. *In the Kingdom of Gorillas.* p. 179.

[303] Fossey Archives. Letter from Dian Fossey to "J.P." (von der Becke) December 7, 1979. f.18: McMaster.

[304] Fossey Archives. Letter from Anita McClellan to Dian Fossey. December 14, 1979. f.18: McMaster.

[305] Ibid

[306] McGreal Files. Letter from Dian Fossey to Heather McGiffin. November 19, 1979.

[307] Fossey Archives. Letter from Dian Fossey to Shirley McGreal. September 13, 1979. f.18: McMaster.

Chapter Sixteen: "1980-1983 Exile"

[308] Fossey Archives. Letter from Dian Fossey To Anita McClellan. January 24, 1980. f. 18: McMaster.

[309] Mowat, Farley. *Woman in the Mists.* p.252.

[310] McGreal Files. Letter from Shirley McGreal to Robinson McIlvaine. July 25, 1980.

[311] McGreal Files. Letter from Dian Fossey to Shirley McGreal. March 1, 1979.

[312] McGreal Files. Letter from Dian Fossey to Shirley McGreal. September 8, 1980.

[313] Mowat Fonds. Interview with Shirley McGreal conducted by Wade Rowland for Woman in the Mists. Box 242. f.17: McMaster.

[314] McGreal Files. Letter from Dian Fossey to Shirley McGreal. May 27, 1980.

[315] Fossey Archive. Contract between Dian Fossey and Stuart Perlmeter. February23, 1980. f.18: McMaster.

[316] Mowat, Farley. *Woman in the Mists.* pp. 250-51.

[317] McGreal Files. Letter from Dian Fossey to "Diane" IPPL. August 9, 1980.

[318] Fossey Archive. Rough Draft-Fossey's Rwandan Trip, by Dian Fossey. f.18. McMaster.

[319] Fossey Archive. Rough Draft-Fossey's Rwandan Trip, by Dian Fossey. f.18: McMaster.

[320] Carr, Rosamond. *Land of a Thousand Hills.* p.52.

[321] Mowat Fonds. Letter from Cdt. Michael Savill to Rosamond Carr. August 29, 1984. Box 240. f. 4: McMaster.

[322] Fossey Archives. Undated note From Sergio Bottazzi. f.10: McMaster.

[323] Fossey Archive. Dian's Obituary for her Old Dog, Cindy. f.5: McMaster.

[324] Mowat Archive. Letter From Dian Fossey to Rosamond Carr. March 1, 1982. Box 241. f.5: McMaster.

[325] Mowat Archive. Letter from Dian Fossey to Rosamond Carr. March 1, 1982. Box 241. f.5: McMaster.

[326] Fossey Archive. Letter from Dian Fossey To Bettie and Frank Crigler. February 15, 1981. f. 18: McMaster.

[327] Fossey Archive. Letter from Dian Fossey To Bettie and Frank Crigler. February 15, 1981. f. 18: McMaster.

[328] Fossey Archive. Letter from Dian Fossey To Dr. A.H. Harcourt. October 27, 1981. f.18. McMaster.

[329] Fossey Archive. Letter from A. H. Harcourt to Professor R.A. Hinde. October 5, 1981. f.18: McMaster.

[330] Fossey Archive. Letter from Dian Fossey to "Sandy" (Harcourt). December 24, 1981. f. 18:McMaster.

[331] Mowat archive. Letter from Dian Fossey To Rosamond Carr. March 1, 1982. Box 242. f. 5: McMaster.

[332] Fossey Archive. Letter from Dian Fossey To Bettie and Frank Crigler. February 15, 1981. f. 18: McMaster.

[333] Mowat, Farley. *Woman in the Mists.* p.281.

[334] Correspondence with Dian Fossey Gorilla Fund International. DFGFI.

[335] McGreal Files. Letter from Dian Fossey to Shirley McGreal. April 8, 1981.

[336] McGreal Files. Letter from Dian Fossey to Shirley McGreal. April 8, 1981.

[337] McGreal Files. Letter from A. H. Harcourt to Shirley McGreal. April 24, 1981.

[338] Mowat Fonds. Letter from Dian Fossey to Anita McClellan. March 4, 1982. Box 241. f.5: McMaster

[339] Mowat Archive. Letter from Dian Fossey to Rosamond Carr. March1, 1982. Box 241. f.5: McMaster.

[340] Ibid.

[341] Mowat Archive. Letter from Dian Fossey to Rosamond Carr. March 1, 1982. Box 241. f.5: McMaster.

[342] Mowat Archive. Letter from Dian Fossey to Rosamond Carr. March 1, 1982. Box 241. f.5: McMaster.

[343] Vedder, Amy. *In The Kingdom of Gorillas*: Simon and Schuster, 2001. p 220.

[344] Letter from Heather Shocker to Georgianne Nienaber. April 19, 2004.

[345] Mowat Fonds. Letter from Dian Fossey To Jane Goodall. February 15, 1982. Box 241. f.5: McMaster.

[346] Fossey Archives. Dian's Obituary for Her Old Dog, Cindy. October 20, 1982. f.5: McMaster.

[347] Mowat Fonds. Letter from Jane Goodall to Dian Fossey. December 20, 1982. Box 241. f.5. McMaster.

Chapter Seventeen: "The Return"

[348] Mowat, Farley. *Woman in the Mists.* p.285.

[349] Fossey Archive. Letter from Dian Fossey to "Susan and Liza." July 18, 1983. f.18: McMaster.

[350] Ibid.

[351] Fossey Archive. Letter from Dian Fossey to "Mother and Father." (Kitty and Richard Price) July, 1983. f.18: McMaster.

[352] Fossey Archive. Letter from Dian Fossey to Susan and Liza. July 18, 1983. f.18: McMaster.

[353] Fossey Archive. Letter from Dian Fossey to "Mother and Father." July, 1983. f.18:McMaster.

[354] Mowat Archive. Letter from Dian Fossey to Stacey Coil. July 15, 1983. Box 240. f.3:

[355] Fossey Archive. Letter From Dian Fossey to "Mother and Father." July, 1983. f.18: McMaster.

[356] Fossey Archive. Letter from Dian Fossey to Anita McClellan. July 11, 1983. f.18: McMaster.

[357] Fossey Archive. Letter from Dian Fossey to Susan and Liza. July 18, 1983. f.18: McMaster.

[358] Fossey Archive. Letter from Dian Fossey to Anita McClellan. July 11, 1983. f.18: McMaster.

[359] Mowat Fonds. Letter from Dian Fossey to M.W. Baumgartel. January 15, 1983. Box 241. f.5: McMaster.

[360] Mowat, Farley. *Woman in the Mists.* pp.292-93.

[361] Mowat Fonds. Letter from Dian Fossey to Stacey Coil. July 15, 1983. Box 240. f.3: McMaster.

[362] Mowat, Farley. *Woman in The Mists.* p. 284.

[363] Interview with Charlene Jendry. July 20, 2004.

[364] Mowat, Farley. *Woman in the Mists.* p. 300.

[365] Preserve on the border between Rwanda and Tanzania.

[366] Mowat, Farley. *Woman in the Mists.* p. 302.

[367] Mowat, Farley. *Woman in the Mists.* p.303.

[368] Mowat, Farley. *Woman in the Mists.* p.304.

[369] Read Grandin, Temple. *Animals in Translation.* New York: Scribner, 2005.

[370] McGreal Files. Letter from Dian Fossey To Shirley McGreal. January 6, 1984.

[371] Ibid.

[372] Fossey Archives. Note from Dian Fossey to Jean Pierre von der Becke.

[373] McGreal Files. Letter from Dian Fossey to Shirley McGreal. April 11, 1984

[374] Fossey Archives. Letter from Dian Fossey to Shirley McGreal. May 6, 1984. f.18: McMaster.

[375] Fossey Archives. Letter from Dian Fossey to Shirley McGreal. May 6, 1984. f.18: McMaster.

[376] Fossey Archive. Letter from Dian Fossey to "Mother and Father." June 26, 1984. f.49: McMaster.

[377] Fossey Archive. Letter from Dian Fossey to Caroline E. G. Tutin. July 30, 1984. f. 18: McMaster.

[378] Fossey Archives. Letter from Dian Fossey to Kay Schaller. August 12, 1984. f.35: McMaster.

[379] Mowat, Farley. *Woman in the Mists.* p. 317.

[380] Fossey Archives. Letter from Dian Fossey to Stacey Coil. September 4, 1984. f.18: McMaster.

[381] Mowat Fonds. Letter from Cdt. Michael Savill to Dian Fossey. August 29, 1984. Box 240 f.3: McMaster.

Chapter Eighteen: "1985 Requiem"

[382] Fossey Archives. Letter from Dian Fossey to Parents. Date Unknown. f.49: McMaster.

[383] Woody plant. Climbs high trees and has a ropelike stem.

[384] Fossey Archives. Letter from Dian Fossey to Louis Leakey. January 13, 1968. f.18: McMaster.

[385] Mowat Fonds. Last Known Article Submitted by Dian Fossey. To Lexikographisches Institute. "Experiences with Gorillas in the Wild." October 30, 1985. Box 241. f. 42: McMaster.

[386] Ibid.

[387] Ibid.

[388] Mowat Fonds. Local brewery cold storage. Cable from American Embassy, Kigali to Secretary of State, Washington, D.C. December 30, 1985. Box 241. f.43.:McMaster.

[389] Interview with Ruth Keesling, August 2004.

[390] Letter from Rosamond Carr to Georgianne Nienaber. August 8, 2004.

[391] Ibid.

[392] Fossey Archives. Letter from Dian Fossey to Shirley McGreal, IPPL. January 20, 1985. f. 18: McMaster.

[393] Mowat Fonds. Letter from Dian Fossey to "Juichi." January 16, 1985. Box 240. f.3: McMaster. (Juichi Yamagiwa of Kyoto University, Japan)

[394] Smyth, Frank. "People in the Mist." January 1995. www.franksmyth.com.

[395] Mowat Fonds. Letter from Kitty Price to Dian Fossey. January 13, 1985. Box 240. f.3: McMaster.

[396] Fossey Archives. Letter from Dian Fossey to Shirley McGreal, IPPL. January 20, 1985. f. 18: McMaster.

[397] Mowat, Farley. *Woman in the Mists.* p. 325.

[398] Ibid. p. 326.

[399] Mowat Fonds. Executive Order From Laurent Habiyaremye, ORTPN, to Dr. Dian Fossey. January 15, 1985. Box 240. f. 3: McMaster.

[400] Mowat, Farley. *Woman in the Mists.* p. 326.

[401] Mowat, Farley. *Woman in the Mists.* p.327.

[402] Mowat, Farley. *Woman in the Mists.* p. 350.

[403] Mowat Fonds. Letter from Kitty Price to Dian Fossey. February 2, 1985. Box 240. f.3: McMaster.

[404] Mowat Fonds. Letter from Dian Fossey to Glenn (Hausfater). February 18, 1985. Box 240. f.3: McMaster.

[405] Ibid

[406] Mowat Fonds. Letter from Dian Fossey to Laurent Habiyaremye. March 18, 1985. Box 240. f.3: McMaster.

[407] Mowat Fonds. Letter from Dian Fossey to "Gina" regarding movie contract. March 25, 1985. Box 240. f. 3: McMaster.

[408] Ibid.

[409] Fossey Archives. Letter From Dian Fossey to Bettie Crigler. March 29, 1985. f.18: McMaster.

[410] Ebert, Roger. Review of Gorillas in the Mist. Chicago Sun-Times. September 23, 1988.

[411] Mowat Fonds. Letter from Dian Fossey to John A. Hoyt: Humane Society of the United States, January 10, 1985. Box 240 f. 3: McMaster.

[412] Mowat, Farley. *Woman in the Mists.* p.318.

[413] Mowat Fonds. Letter from Kitty Price to Dian Fossey. April 20, 1985. Box 240 f. 3: McMaster.

[414] Congo

[415] Gordon, Nicholas. *Murders in the Mists.*

[416] Mowat Fonds. Dian Fossey's Notes Concerning the Capture of Sebahutu. May 3, 1985. Box 240. f. 3: McMaster.

[417] Mowat, Farley. *Woman in the Mists.* p.334.

[418] Mowat Fonds. Letter from Mark Condiotti to Dian Fossey. May 7, 1985. Box 240. f.3. McMaster.

[419] Ibid.

[420] Mowat Fonds. Letter from Dian Fossey to "John." May 19, 1985. Box 240. f.3: McMaster

[421] Mowat Fonds. Letter from Dian Fossey To Mark Condiotti. May 8, 1985. Box 240. f. 3: McMaster.

[422] Mowat Fonds. Note from Mark Condiotti to Dian Fossey. May 6, 1985. Box 240. f.3: McMaster.

[423] Mowat Fonds. Letter from Dian Fossey to Mark Condiotti. No date, but in response to Condiotti note of May 6, 1985. Box 240. f.3: McMaster.

[424] Mowat Fonds. Note From Dian Fossey to Mark Condiotti. Box 240. f. 3: McMaster.

[425] Mowat Fonds. Farley Mowat's notes on "African Staff at Karisoke." Box 242. f. 5: McMaster.

[426] Mowat Fonds. Letter from Dian Fossey to Mr. and Mrs., Harold Price (Digit Fund benefactors). May 13, 1985. Box 240. f.3. McMaster.

[427] Mowat Fonds. Letter from Mark Condiotti to Dian Fossey. May 8, 1985. Box 240. f.3: McMaster.

[428] Mowat, Farley. *Woman in the Mists.* p.338.

[429] Mowat Fonds. Letter from Dian Fossey To "Martha." May 15, 1985. Box 240. f. 3: McMaster.

[430] Mowat Fonds. Notes for *Woman in the Mists.* Quote from Letter from Dian Fossey To W.B. Mager. No Date. Box 242. f.4. McMaster.

[431] Mowat Fonds. Letter from Dian Fossey to "John." May 19, 1985. Box 240. f. 3: McMaster.

[432] Mowat Fonds. Letter from Dian Fossey to "John." May 19, 1985. Box 240. f. 3: McMaster.

[433] Mowat, Farley. *Woman in the Mists.* p.336.

[434] Mowat Fonds. Letter from Dian Fossey to Stacy Coil. August 18, 1985. Box 240. f.24: McMaster.

[435] Mowat Fonds. Letter from Dian Fossey to "Gina." (Maccoby-agent)August 1, 1985. Box 240. f.3: McMaster.

[436] Mowat Fonds. Letter from Dian Fossey to "Gina." (Maccoby-agent)August 1, 1985. Box 240. f.3: McMaster.

[437] Froelich, Warren. "Life Is Much Better Among the Gorillas." San Diego Union-Tribune. June 27, 1985.

[438] Fossey Archives. Oslerwelch Labs. July 2, 1985. f. 47: McMaster.

[439] Mowat Fonds. Letter from Rosamond Carr to Dian Fossey. August 22, 1985. Box 240. f. 3: McMaster.

[440] State department directives encouraged the use of Fansidar™, which has since been taken off the market for liver complications. Weinland, Helen. *Living Abroad With Uncle Sam.*

[441] Mowat Fonds Letter from Dian Fossey To Stacey Coil. September 14, 1985. Box 240. f. 24: McMaster.

[442] Mowat Fonds. Letter from Dian Fossey to "Linda." August 1, 1985. Box 240. f. 24: McMaster.

[443] Mowat, Farley. *Woman in the Mists.* p.342.

[444] Mowat Fonds. Letter from Dian Fossey to Canisius Shyirambere. July 22, 1985. Box 240. f. 3: McMaster.

[445] Key Documents of the Ramsar Convention. 1980. www.ramsar.org/cop1_participants.htm

[446] Mowat Fonds. Letter from Canisius Shyirambere to Dian Fossey. May 30, 1985. Box 240 f. 3: McMaster.

447 Mowat Fonds. Letter from Dian Fossey to "Linda." August 1, 1985. Box 240. f.24: McMaster.

448 Carr, Rosamond. *Land of a Thousand Hills*. p.176.

449 Carr, Rosamond. *Land of a Thousand Hills* p. 176.

450 Mowat Farley. *Woman in the Mists*. p. 343.

451 Helen Weinland was the official who made the call, but says that Dian exaggerated her role. Weinland maintains that she was diplomatic in her request that the Rwandans recognize the contribution Fossey made instead of exhibiting obstinacy in their refusal to expeditiously grant the visa request.

452 Mowat Fonds. Letter from Dian Fossey To Stacey Coil. September 14, 1985. Box 240. f. 24. McMaster.

453 Mowat Fonds. Letter from Dian Fossey to Mrs. Price (not mother). September 19, 1985. Box 240. f.3: McMaster.

454 Charged in absentia with Fossey's murder

455 Jorge Hess from Switzerland

456 Mowat Fonds. Letter from Dian Fossey To Stacey Coil. September 14, 1985. Box 240. f. 24: McMaster.

457 Mowat Fonds. Letter from Dian Fossey to Anita McClellan. October 5, 1985. Box 240. f. 24: McMaster.

458 Email from Evelyn Gallardo to Georgianne Nienaber. September, 2004.

459 Fossey Archives. Letter from Dian Fossey to Evelyn Gallardo. September 20, 1985. f.18: McMaster.

460 Mowat Fonds. Letter from Dian Fossey to W. Allen Royce. October 17, 1985. Box 240 f. 3: McMaster.

461 Telephone conversation between Evelyn Gallardo and Georgianne Nienaber, Saturday August 28, 2004.

[462] Mowat Fonds. McGuire, Wayne. "I Didn't Kill Dian, She Was My Friend." Discover Magazine. February, 1987. p.37. Box 241. f. 42: McMaster.

[463] Email From Evelyn Gallardo to Georgianne Nienaber, September, 2004.

[464] Mowat Fonds. Letter From Dian Fossey to "Pat." September 12, 1985. Box 240. f. 24: McMaster.

[465] Mowat Fonds. Letter from Dian Fossey to "Pat." September 12, 1985. Box 240. f. 24: McMaster.

[466] Mowat Fonds. Letter from Dian Fossey to "Pat." September 12, 1985. Box 240. f. 24: McMaster.

[467] Possibly Jean-Baptiste of ORINFOR, the state news agency. Says he quit because he had to vet all of his copy with Protais Zigiranyiirazo, Prefect of Ruhengeri. See Gordon, p. 149. Possibly Aloys Mundere.

[468] Probably Augustin Nduwayezu of the National Police Surete (Secret Service). See Gordon, pp. 109-110.

[469] Mowat Fonds. Letter from Dian Fossey to "Pat." September 12, 1985. Box 240. f. 24: McMaster.

[470] Mowat Fonds. Letter from Dian Fossey to Anita McClellan. October 5, 1985. Box 240. f. 24: McMaster.

[471] Fossey often used the word "autopsy" instead of the more correct term, "necropsy."

[472] Fossey Archives. Letter from Dian Fossey to Evelyn Gallardo. September 20, 1985. f.18: McMaster.

[473] Mowat Fonds. Letter from Dian Fossey to Rane Randolf (accountant). September 30, 1985. Box 240. f. 3: McMaster.

[474] Mowat, Farley. *Woman in the Mists.* p. 349.

[475] Mowat, Farley. *Woman in the Mists.* p.356. Carved puff adder. Curse of death.

[476] Fossey Archives. Letter from Dian Fossey to "Pat." November 21, 1985. f. 18: McMaster.

[477] Mowat Fonds. Letter From Karl Hoffman, US Embassy in Kigali, to Wade Rowland. November 19, 1986. Box 241. f. 43: McMaster.

[478] Mowat, Farley. *Woman in the Mists.* p. 359.

[479] Mowat Fonds. Dian Fossey's 1985 Diary excerpt. Box 241. f. 41. McMaster.

[480] Dian Fossey's spelling. BAZIMU is actually an African belief that the dead are not dead, but live on in spiritual form. It is not known what Fossey meant when she described Basimu as a hereditary disease.

[481] Fossey Archives. Letter from Dian Fossey to "Pat." November 21, 1985. f. 18: McMaster.

[482] Gourevitch, Philip. *We Wish to Inform You That Tomorrow We Will Be Killed with Our Families.* New York: Picador, 1998, pp. 77-78.

[483] Fossey Archives. Letter from Dian Fossey to "Pat." November 21, 1985. f. 18: McMaster.

[484] Ibid.

[485] Mowat Fonds. Dian Fossey's Christmas List, 1985. Box 240. f. 5. McMaster.

[486] Mowat Fonds. Dian Fossey Diary 1985. Box 241. f. 41: McMaster.

[487] Sjaak Van de Nieuwendijik. Dian met him in 1984 during a brief visit to Holland. He took leave from his job as a gorilla keeper to learn more about gorillas in the wild.

[488] Mowat Fonds. Dian Fossey Diary for 1985. Box 241. f.41: McMaster.

[489] Mowat, Farley. *Woman in the Mists.* p.362.

[490] Gordon, Nicholas. *Murders in the Mist.* p.110.

[491] Mowat, Farley. *Woman in the Mists.* p. 363.

[492] Yamagiwa, Juichi. *War and Tropical Forests: Conservation in Areas of Armed Conflict.* "Bushmeat Poaching and the Conservation Crisis in Kahuzi-Biega National Park, Democratic Republic of the Congo." pp.115-135.

[493] Congressional Testimony of Wayne Madsen. Office of Congresswoman Cynthia McKinney. www.muhammadfarms.com/Covert_Action_in_Africa.htm.

[494] Rosamond Carr to Georgianne Nienaber, March 15, 2005.

[495] Telephone interview with Ruth Keesling. August, 2004.

[496] Mowat Fonds. Dian Fossey Diary Entry 1985. Box 241. f. 41: McMaster.

[497] Mowat Fonds. Farley Mowat's notes on "The Window of Opportunity." Box 242. f.18: McMaster.

[498] Mowat Fonds. Dian Fossey's Diary, 1985. Box 241. f.41: McMaster

[499] Mowat Fonds. Dian Fossey's Last Diary Entry, 1985. Box 241. f.41: McMaster.

[500] Vollers, Maryanne. "The Strange Death of Dian Fossey." People Weekly. February 17, 1986.

[501] Carr, Rosamond. *Land of a Thousand Hills.* p.176.

[502] Vedder, Amy. *In the Kingdom of Gorillas.* p.236.

[503] Duty officer at US Embassy

[504] Vedder, Amy. *In the Kingdom of the Gorillas.* p. 254.

Chapter Nineteen: "Coda"

[505] Letter from Rosamond Carr to Georgianne Nienaber. August 8, 2004.

[506] Hayes, Harold T.P., *The Dark Romance of Dian Fossey*, p.33.

[507] Vedder, Amy. *In the Kingdom of the Gorillas.* p.260.

[508] Mowat Fonds. Actualite Nationale, daily bulletin of the Agence Rwandais de Presse. December 12, 1986. Box 241. f.43: McMaster.

[509] Fossey Archives. Letter from Dian Fossey to Ric Krammer. November 30, 1979. f. 18: McMaster.

[510] Deutsch, Linda." Researcher Proclaims Innocence in Fossey Murder." August 29, 1986.

[511] Deutsch, Linda." Researcher Proclaims Innocence in Fossey Murder." August 29, 1986.

[512] Faul, Michelle. "Rwandan Official Confirms N.J. Man Sought in Fossey Murder." August 2, 1986.

[513] As the acting chargé d' affaires, Weinland was in charge of business at the embassy during the absence of the ambassador. Ambassador John Blane had been transferred to Chad

[514] Crary, David. "Rwanda Officials Praised for Response to Dian Fossey's Murder." December 29, 1985.

[515] Weinland, Helen. *Living Abroad with Uncle Sam.* 1st Books: 2003. p.103.

[516] Ibid

[517] Mowat Fonds. McGuire, Wayne." I Did Not Kill Dian, She Was My Friend." Discover Magazine. February, 1987. Box 241. f. 42: McMaster.

[518] Dwight Nelson. Hired by Ruth Keesling on behalf of the Morris Animal Foundation to rebuild the camp. Telephone conversation with Ruth Keesling. July, 2004.

[519] Gordon, Nicholas. *Murders in the Mist.* p. 93.

[520] Vollers, Maryanne. *People Weekly.* February 17, 1986.

[521] Gordon, Nicholas. *Murders in the Mist.* p.111.

[522] FOIA Report.

[523] Gordon, Nicholas. Murders in the Mist. p. 157.

[524] Fossey, Dian. *Gorillas in the Mist.* p. 16.

[525] Mowat, Farley. *Woman in the Mists.* p. 300.

[526] 9mmWalther PPK/S

[527] Astra Constable .380. Photo © Georgianne Nienaber.

[528] Boyd, Matthew J. Email to Georgianne Nienaber. September 30, 2004. Boyd is a computer technician with military experience. He researches firearms, ballistics, and ammunition as a hobby.

[529] Located in Brainerd, MN USA.

[530] Interview with Terry Fairbanks. Central Lakes College Criminology Department. Brainerd, MN.

[531] Mowat Fonds. Letter from Karl Hoffman to Wade Rowlands. November 19, 1986: McMaster.

[532] Borst, Barbara A. "Rwandan Justice: A Show of Pomp and Circumstantial Evidence," Discover Magazine. February, 1987.

[533] Gun's World. "Astra M900 Pistol." Aviable. Online: http://www.gunsworld.com/spain/astra900_us.html

[534] Gordon, Nicholas. *Murders in the Mist.* p.57.

[535] Letter from Rosamond Carr to Georgianne Nienaber, November, 2005.

[536] Telephone interview with Ruth Keesling. July, 2004.

[537] Mowat Fonds. McGuire, Wayne." I Did Not Kill Dian, She Was My Friend." Discover Magazine. February, 1987. Box 241. f.42: McMaster.

[538] Gordon, Nicholas. *Murders in the Mist.* p.110.

[539] Vedder, Amy. *In the Kingdom of Gorillas.* p. 236.

[540] Gordon, Nicholas. *Murders in the Mist.* p. 32; 56-60.

[541] FOIA Report

[542] Gordon, Nicholas. *Murders in The Mist.* p.90.

[543] Verbatim text. Should be *gorilla beringei beringei* by recent classification.

[544] Fossey Archives. State Department Cable from Kigali Embassy to Secretary of State, Washington, DC. f.40: McMaster.

[545] Mowat Fonds. Cable from U.S. Embassy in Kigali to State Department. Box 241. f. 43: McMaster.

[546] Kelly, Sean. "American Naturalist Buried Among her Beloved Gorillas." January 1, 1986.

[547] Hirondelle News Agency. Foundation Hirondelle. Lausanne, Switzerland. July 27, 2001.

[548] Hirondelle News Agency. November 25, 2003.

[549] Minutes of the International Criminal Tribunal for Rwanda. "The Prosecutor vs. Protais Zigiranyirazo." Case no. ICTR-2001-73-I. February 25, 2003.

[550] Goodall, Jane. "Dedication, Courage, and Love." Reprint from International Primate Protection League

For information: info@thelegacyofdianfossey.com

Webpage: www.thelegacyofdianfossey.com

978-0-595-37669-8
0-595-37669-X

CPSIA information can be obtained at www.ICGtesting.com
Printed in the USA
LVOW041733081211

258482LV00002B/60/A